Political Perversion

President Trump prepares to welcome the Clemson Tigers to the White House on Monday, January 14, 2019. Official White House photo by Joyce N. Boghosian, courtesy of the White House.

Political Perversion

RHETORICAL ABERRATION IN THE TIME OF TRUMPETEERING

Joshua Gunn

The University of Chicago Press CHICAGO & LONDON

The University of Chicago Press, Chicago 60637
The University of Chicago Press, Ltd., London
© 2020 by The University of Chicago
Published 2020

29 28 27 26 25 24 23 22 21 20   1 2 3 4 5

ISBN-13: 978-0-226-71330-4 (cloth)
ISBN-13: 978-0-226-71344-1 (paper)
ISBN-13: 978-0-226-71358-8 (e-book)
DOI: https://doi.org/10.7208/chicago/9780226713588.001.0001

Library of Congress Cataloging-in-Publication Data

Names: Gunn, Joshua, 1973– author.
Title: Political perversion : rhetorical aberration in the time of Trumpeteering / Joshua Gunn.
Description: Chicago : The University of Chicago Press, 2020. |
Includes bibliographical references and index.
Identifiers: LCCN 2019044399 | ISBN 9780226713304 (cloth : alk. paper) |
ISBN 9780226713441 (pbk. : alk. paper) | ISBN 9780226713588 (e-book)
Subjects: LCSH: Communication—Political aspects—United States. |
Rhetoric—Political aspects—United States—History—21st century.
Classification: LCC P95.82.U6 G885 2020 | DDC 302.2/09730905—dc23
LC record available at https://lccn.loc.gov/2019044399

For my mentors, Barb, Barry, Ed, and Tom

Da mihi castitatem et continentiam, sed noli modo!

SAINT AUGUSTINE OF HIPPO, *The Confessions*

To acknowledge today that there is failure—not an end, nothing is finished—is to recognize that there is hope. My logic here, don't forget, is also the logic of Augustine: as long as there is anxiety, there is hope.

PAUL VIRILIO, *The Accident of Art*

CONTENTS

FIGURE 1. Artist Mitch O'Connell's *Alien Trump*. Courtesy of Mitch O'Connell.

PREAMBLING TOWARD PROFLIGACY

I cannot think of a time when there were more upset people in my living room than on the evening of July 21, 2016. Clutching what amounts to over-the-counter Xanax in salt-rimmed glasses, we assembled to watch the Republican presidential nominee deliver his acceptance speech at the national convention in Cleveland. As with any political spectacle worthy of a drinking game, we had expected to laugh and jeer, but it turned out that what he said wasn't funny (at least anymore).[1] Our experience watching the speech was unexpectedly traumatic. But why the shock? Whence the surprise? Ivanka Trump delivered a pitch-perfect spousal send-up as an introduction to candidate Trump, at least in regard to historical norms.[2] Annexing the podium, The Donald barked a series of authoritarian commonplaces: conventionalism; aggression toward the unconventional; mystical stereotyping; tropes of "strong" and "weak"; generalized hostility; projection (about nonwhite others and Islam); and sexual obsessiveness—all of it was there.[3] So, too, was Theodor W. Adorno's elaboration of the autocrat as a "rabble rouser" who lacks any positive policies and whose rhetoric is "so monotonous that one meets with endless repetitions as soon as one is acquainted with the very limited number of stock devices."[4] No surprise there either.

Nor should we have been startled that the Grand Ol' Party promoted and voted for the vacuous repetitions of a demagogue.[5] Since the First World War, the West has become quite familiar with theories of mass psychology and political governance, many of which explain Trump's appeal. For example, Sigmund Freud elegantly described social movements, especially populist ones, as ways of mollifying conflicts internal to every person through collective experience. Although the details are complex, the general story Freud tells is rather simple: most people's egos are frail, and we do all sorts of things to shore them up. Such "normal" fragility is a consequence of an internalized "over-I" (or superego) that comes from our families, communities, and societies, demanding conformity and often inspiring a punishing guilt.[6] So, for example, Freud says the command to "love thy neighbor as thyself" is a punishing one because it is impossible.[7] Humans have therefore developed all sorts of techniques, especially the use of drugs, legal and otherwise, to provide relief from social demands. Love is such an intoxicant; so, too, is watching movies, enjoying music, the joy of schadenfreude (or taking pleasure in others' misfortune, the typical plot of "reality television"), and, of course, sipping margaritas.[8]

The simple story or syrup, then, is that authoritarian leaders are intoxicants, mediating the cultural superego or, as is the case with fascism, installing themselves in its place.[9] One could argue that the Trump campaign (and presidency to follow) was a kind of drug, and that Trump's supporters are cinched to him with a powerfully affective bond. Adorno argued such a bond is often achieved through repetition, much like the refrain of a pop song; during Trump's rambling, seventy-five-minute screed, audiences got a recounting of his worst hits ("America first," "Build a wall," "Repeal Obamacare," and so on). Relatedly, for a summer class in cinema theory, I had also recently screened a part of Leni Riefenstahl's propaganda film of the 1934 Nazi Party Congress in Nuremberg, *Triumph of the Will.* Watching the RNC rally, I was reminded of this film. So was Trump's speech shocking because it recalled a fascist aesthetics that many believed to be long abandoned?

Debriefing with tobacco on the patio—which is what alcohol permitted us to do that night without too much guilt—my guests and I took up the *f* question. The term "fascist" is muddy, mostly used as an epithet these days, as George Orwell predicted.[10] More than a few commentators and critics have hedged against using the term. "Fascism," some say, should be the word for an authoritarian personality who encourages a violent coup or genocide. "Trump is, fundamentally, a blustering political opportunist courting votes in a democratic system," argued Gianni Riotta in 2016, and "he has not called for the violent overthrow of the system itself."[11] Since 2016 there have been numerous federal and state investigations of President Trump and his entourage, a book by former US secretary of state Madeleine Albright titled *Fascism: A Warning*, and a government-sponsored mistreatment of migrants from Mexico and Central America. Still, Riotta was right to underscore that no one has advocated a violent overthrow of "the system." Yet. But how does "yet" metamorphose to "now?" in a sense that is real but not recognized as such?

I sympathize with those who hesitate using the *f*-word, but for reasons different than Riotta's: labeling Trump and his ilk as "fascist" displaces our collective responsibility for their ascent to national power; the "system" includes us, and at a number of levels we cultivate a painful pleasure for the violence that these political figures enable—verbal and otherwise—that has become a weekly event on our screens. In the United States, our general tendency to focus on any one person as a "fascist" is a misstep because it is a failure to understand the authoritarian mood of our time as *cultural and systemic*. Following the insights of a number of scholars in the humanities, I think we would do better to focus on relationships, on the connections between bodies, on the relation between publics and personae, on the links between relations among people and the forces of production (e.g., technology), and on the bond that an electorate imagines between itself and its leaders (a fantasy with consequences). I think and feel that the reason my friends and I were traumatized in my living room has more to do with the realization that Trump is less a discrete person than he is a kind of cultural gallbladder on autosecretion. I think that our fear is about a realization that the Trump campaign was an uncanny channeling and redirecting of social bile, but not in any studied way. What frightened us is that Trump is epiphenomenal, that he is a fungible figure. Having had some time for reflection, I will argue that our nauseating anxiety that night had more to do with the truth that Trump's rhetoric and person are better understood as replicating a style and genre of political discourse originally conceived in the name of authoritarianism or fascism or demagoguery but now better described as a structural perversion.

So here it is: the primary argument of *Political Perversion* is that as US technoculture trends toward what I term "psychosis" (a kind of hypermediated chaos), it innervates increasingly conspicuous eruptions of perversity in popular conversations. To put this more crudely—and I insist that there's nothing wrong with crudeness when warranted—an increasingly bewildering world makes for speech that is both nutty and predictable *at the same time*. I argue that "perversion" is the best word for this doubling political discourse. The rhetoric and figure of Donald J. Trump is my primary example, but I stress that his figure and rhetoric comprise only *one* example; the book mostly pertains to the conditions of possibility for perniciously perverse rhetorics (as I'll note in a later chapter, this project originally began as an analysis of the resurgence of horror television programming).

I also do not (necessarily) mean "psychosis" or "perversion" in a bad way—which is the most popular reception for both—but rather in a more cultural way described by psychoanalytic thinkers in the twentieth century. My study describes and explains psychosis and perversion to offer a vocabulary that enriches our discussions of what seems to be dominating our speakers and screens. In so doing, I complicate the cynical and sometimes dismissive, gonad-clutching character of what often passes as "political analysis" in mainstream news and social media, which often sounds like a lala-poll-ooze-ugh party or an overly serious, partisan sing-along of catchwords ("double down" makes me clutch my own pearls). There are alternate ways of thinking and talking about public figures as expressions of our social context.

I am primarily interested in describing how a perceived deviancy in popular discourse *cannot* be reduced to the individual or the personal. I also suggest that we cannot always postulate that profound perversions of propriety index seismic shifts in a culture or community either. Sometimes an aberration is a revelation, a peek at rearrangements of power, a glimpse of systemic ills that were already murmuring. In the case of contemporary political rhetoric, to quote a more reliable Talking Head, I argue "Same as it ever was," but I add, "only more so." *Political Perversion* is mostly an account of the "more so" and, in the end, how this "more so" is hurting people.

Finally, two more caveats in the interest of playing with a broader readership. (I should note that both the publisher and I hope to reach readers outside of the academy. I pledge to tell those of you not reading this book for scholarly reasons when there is something you probably can skip, such as the first chapter on critical method.) First, as a behavior, event, or endurance sport, perversion is not actually an aberration; it's only perceived as such. Life as such *is perverse*. Period. To realize this is to take a step on the path toward becoming a "grown-up." As I will detail, Freud argued that perversion is common and universal, even fun. It's the perversion of perversion—the failure to regard others as subjects worthy of respect and recognition—that leads to meanness and harm. In the spirit of the double character of perversion, the harmless and universal on the one hand and the horrible and mean on the other, both the cover of this book and my writing are deliberately playful, trending toward the serious. Figure 1 references John Carpenter's 1988 "horror comedy" *They Live*, which tells the story of the itinerant construction worker Nada (Nope!), who discovers a box of sunglasses. When worn, the sunglasses reveal that the world is actually peopled by aliens who control humans through subliminal messaging. The commentary of Mitch O'Connell's art should be obvious, with its melding of the civil religion and profane alienation: my deliberately playful or "performative" writing may not be initially as succinct as Mitch's imagination, but as the book progresses, I promise that the sunglasses do go on. In short, I'm writing perversely on purpose, punning and juxtaposing the permitted and the taboo as I go. As I work toward more serious topics, however, my prose gradually sobers up. I mean to celebrate our common perversion while eventually condemning the kind that is hurting us. It's a tricky pickle, but worth it, given the stakes of political perversion that have come to dominate publics.

Second, insofar as we are slouching toward Sodom, permit me to ruin the salty ending: other than the cultivation of charity, *I do not propose a solution* to the political and cultural problems described here. There is a need for addressing these problems in practice, but before we can be pragmatic there has to be some space and time for reflection, and perhaps then some agreement about *what the hell* it is we are addressing.

Eating Poorly, or Ketchup on a Steak

The chief (*chef*) must be an eater of the flesh.

JACQUES DERRIDA[1]

Not too long after he founded his company in Pittsburgh, Henry John Heinz introduced his famous ketchup in 1876, which is now the best-selling brand in the world.[2] As culinary histories go, we probably should not be surprised that a seventeenth-century Asian table sauce—made of pickled fish!—would turn up in the United States in an octagonal bottle of sugary red pulp, the butt of which one . . . Must. Relentlessly. Pound. To. Release. The. Tangy. Treacle.[3] Such a contest of the comestible recalls Saint Jerome's regard for infants, who wondered why anyone would enjoy "brat[wurst]s . . . crawling upon his breast and soiling his neck with nastiness."[4] Eating with ketchup, like burping a baby, is a potentially gross brand or breed of labor.

"Bussoftlhee, mememormee! . . . A way a lone a last a loved a long the riverrun, past Eve and Adam's, from swerve of shore to bend of bay, brings us by commodius vicus of recirculation back" to the Southern White House.[5] Mara-Lago, that is—sand bunkers, fancy cars—the lavish, six-star resort where Hair Führer retreats after golfing at his club in Palm Beach, Florida.[6] The resort was built by General Foods cereal queen Marjorie Merriweather Post. Post owed her familial fortune to her father, whose adventures in sanity landed him in a religious "health club" (that is, a sanatorium) run by Seventh-Day Adventist John Harvey Kellogg, whose healthy eating ideology influenced his brother and future foodie rival Will Keith Kellogg to found the Kellogg company.[7] Inspired by the cereal foods the elder Kellogg served up to rescript the burned-out in *sola cereālis*, Papa Post formulated Grape-Nuts to help soothe the nerves of men on the verge of a mental collapse; one early ad for the cereal reads,

Grape-Nuts "steadies a Man. All of a man's real power comes from steady nerves and a keen, clear brain."[8]

Despite the dubious mental health claims of Grape-Nuts advertisements, it is consequential, at least for *Political Perversion*, that the self-professed "stable genius,"[9] Donald John Trump, is *the* junk food of presidents in many senses.[10] His decision to serve burgers and fries from Wendy's and Burger King to the 2019 national college football champions was widely derided as made in bad taste.[11] Although his preference for the "clean" (which is to say, less poisonous) cuisine of McDonald's and Kentucky Fried Chicken is well known,[12] it is his penchant for eating his steaks well done with a side of ketchup that first inspired popular indigestion and gobs of gastronomic grievances, many in the form of social media memes.[13] For example, Trump's dietary druthers have been rather distasteful to cosmopolitan culinarians across the country, such as *New Yorker* food correspondent Helen Rosner, who wrote that "adults who won't eat pink-hearted steaks" are risk averse and display "an unwillingness to trust the validity and goodwill of any experiences beyond the limited sphere of [their] own."[14]

Rosner reminds us that the addition of ketchup to rubberized meat is compensatory,[15] returning flavor to a body squeezed of its blood by pounding on the backside of another. One could argue that in a peculiar, perverse sense, ketchup on a well-done steak is homologous to our piquant political diet these days and the consequent "both-sides" logic of moral equivalency particular to Trump's expressed worldview. This is to suggest, for example, that there are underlying, structural links between spectatorship and the consoler in chief's remarks after a "Unite the Right" march led by white supremacists in Charlottesville, Virginia, on August 11, 2017.[16] Some readers may remember that after the illiberal unleashed violence on counterprotesters—a neo-Nazi plowed into a crowd with his car, killing one and injuring nineteen others—Trump remarked in a curiously hostile press engagement that "I think there is blame on both sides. . . . You had a group on one side that was bad. You had a group on the other side that was also very violent. Nobody wants to say that. I'll say it right now."[17] In the context of our contemporary era of "laissez-faire racism,"[18] Trump questioned journalists' failure to consider the violence of the "alt-left," confirming a congruity that outraged people across the political spectrum—except, of course, hush-mouthed and vocally avowed bigots.

Trump's expressed feelings about racist violence are perverse in the common or popular notion "of a person . . . disposed to go against what is reasonable, logical, expected, or required," but this is *not* to say that the commonsense understanding of perversion is necessarily deviant, especially when extending the contextual horizon beyond the current conjuncture to include the conscious and unconscious mores of publics and counterenclaves.[19] For some, Trump's remarks demonstrate a common perversion because they reflect a *knowing* violation of widespread expectations regarding presidential speech and behavior, at least as indexed by the popular news media pundits (and certainly the largest readership of an academic monograph). As the electoral results of the 2016 presidential campaign underscore, however, such expectations are neither immutable nor universal, reflecting increasingly inefficient, conversational commonplaces and a perceived erosion of a shared sense of civic authority (e.g., a president is trustworthy and consistent, a president should condemn discrimination and violence as "un-American," and so on). The now familiar discrepancies between the popular vote and the Electoral College in the United States suggest that common perceptions of perversion vary from one party to the next *in many senses*.

At least one of those senses is that the swollen success of Trump's species of electoral perversion reckons on a well-worn, bigoted (home) base. Numerous scholars and cultural critics have long observed that racism and white supremacy have been constitutive norms since the beginning of the country, as the "United States was founded on hate—the hatred that justified colonial annihilation of American Indians and that perpetuated the enslavement of Africans."[20] Charles W. Mills has dubbed one footing of this foundation "the Racial Contract," a perverse expression of the Western idealism of the social contract, which is *supposed* to include and guarantee equality and participation for everyone (e.g., the US Constitution, the rule of law, and so on). In a political context—that is, in the field of power principally but not solely concerned with the use of force—a social contract is forged over some object, typically a resource like food, shelter, land, and so on. But an attention to sociocultural and economic history demonstrates contractarian thinking as such, closely linked to a universalizing impulse, depends on a gesture of exclusion in one way or another. This "primal exclusion" inevitably trends toward alliances over the object of a *people* who are removed, owned, and/or killed.[21] For Mills, the Racial Contract in the United States is "just for the people who count, the people who are really people ('we the white people')."[22] Unsurprisingly, Mills suggests that the Racial Contract works in tandem with another foundational footing that Carole Pateman terms the "Sexual Contract," a form of promise making that excludes women for the benefit and self-fashioning of men (bell hooks has taught us, of course, that multiple foundations of exclusion comprise an interlocking, politico-cultural system).[23] To wit: if Trump is perverse in the popular sense of violating civic expectations, such violations only begin to make sense as such when the racist and sexist norms of US culture are foreclosed, disavowed, or repressed: "I'm not racist, but . . ."

Although *Political Perversion* is not directly concerned with social contract theory, the study does begin with the assumption that such thinking provides a coherent and complementary vocabulary for grappling with an increasingly conspicuous culture of civic duplicity—a contemporary swerve toward a more "generalized perversity."[24] In this respect *Political Perversion* is an attempt to advance a correlative psychoanalytic and rhetorical vocabulary for the structures and *affective* motors driving the conventions and ideological habits of our time. In the chapters that follow, I will argue that we can locate Trump's perversion not only in the common sense of violating expectations but also in a deeper, structural sense indicated by the inevitably exclusionary logic of a moral equivalency yoked to death: suggesting that the violence of white supremacy is akin to social justice advocacy, aggressive or not, points up a particularly privileged and infantile ethic of provocation or (foul) play—underwritten by the exclusion of women, persons of color, non- or antinormative gender and sexual identities, and so on—that is hardly subversive; rather, it denotes an orientation toward others that is radically conformist in the United States.[25] Trump's "both sides" logic indexes an obscene, semiconscious form of loyalty to a systemic racism and sexism.[26]

To some extent, such a perspective depends on homological thinking,[27] or the perception of structural similarities among different strata of experiences or events: putting ketchup on an overdone steak—or on anything, really—is a culinary conformity commonly associated with children complying with the demands to "stop playing with your food" and "finish your plate."[28] The nutritional value of protein is both accepted and negated at the same time by recourse to a sugared hegemony (Mary Poppins approves!).[29] To couple racist, presidential policy to culinary infantilism is not so much a perspective by incongruity as it is an ontological equivocation; dressing dead meat is just another way of screening strange fruit. *Political Perversion* endeavors to elaborate, as opposed to alleviate, the indigestion that inevitably ensues.

AFTER THE AMUSE-BOUCHE (A THESIS)

Unquestionably, by the time readers finish sampling this introduction, the president of the United States will have vomited something more (ob)noxious than when starting. This is because, I will argue, Trump is perverse in a structural and uncommon sense, and as such his person betrays a *compulsive* need to violate perceived norms as a core component of his character. My moderate thesis is simply that Trump's public discourse represents *political perversion*, a composite style and genre of rhetoric that is not particular to Trump, just more conspicuous to us after his chaotic campaign and presidency began. While not unique to Trump, I suggest that just having a sense of the contours and commonplaces of the political perversion of his example will help us to grapple better with the political rhetoric of the past and future. Ultimately, however, my supersized speculation—more of a (hypo)thesis, really—is that we can most profitably read Trump's version of political perversion as an omen that "America" is becoming more generally perverse or culturally pyretic, rejecting the adage that you "can't always get what you want," as the Stones once sang, in favor of uncomfortably belting out Veruca Salt's demanding refrain in the first filmic version of *Willy Wonka and the Chocolate Factory*: "I want it now!" As an expression of US culture, the figure of Trump represents a more general decline of playfulness, creativity, and compromise and the ascent of a spiteful, scripted sentiment of demand in the popular imaginary. If perverse rhetorics are on the rise, I think cultural critics are obliged to better describe and understand their rhythms and influence.

Now, I stress that I do appreciate the commonplace connotations of perversity, and there may be politically or culturally strategic reasons to solicit them depending on the project—a point to which I will return in chapter 4. But, given the contradictions common perversion exposes in the context of racist and sexist cultural norms, the concept I mean to evoke most frequently is a psychoanalytic one that is more suggestive of a cultural structure or stylized habit for relating to others than it is a mere deviance. I should also be careful to underscore that I am less concerned with Trump's singularity than I am with what his figure represents and helps to organize for discussion: perversion understood as a structured *disavowal* of consensus reality at the core of a political ecology, which is both exacerbated and exposed by speakers, screens, and (communicative) speed. In addition to the deregulating arrhythmia of the 2016 presidential campaign, one can also smell political perversion cooking in the failures of environmental protections, "commonsense" gun control, and the successfully deceptive influence of "fake news," all of which will be taken up in subsequent chapters. The focus of the book, then, is not Trump. Rather, *Political Perversion* is an elaboration of, well, political perversion, a style and genre of perverse discourse in general, with the example of Trump and the rhetoric associated with his presidency in particular. Whether by term limits or impeachment, electile dysfunction or resignation, Trump will disappear from office—perhaps even before this book is published. *Political perversion will not.*

As the most conspicuous example of political perversion in our time, I will be arguing that the best label for the figure of Trump is "pervert." Numerous commentators, pundits, and scholars have been quick to describe Trump as a redneck, a demagogue, a fascist, and a psycho; however, *Political Perversion* advances the argument that such labels fail to stick, not because Trump shares Ronald Reagan's elusive "Teflon factor" but because these descriptions do not effectively identify the dynamic that animates him and fascinates us.[30] Trump evinces a *structure* of perversion that recalls a long-standing cultivation of certain modes of spectatorship, or culturally learned ways of "looking" at others, especially those of watching and listening to films, television programs, and various forms of Internet-based entertainment. Such a perspective may appear more cultural than clinical; however, from the Lacanian psychoanalytic vantage I adopt, these two actually start to look the same the more you keep staring. To a great extent, then, much of this study is an argument of definition, guided by the hope that once we name and describe the character of a person or event or a discourse, we are better able judge it, manage it, challenge it, and perhaps even change it. Thinking about how one should name and describe an object for critical insight is the task of methodology,[31] and so part of my project takes up the problem of how one does psychoanalytic rhetorical criticism, primarily by example but discussed most explicitly in chapter 1. (I note that readers relatively uninterested in the art of academic criticism and its challenges can skip the first chapter without missing the book's primary argument.)

To begin to state my case (file) here, however, I should first make good on the promise of the title by more directly defining rhetoric and perversion, explaining why popular perceptions of both are often but never wholly erroneous, moving toward an elaboration of my critical perspective and the anticipated overview of chapters.

RHETORIC

The study of rhetoric began over two thousand years ago and, at least in the West, was most famously and formally systematized as an academic subject by Aristotle. Today we call it "rhetorical studies" because its scope has expanded dramatically beyond any one approach. For the ancient Greeks, as an object "rhetoric" referred to persuasive oratory or speechmaking in community contexts: political fora, law courts, and celebrations like funerals or weddings. Aristotle preferred to think about rhetoric as the name of a body of study (akin to philosophy or biology), defining it as "an ability, in each [particular] case, to see [*theōrēsai*] the available means of persuasion."[32] In this sense, "rhetoric" is a word for *theories of persuasion* (to imagine or grasp the purpose of persuasion), which renders the term "rhetorical theory" somewhat redundant. Although since Aristotle's time definitions of rhetoric have proliferated and changed dramatically in ways that the ancients would hardly recognize, today scholars of the subject tend to think of rhetoric, first, as a theoretical enterprise that frequently derives its insights through the analysis or criticism of cases (that is, rhetoric is a "field") and, second, as something artful or expressive, a thing that is created or produced (e.g., literature, a presidential speech, Twitter melees, and so on). My approach participates in this two-rhetorics tradition, and contextual clues will help to indicate when I mean rhetoric *as a field of study* and rhetoric *as a thing produced*.

Speaking of things produced, the term "rhetoric" is used in popular discourse in frequently dismissive ways, often as a synonym for bullshit, as in the phrases "mere rhetoric" or "empty rhetoric."[33] The contemporary olfactory use of the term outside of academic circles is not without precedent—an ancient one, even. Aristotle defended rhetoric as an art and field of study that was amoral, much like the National Rifle Association defends guns ("Rhetoric doesn't harm people, bad people harm others with rhetoric"). This defense, however, is in some sense a patricidal gesture toward Aristotle's longtime mentor Plato, one of the earliest critics of studied oratory. It is likely Plato even coined the term "rhetoric" to refer to what he regarded as the immoral sophistry of his time.[34] In Plato's dialogue the *Gorgias*, for example, Socrates compares rhetoric to "cookery"—the equivalent of junk food—and observes that although some rhetoric might taste good, consuming it too readily or mindlessly could condemn your soul to an overweight hell of reincarnation.[35] Unlike the more vaunted value Plato accords "the true art of discourse" (by which he means dialectics), the analogy here is that political rhetoric is akin to the civics of a Big Mac or a bucket of KFC Popcorn Nuggets—or a stiff steak submerged in pickled fish sauce. As either a field or a thing, rhetoric has always been given, in one sense or another, a bad rap.

Like most rhetorical scholars, I understand rhetoric primarily to mean the study and theory of influence and secondarily discourse that moves people, sweet or stinky. Whether this influence is conscious or unconscious, I am particularly interested to understand influence as a modality of power in or across contexts of representation and, for lack of a better term, speech.[36] I share some of Plato's concerns about rhetoric as a technology of intemperance and deceit,[37] but we differ greatly regarding the power of the individual to control language. Social, political, and cultural influence today is not necessarily by the mouth or pen of a particular person; specific persons are to a large extent the playthings of language, broadly construed, a perspective that is often elabo-rated in respect to "the linguistic turn" or sometimes "posthumanism."[38] This is not to say that individuals cannot make decisions or judgments or do not have a degree of agency, only that the *meaning* of such is constrained by vo-cabularies and animated by structures of which we are only partially aware.[39] For me, a rhetorical approach to understanding culture attempts to limn the range of agency and various structures of influence through an analysis of the language-related forms, patterns, and textures that index them. For this reason, looking for ruptures or contradictions in discourse is commonplace in rhe-torical analysis, as these provide conspicuous inroads into the often ethereal undulations of the heretofore unnoticed or forgotten. But what is rhetorical analysis or criticism exactly, and where did it come from?

RHETORIC AND CULTURAL STUDIES

> Literary criticism, to survive, must abandon the universities, where "cultural criticism" is a triumphant beast not to be expelled. The anatomies issuing from the academies con-cern themselves with the intricate secrets of Victorian women's underwear and the nar-rative histories of the female bosom. Critical reading, the discipline of how to read and why, will survive in those solitary scholars, out in society, whose single candles Emerson prophesied and Wallace Stevens celebrated.
>
> HAROLD BLOOM[40]

In the academic humanities, both rhetorical and cultural studies have of-ten served as foils for more literary foci of criticism, particularly as criticism emerged and was disciplined in the private Ivy League universities. As a self-professed elitist, Bloom's regard for colleagues who study popular or "low" culture still reflects an entrenched class system particular to the humanities that few are willing to explicitly discuss (having a book published with Chi-cago or Oxford University Press, for example, is more "prestigious" than hav-ing one published by a land-grant public university press). The centuries-long bad rap the study and practice of rhetoric has received, as well as the more contemporary castigation of cultural studies, participates in this academic class hierarchy. Because *Political Perversion* is a critical study of culture with a particular attention to the persuasive dynamics of the popular, it is important to take a few pages to explain why I have nested the book in a particular way: the central kind of critical cookery practiced here is often termed "rhetorical" or "cultural criticism," today two different but often confused, promiscuous practices that draw from and build upon a number of traditions, especially philosophy. Rhetorical studies is typified by modes of interpretation, while many would argue cultural studies is driven toward contextual and ideological analyses (historically and sociologically especially). *Political Perversion* is uneasily situated between both interdisciplines because of their shared commitments and values, as opposed to objects or methods, and it is helpful to rehearse why this is the case (readers less concerned with academic disciplines can skip ahead to the "Perversion" section below).

Although origin narratives differ widely, rhetorical criticism is usually said to begin with the analysis of speeches and related forms of public address in the early twentieth century,[41] gradually changing out "speech criticism" for "rhetorical criticism" in the 1950s and '60s to better reflect the widened domain of objects studied as artifacts (at that time, various technologies and cultural shifts were challenging formal oratory as a primary means of influence, most especially television).[42] Despite the changing modalities of public address, many traditional, centuries-old coordinates of analysis animate rhetorical criticism: the organization and arrangement of discourse; the recurrence of patterns such as form and genre; ethical "proofs" and the use of evidence; speech styles and rhythms; the use of tropes like metaphor and metonymy; and so on. What's different today from the study of rhetoric in past centuries is that the object domain of the field is rather vast, including written or spoken speeches, of course, but also the "texts" appearing on various screens— even brain scans![43] Consequently, the coordinates of rhetorical criticism have expanded considerably to include the analysis of fantasy and ideology, the discursive modalities of power, critiques of race and gender dynamics, an attention to affect, and a litany of post-isms in ways that parallel cognate forms of criticism in the humanities in general. As it is commonly practiced today, rhetorical criticism is coherent as an approach to understanding and critiquing culture only insofar as it has an institutional history and commonly disciplined habits of reading; it no longer makes sense to say rhetorical criticism is understood by reference to a particular object or text.[44]

Although a survey of the history and habits of rhetorical studies as a field would provide the best understanding of rhetorical criticism for unfamiliar readers, it would be impossibly unwieldy. Rather than rehearse this history and these habits in detail, however, I gamble that a more economical approach can take a comparative peep at the complementary *institutional exigencies* of rhetorical and cultural studies. The origin narratives of these two "studies" fields differ as well, of course, but it's worth underscoring the common cause of rhetorical criticism and cultural studies and their convergences today, as theorists and critics from both traditions increasingly intermingle, sharing certain habits and attending the same house parties. That cause, I argue, is an interest in everyday and excluded persons, originally the "industrial classes" and their cultures and the political allegiances and tensions such an interest inevitably entails for the classroom and scholarship.

In the United States, what was to become rhetorical criticism was a pedagogical and scholarly practice that emerged in response to the birth of the public university and the new kind of college student that it produced. After the Civil War, the students coming to the new land- and sea-grant universities were not as literate as more privileged young persons heading to the Ivy Leagues, requiring the creation of less advanced textbooks and introductory courses that addressed basic writing and speaking needs. As the number of these skill-based courses increased, rhetoric, composition, and speech departments came to be (the latter evolved into speech communication and, finally, communication or communication studies). In order to defend their working with the public university student, as well as address the need to produce research for institutional legitimacy, early speech scholars in the 1920s, such as Herbert A. Wichelns, called for, and eventually established, the "literary criticism of oratory," a counterpart to the respected criticism of written literature that was already well established.[45] The initial argument for taking oratory seriously was that it was as aesthetically rich, if not more culturally influential, as literature, which are claims that would be repeated by David Bordwell and others decades later to justify film studies too.[46] Gradually, however, speech critics would succumb to the more widespread critique of the elitism of "great art" and the so-called Western canon, increasingly turning their attention away from "great speeches" to discourse of the popular, the political, and the everyday. Today, rhetorical critics continue to find interest in speeches (especially the presidential) but also in films, music, and other objects of quotidian culture, eschewing in some sense the "high culture" aspirations of more conservative and entrenched approaches in the humanities (particularly literary criticism).

Cultural studies have a similar origin narrative, albeit in postwar Britain, through its various attempts to teach nontraditional (or adult) students critical thinking through objects encountered in everyday life or mass culture (television, popular music, fashion, and so on). Many accounts identify Richard Hoggart's and Raymond Williams's work as providing the intellectual and political foundation of cultural studies, both of whom began turning their critical training toward objects of popular culture as a way of reaching and understanding their adult students.[47] With the assistance of Stuart Hall, Hoggart set up the Centre for Contemporary Cultural Studies at the University of Birmingham (the "Birmingham School") in 1964. Unlike the many communication studies established in the United States some thirty or forty years earlier in departments of English, journalism, and/or mass communications and speech, however, many scholars associated with the center designed their teaching and research to be explicitly *political*, an unusual position for many academic organizations at the time. Stateside, notable academic exceptions include Wilbur Schramm's Institute for Communications Research, established at the University of Illinois in 1947, which was organized to study the growing dominance of mass media and communication technologies in the postwar period, as well as the work and activism of various feminist, new left, and counterculture thinkers with no one disciplinary home.

If rhetorical scholarship can be said to begin with oratory and writing as its original critical object, in some sense the touchstone text for cultural studies was originally literature, but only because Hoggart and Williams were trained in this academic tradition and published their first works inside its frame. Hoggart's second book, however, is particularly concerned with the "massification" of UK culture and the eclipse of the kind of folk culture that is a consequence of face-to-face and hand-to-hand intercourse. The "drift" toward mass culture, for example, was reflected in junk periodicals and pulp stories (and eventually television) for Hoggart.[48] This deliberate break with a singular kind of critical object in the Birmingham School means that "cultural studies is not defined by a particular sort of text . . . nor can it be defined by a particular set of methods,"[49] observes Lawrence Grossberg, because the object of cultural studies "is always context."[50] Because culture is constantly reconfiguring, Grossberg argues that cultural studies on both continents had to—and must continue to—revolutionize themselves in response to sociocultural and economic changes, even though its institutional inspirations reflect "a particular commitment to a particular style of intellectual work."[51] That "style" has typically been more sociological and Marxist in orientation (and more recently, Deleuzian), expressing a commitment to the working class and marginalized peoples, a commitment continued by Grossberg and others who helped to introduce the Birmingham approach to communication studies in the United States—as well as the studies in media ecology coming down from Canada.[52] Today, many media and cultural studies scholars have joined rhetorical and communication scholars in the largest communication professional organization in the United States, the National Communication Association, perhaps a growing rapprochement signified by their (juke) joint journal, *Communication and Critical/Cultural Studies*.[53]

It goes without saying that in the United States there are other impactful critical and cultural studies traditions in comparative literature programs and departments of English and philosophy and so on, in particular, studies of contemporary objects and events as they intersect with continental theory (as represented, for example, in the work pursued in journals like *Critical Inquiry* and *Cultural Critique*). These critical and cultural studies, however, derive from the private university tradition and possess a more cultivated and literary character. Regardless, in our so-called digitized life, today many of us working in the critical humanities are increasingly writing, reading, teaching, and thinking in the same places and spaces as higher education continues to digitize, corporatize, and corral the liberal arts, making virtual spaces into computerized commons.[54] It's also unquestionably the case that rhetorical and cultural studies in the United States, while loosely intertwined institutionally,[55] are nevertheless methodologically diverse and marked by strong disagreements (e.g., the utility of dialectics or polemics, the role of the political in scholarship, the place of Althusser or psychoanalysis, and so on).[56] Nevertheless, rhetorical and cultural studies' approaches to communication and culture historically and institutionally begin with a commitment to the less advantaged student and by taking the objects of popular and everyday culture seriously. *Political Perversion* claims a common cause with both because it aims to analyze and clarify the (ob)scene of perversion, the political rhetoric of our contemporary conjuncture, which is anything but proper or respectable.

PERVERSION

Peek-a-boo! / I know what you do / 'cause I do it too.

DEVO[57]

Because the common conception of perversion is presumably profane and marked by an excess or violation (usually both), perverse rhetoric provides a conspicuous opening for inspecting the larger logics of the cultural influence it both disseminates and distorts. I opened with a rumination on junk food because its discourse is a fecund field of perverted fulsomeness, especially in contrast to its provenance: At the crest of processed foodstuffs and the emergence of the "industrial diet" at the turn of the twentieth century, Upton Sinclair published *The Jungle* in 1906, a scathing critique of the meatpacking industry that "signaled the generalized anxiety and distrust consumers had with food produced in anonymous places."[58] It is in the context of a general dis-ease over food sourcing in the United States that the pseudoscientific and quasi-religious character of convenient comestibles came to be: Grape-Nuts was originally marketed for mental (and masculine) well-being, "a food for brain and nerve centres" that was already "predigested" for easy, nutritional uptake.[59] Similarly, "Henry Heinz's religious convictions inspired him to construct purity as a moral imperative" for his products; Heinz's ketchup was marketed as wholesome and natural, and like all of the company's products, Heinz boasted its "preparation purity has always been the first consideration, and with it is combined the most rigid care and inspection of every department."[60] The purity rhetoric of mass-produced processed foods in the early twentieth century bears the trace of a popular obsession with "mental hygiene" and "social adjustment," which diverges significantly from the indulgent binge banter of our time.[61] Heinz originally marketed its ketchup as pure and healthy; by the 1980s the company was touting the ketchup's "thick and rich" superiority to competing runny brands.[62]

Over the twentieth century food marketing became increasingly thick and grandiloquent in the United States, creeping toward an immoderate ideology of conspicuous overconsumption and self-indulgence—including advertising urging the infelicitous use of ketchup on everything, of course, but also broadcasted banter beseeching benders with a bacterial bubbler that the chow-mart chain Golden Corral ballyhoos as the "Chocolate Wonderfall." (It is unclear whether the wonder is inspired by what is to be consumed or the speedy side effects of listeria.) As one would expect of bio- or necropolitical dynamics—we are unsure which—our ecology of consumptive enjoyment has been repelled by "obesity epidemic" jeremiads and pop soda bans, but apparently to little effect on the bottom line or waistline.[63] Although it is only a segment of the junk food industry, in the United States alone fast food franchises account for approximately $199 billion in revenue annually;[64] at the time of my writing, the industry is apparently "growing faster than the U.S. economy."[65] All of this is simply to say that, at least in the United States, we know very well some food is bad for us, but we eat it anyway because its influence—its physical *and symbolic* affect or force—seems to help us pilot the penumbra of personhood, at least temporarily. Junk food is pleasurable or exciting or intoxicating, at least until the first swallow. At least until the burps of shame come up.

The compulsive and often secret enjoyment of junk food can help us to understand better the perverse dimensions of rhetoric and the rhetorical dimensions of perversion, either coming or going, because of their mutual relation to, and cultivation of, the *appetites* Plato warned us about. As both Francis Bacon and Jacques Lacan observed,[66] left unchecked the "affections" or appetites—like these sentences—trend toward excess.[67] Despite a veritable c(l)ottage industry of *Supersize Me*-style condemnation, many of us in the United States continue enjoy mass-produced food that we *know* is unhealthy.[68] To ease the guilt of readers currently snacking, I offer a self-referential example: I often find myself in a local food chain, Torchy's Tacos, on a regular basis ordering a caloric catastrophe from the "secret menu": the Ace of Spades, a coma-inducing heavy-metal taco tribute to the late Motörhead luminary Lemmy, which includes a jalapeño sausage link, chopped brisket, green-chili queso, cotija cheese, sour cream, and a fried egg. Now, eating junk food might seem somewhat subversive within earshot of the liturgies of CrossFit cults, but the reality is that my enjoyment is in perfect compliance with the crushing demand of consumerism: *Enjoy, or else!*[69] I certainly enjoy the Ace of Spades despite my better judgment, despite the ensuing guilt, and despite a decade-long prescription for beta-adrenergic blocking agents—indeed, all the more so *because* of these. Popular pleas for a purity of provisioning persist only insofar as a public is concurrently pushed to "treat yo' self!" to the point of a nauseating nimiety.[70] (And then dieting.)

Moderation is a Janus-faced norm that invites its own violation by distraction. The ceaseless, almost obscene demand to "Enjoy!" and look the other way is richly represented in the 2015 merger of Kraft and Heinz into one of the largest crap food conglomerates in the world, the Kraft Heinz Company, bankrolled in part by that bastion of fiscal restraint and wisdom, that vaunted CEO of Berkshire Hathaway, Warren Buffet. Concerned that they were underperforming in the $7 billion frozen food market, Kraft Heinz crafted a new, somewhat upscale frozen food line called "Devour" targeted specifically for the twenty- to thirty-something bachelor market.[71] For its rollout, one of the first Devour television ads utilized popular perversion—an appeal to eroticized excess—in a salacious sales strategy. In the commercial, which I'll dub the "Auto Mechanic Dungeon," a twentysomething man in blue auto-mechanic garb stands in a break room holding a recently heated frozen meal in his left hand and a fork in his right. A sewn nametag tells us he is "Nelson." While Nelson delivers a dirty-talking monologue to his meal—a warped take on Prince Hamlet's soliloquy—a much older (noble)man named "Gus" catches him by surprise:

NELSON: Ummmmmm, Devour, say my name! I'm talking to you, creamy, white, cheddar mac and cheese with bacon. Can you feel it? You like that don't you? Oh, you taste so creamy! Lil' sounds your crispy bacon makes drive me crazy. Naughty little—*[smacks his meal with his fork]*
GUS: Did you just spank your lunch?
NELSON: *[sheepishly]* Yes.
GUS: Niiiiiice!

Jump cut to a series of frozen meals in a domino line; a seductive female phone-sex voice says, "Food you wanna fork!" as the same words appear on the screen in capital letters. "Introducing Devour," concludes an oversexed Ophelia.

In some ways the Devour commercial represents a triumph of Freud's arguments concerning the perversions. In Freud's time perversion was a term frequently used for characterizing homosexuality or gender nonconformity ("inversion") as unnatural and immoral, which Freud thought was terribly misguided and exposed private bedrooms to public life with the outmoded moral censure of religious illusion. The "extraordinarily wide dissemination of the perversions," observed Freud, "forces us to suppose that the disposition to perversions is itself of no great rarity but must form a part of what passes as the normal constitution."[72] Freud arrived at this conclusion because of his view that the objects of our compulsions, appetites, or simply "drives"—toys, food, body parts, and so on—were in some sense epiphenomenal as long as they continue to catalyze *and* moderate the drives' aims (usually satisfaction or death, whichever comes first). In regard to the sex drive, for example, Freud said that "all human beings are capable of making a homosexual object-choice and in fact have made one in their unconscious."[73] As we grow older, appropriate object choice is increasingly (en)forced by culture. For these reasons, to say that queer compulsions are morally or unnaturally perverse is to suggest the objects of the drives are somehow biologically or genetically *fixed*. Because so-called perversions are so widespread, however, Freud argued that this hard-wiring thesis gets it exactly backward, thereby rendering a default "constitution" of the human condition pathological (cf. the doctrine of "original sin"). To the contrary, everyone plays with their food, so to speak.

Although there is increasing evidence today that extra- or nonhuman animals experience affects and communicate in complex ways,[74] Freud's views on the symbol-using uniqueness of the human was typical of the humanist views his time.[75] Regardless, the startling claims Freud advances in his 1905 bombshell *Three Essays on the Theory of Sexuality* hinge on the fundamental role that human symbolicity plays in sexual development, including the organization of gender and sexual orientation.[76] Culture, first represented by a caregiver, regulates when our mouths can suck (either a breast or bottle or cigar will do, but only two will work long term) and the proper biphasing functioning of the anal sphincter (that is, potty training), which is to say "society" influences what objects *should be* chosen to satisfy a drive's aim. The gist is that there is no "normal," essential, gendered, sexual disposition: because humans engage in sexual behavior that is *not for the purpose of reproduction*, we are all perverse. For this reason, Gus commends Nelson's perverse food play as exemplary, a permissible excess of enjoyment that appears to champion Freud's views.

The commercial's commendation of a common or universal perversion, however, distorts Freud's argument on the side of heteronormativity. Freud's argument is more radical than is commonly supposed because it suggests that the default human condition is a sort of tangle of half-baked, "polymorphous" instincts that only find expression through symbolic mediation, thereby becoming what he termed the "drives" (*Triebe*). As Tim Dean and Christopher Lane observe, from this point of view "Freud was led to argue that human sexuality is constituted as perverse because it emerges in the drive's separation from natural functions [e.g., reproduction]. By defining the drive as unnatural, as operating *contra naturem*, Freud effectively 'queers' all sexuality."[77] The consequence, as Astrid Gessert puts it, is that one's sexuality progresses from a " 'homebase' of perversion in infancy toward 'normality,' not the other way round."[78] With regards to Simone de Beauvoir, one is not born but rather becomes a "normal." In the United States this has often meant getting straightened out in one way or another.

THE PERVERSION PICKLE

After the influence of Freud, by the end of the twentieth century common perversion paradoxically expanded to encompass the conventional: not only does perversion denote an act or behavior that violates or transgresses the presumed expectations or norms of a given culture, but also that *such violations and transgressions are to be expected.* This more permissive view of perversion is illustrated by the rather swift depathologization of queerness in 1973: the American Psychiatric Association ultimately removed "homosexuality" as a diagnosis from its internationally known and widely used *Diagnostic and Statistical Manual*,[79] an institutional power play that is no longer controversial among the medical or legal establishment but that has yet to achieve hegemony at the popular levels of government and culture. At least for the psychological, psychoanalytic, and psychiatric communities, queer desire is "normal."

It is still likely the case that most people do not subscribe to a belief in a universal perversity as Freud proposed. Today, however, there is nevertheless a pervasive and palpable permissibility for all sorts of perversions, particularly in popular entertainment. The decidedly sexual character of the Devour commercial certainly fits the bill, but so does the increasingly intense violence depicted in popular serial programs and cinema, such as the cheerful cannibalism depicted in the *Hannibal* franchise or even the smutty, sadomasochistic torture fantasies depicted in Mel Gibson's film *The Passion of the Christ*.[80] One could also argue that the emergence of rating systems for film, video games, and television programs are ultimately designed to index degrees of deviance, locating the enjoyment of exposure on an age-bound continuum beginning in youthful trauma and ending in adult fun.

There remain, of course, more extreme, unacceptable deviations from commonplace or assumed norms that we *judge* as pathological and/or criminal, such as incest. This "bad perversion" not only points up a problem with the ambiguities of the term "perversion" itself but also rehearses a well-known pickle that Freud fully acknowledged: as Gessert puts it, where perversion is concerned, "there exists an insoluble difficulty in drawing a sharp line between mere variations of sexual aims and pathological symptoms."[81] Freud's solution to the pickle was to suggest that clinical perversion is noted by the presence of "fixation," such that a pathological pervert is obsessed with a particular object that dominates their sexuality or life in such a way that it causes harm. An obsession with high-heel shoes, for example, is a fetish, but someone who can only get off in the presence of such shoes has a fixation that could result in hoarding or theft—or poking out someone's eye.

Of course, the fixation solution kicks the conceptual can into the juridical domain, still leaving us with the "conundrum that an exclusive fixation on heterosexual genital intercourse should also be considered as perverse," as Gessert, Dean, and Lane suggest.[82] In chorus with these scholars, James Penney opines that despite the radical clinical and moral reorientation his theories inspired, Freud was "unable to coin a satisfactory theoretical definition of perversion on the empirical level of the classification of sexual behavior."[83] As we will explore in subsequent chapters, a more satisfying solution to the problem of the continuum perversion is to distinguish between perverse structures and perverse behaviors or traits.[84]

For this introductory instant it is useful to consider how the state—by which I reference institutions that have the power to use force, including the health care industry, media corporations, and so on—determines pathology or criminality at the farther reaches of the perversity continuum. At least in the clinic, Freud's fixation solution worked for a while, which is ultimately reflected in the behavioral bent of North American professionals, relocating bad perversion at the horizon of criminality in terms of "paraphilia," presumably to get away from the moralistic history and connotations of "perversion." A diagnosis of paraphilia is focused on behavior, "and more specifically on that aspect of behavior that transgresses the *legal* norm" (my emphasis).[85] The shift to legality is a consequence of more catholic views of sexuality (or food play) in an "increasingly permissive society," as Paul Verhaeghe explains. Bad perversion is imagined as a fixation plot involving "the private norms of the (potentially short-lived) couple. 'The' norm then becomes the famous 'informed mutual consent': anything is permitted, on condition that the partners agree—penal law interferes little in private matters. As a result, the chief forms of perversion these days, practically the only ones left, are pedophilia and incest, followed by 'sexual harassment' in quick succession. This is because in such cases informed mutual consent is missing."[86] Punishable perversion differs from a permitted or common perversion because it concerns harm to another person without their conscious agreement. At the time of my writing, the most protrusive, juridical perversion in the news is that of Bill Cosby, the disgraced comedian and community activist convicted of sexually molesting a woman after drugging her senseless—and he is accused of doing the same to fifty-nine others.[87] Cosby's apparently decades-long fixation on drugging and molesting women veers toward the necrophilic; however, it is also demonstrative of a patriarchal sexual right over the bodies of women, a well-known and much studied *ideological* perversion structuring social relations in the United States, often described as "rape culture."[88]

At this juncture, then, we can distinguish among three categories of perversion plotted along Freud's postnatural continuum: a *common perversion*, which is universal and orbits permitted forms enjoyment, culturally cultivated and moderated; a *juridical perversion*, which is identified through fixation and the lack of mutual informed consent; and an *ideological perversion*, which concerns aberrations in the unspoken beliefs, attitudes, and values of a given community (e.g., misogyny). Although juridical perversion is most visible because it arrives most surprisingly as a violation of penal codes, it is not limited to the machinations of state institutions or governments, for we can think of laws and rules that may or may not be backed by state power (e.g., exogamy or marrying a cousin, unpunishable ethical violations, and so on). Whether state-enforced or culturally coerced, juridical perversion reflects generalized structures of socialization (e.g., the nuclear family and sexuality) and the law writ large, which Freud dedicated himself to describing over the course of his career, moving from the individual to the group and, in the end, civilization itself. As a kind conceptual threshold between the common and the ideological, juridical perversion proves to be the most visible rupture of expectation violation.

The Devour commercial helpfully illustrates all three forms perversion as well as their connectedness, albeit the common more clearly than the juridical and ideological. Or rather, I would argue that a presumably naughty "fun" of

F I G U R E 2. Screen shot from Devour television commercial. Gus spies Nelson "spanking" his macaroni.

common perversion *is made to run cover for a juridico-ideological perversion* that reinscribes heteronormative "laws."

First, Nelson's perverse behavior is seen as inconsequential by Gus because there is no moral censure (Nice!). The dirty talk and fork-spanking of food denotes something excessive yet enjoyable at some level; again, inasmuch as human sexual enjoyment exceeds the purpose of biological reproduction, devouring (or punishing) one's food is not for the purpose of nourishment. Playing with or worshiping your food is a well-recognized, infantile perversion heralded as "food porn" by grown-ups on the Intertubes; the term "porn" indexes this perverse dimension by virtue of its presumed incongruity with "food." Similarly, "binge" rhetoric, whether it concerns comestibles or the addictive streaming of Netflix shows, connotes a kind of permitted excessiveness or "guilty pleasure" common to North American culture. The presumed naughtiness of such excessive playfulness—be it fuzzy handcuffs in the bedroom or spanking one's macaroni and cheese—dialectically sustains an illusion of normalcy by virtue of its faux transgressions. The default condition of perversion, now more widely permitted, is still in the realm of common perversion, and it represents the success of Freud's intervention: perversion is no longer the signature of moral depravity that it once was, and it is certainly no longer articulated to LGBTQ persons. Perversion is for everyone!

The juridical and ideological perversion evinced by the commercial is more complicated and is presented as an informal pact—literally a verbal contract noted in the key of "Nice." No illegal act is performed, but the juridical is certainly in play: the recognition of "nice" intones, *"Although playing with your food is naughty, the Law permits it."* At this structural level, the relation between Gus and Nelson exemplifies what Freud advanced as the "Oedipus complex" or the Oedipal triangle, which I will dub simply as the "Oedipal relation" or "Oedipal" for short. As is commonly known, Freud's theory of sexual development concerns a young person's desire for the mother and a father figure's denial of that exclusive relation, usually with the threat of "castration," in effect laying down the law ("No! You cannot have mommy all to yourself!"). I will elaborate the Oedipal structure in the next chapter in more detail, but here it is important to underscore an acceptance of the paternal figure's denial entails a metaphorical substitution: the child, denied the love object of mother, is resigned to seeking out alternative love objects outside of the family structure. The Devour commercial restages an Oedipal contract between a father figure and a son over a substitute object. When caught by Gus, Nelson looks sheepish and guilty, fearing a paternal judgment over his choice. But the father approves! It's not a violation of his prohibitions! In this way, then, Nelson is happily confirmed in his perverse enjoyment and sustains his identity as master of his own object/food/lover. The mute third figure in this scenario, the macaroni, functions as the object of a contract between these two men. As is the case with most contracts, a third party must be excluded and silent.

Few products are actually advertised these days, as products function as substitutes for traits or lifestyles or some sort of object of identity: we know that selling beer is often about the promise of sex, and selling cars is often about the purchase of class mobility or gender identity (a feminine Kia versus, say, a masculine Ford F-150). Understanding the juridical pact of the commercial between the figures of father and son implicates the macaroni in an ideological scenario; the macaroni is *not* simply macaroni; it is a love object that forges a bond between men. Given the target demographic for the Kraft Heinz concoction, at one level the commonly perverse sexuality staged in a breakroom dungeon is a screen for the *ob*-scene desire of the "male" consumer for a father's approval in a context of an oppressive masculinity: Heinz Kraft is selling an alternative form of masculine approval. This tacit argument leads us to ask a rather ridiculous question: *Did the macaroni consent to being spanked?* The question of consent, and at another implied horizon, the question of *marriage*, underwrites the spot's intended, quasi-conscious appeal.

The ludicrous question of the macaroni's consent limns the horizon of the perverse ideology of the Sexual Contract elaborated by Pateman: in the West, the social contract advanced by Hobbes, Locke, and others historically excluded women, or rather, contracted over their bodies as property (e.g., the marriage contract, "Who gives this woman to this man?").[89] That the commercial is homosocial and explicitly about sex ("Food you wanna fork!") clues us into troublesome gender dynamics, rehearsing the logic of exchange or "trafficking" elaborated by Gayle Rubin in her landmark essay "The Traffic in Women: Notes on the 'Political Economy' of Sex." In her insightful reinterpretation of Freud, Lacan, Lévi-Strauss, Marx, and Mauss, Rubin argues a "sex/gender system" or economy has been established in which women are exchanged "as a fundamental principle of kinship."[90] Rubin argues that a concept of contractual exchange

> is attractive in that it places the oppression of women within social systems, rather than biology. Moreover, it suggests that we look for the ultimate locus of women's oppression within the traffic of women, rather than within traffic in merchandise. Women are given in marriage, taken in battle, exchanged for favors, sent as tribute, traded, bought, and sold. Far from being confined to the "primitive" world, these practices seem only to become more pronounced and commercialized in more "civilized" societies. Men are of course also trafficked—but as slaves, hustlers, athletic stars . . . rather than as men. Women are transacted as slaves, serfs, and prostitutes, but also simply as women.[91]

The Devour commercial figures such traffic, fittingly in an auto mechanics' garage: in its passive submission, the macaroni is a feminized object that becomes a vehicle of communication between men.[92] It doesn't matter if the punished pasta consents to forking; what's ultimately important in the diegetic scene is the kinship between father and son. In this way, the Devour commercial links up common, juridical, and ideological perversions in a thirty-second Oedipal tangle. Prima facie, the commercial appears perverse in the common, harmless sense, but only insofar as the sexist norms of US culture are foreclosed, disavowed, or repressed at the moment of their promotion: "I'm not sexist, but . . . nice!"

NEUROTICALLY YOURS, OR, LEADING FROM PSYCHOSIS TO PERVERSION

So far I have served up a perverse homology between contemporary junk food and the presidency of Trump, noting that the rhetoric orbiting both is conspicuous because of its compulsive and excessive character. I also described what I mean by rhetoric and perversion in a bit more detail. Rhetoric is primarily a field of study concerning theories of influence, especially in relation to language and speech, and secondarily a discourse produced. However, to make sense of the many ways "perversion" signifies everything from harmless fun to injurious meanness, I've had to distinguish among common, juridical, and ideological profiles to help detangle their complexity and to prepare the way for discussing structural perversities in the pages to come (particularly those intersecting with larger cultural cruelties regarding race, gender, and sexuality). Along the way, I hope I have provided a taste of the kind of critical cookery central to *Political Perversion* with the brief analysis of the Devour commercial: a media "text" with visual and aural qualities invites a theoretical perspective (in this case, queer/psychoanalytic theory) in order to advance a particular "reading." The reading is not definitive but one of many possible readings. For the purposes of this introduction, I am particularly interested in showing how the common perversion staged by the television commercial obscures a more insidious, juridico-ideological one (the Sexual Contract), as much of the analyses that follow concern similar or analogous misidentifications. The criticism is *rhetorical* because of its focus on the linguistic, iconic, or related representational textures of everyday life, as opposed to its siblings in art and literary criticism, which have been more traditionally conjoined with "high culture."[93] And as I discuss in the next chapter, the criticism is *psychoanalytic* in character because it reads the commercial for the intent of neither the producers nor the audiences but, rather, symptomatically as an expression of unconscious and semiconscious forms and structures that comprise or inhere in the popular imaginary.

I approach my theses regarding political perversion somewhat inductively, moving from a wider, more contextual view in chapter 2 to particular statements, events, and structures in chapters 3 and 4 and finally pull out for a more panoptic view of political dynamics *at play* in the conclusion; the conceptual structure of the book is meant to resemble the curves of an hourglass. This organization is inspired by the cabalistic or dialectical approaches ("As above, so below") advanced by the thought of pioneering media ecology materialists, particularly Walter Benjamin and Paul Virilio, implicating the important dynamic of *speed* and the fading of authorial force as technologically induced governing factors in Western culture, moving from mechanical reproduction (mass-produced food, serialization) to digital (re)production (real-time, circulatory logistics). As with many materialist approaches, I begin with the assumption that the basic arrangements of resources and power in a society influence, constrain, or produce (as opposed to wholly determine) cultural expression, including ideology and politics. If we are going to explain how a hyperactive Hierophant like Trump is possible at all, an account of rapid, technological change and the transformation of communicative networks seems crucial. Trump's style is so closely associated with Twitter, for example, that it is pivotal to ponder how the almost instantaneous, global reach of this contemporary mode of telegraphy has transformed how people in the United States interface with and modify their worlds. With the example of social networking, I suggest that our newfangled, networked environment has become characteristically *psychotic*.

Chapter 3 focuses on perversion as a style of public address enabled, constrained, and ultimately catalyzed by the increasingly psychotic environment described in chapter 2. A hypermediated habitat governed more by speed than reflection is productive of the demanding or righteously insistent citizen-spectator. Insofar as a demanding subject both knows *and* disavows an impulsive statement or deed is harmful to others, the subject is *structurally* perverse. Here I focus on Trump's rhetoric as an example of the perverse structure on two levels: first at the level of the statement or spoken discourse and second at the level of *style*, or how a rhetorical repertoire accrues and coheres through repeated statements that are both verbal (speech, tweets, tone) and visual (looks, body comportment, gesture, and so on). With reference to Tim Burton's 1985 classic *Pee-wee's Big Adventure*, I conclude by arguing that the perverse style is characterized not only by the mechanism of disavowal but also by the simultaneous invention of insatiable demands.

At least for me, the most theoretically challenging and difficult issues are consigned to chapter 4, which mediates the conceptions of genre and judgment with the help of psychoanalytic theory in a posthuman mood. It is also here the final, robust articulation of *political perversion* appears as a form of rhetoric that displays perverse behavior (statements, style) and structure (genre) in a remarkably coherent and homological manner. The largest question the chapter takes up is, *What does it mean to say Donald Trump is a pervert?* Here we must confront the perversion pickle again—the ethical dimension of perversion usually consigned to the penal—in relationship to critical protocols that resemble, more or less, the so-called Goldwater Rule established by the American Psychiatric Association in 1973: it is unprofessional and unethical to psychoanalyze public figures whom you have not analyzed personally. I challenge such restraint in *criticism* by arguing that this reticence is underwritten by romantic conceptions of autonomous personhood that we have long abandoned in the theoretical humanities (the *cogito*, the transcendental subject, and so on). The structures of neurosis, psychosis, and perversion adopted by subjects for a sense of identity inhere in *culture*, not individuals, which is why Trump is not simply a biological individual but a figural expression of US political/popular culture. To this end I examine how the cultural norms of disavowal and demand are baked into genres of spectatorship, particularly those of "reality television" and "fake news," the junk food of our so-called screened life. I argue that perverse genres have cultivated aggressive attitudes for apprehending others, including voting. I term one recent consequence of this cultivation the ironic or "Fuck it" electorate.

Building on the discussion of the emergence of an ironic electorate, I conclude *Political Perversion* by arguing that political perversion can be understood as a form of playfulness gone wrong, turning from my emphasis on Lacanian ideas to D. W. Winnicott's conceptions of play, object relations, and "transitional zones." In some sense, we can understand the 2016 presidential election as a kind of transitional zone–cum–video game in which voters exercised their right to blow up the system without regard to consequence—a kind of magical voluntarism, as if two lives still remain to play.[94] This right to destruction, I suggest, is eerily similar to the now all-too-common scripts of mass shootings and suicide bombings. As a concept, play is typically understood as a creative activity in which people engage one another to test, negotiate, and establish boundaries. Play is perverted, however, when boundaries become rigid and creativity is exchanged for order and the demand for others to "play by the rules." Political perversion is gleaned when perverse behaviors and structures seem to coincide in a particular figure or discourse, but often in the context of a mood or affective mist that smells like play gone bad, a fulsome, bovine bouquet of bitter char and sweet pickles.

CHAPTER 1

On Critical Violence

Because in Deconstruction there is always a disparity between the conscious intention of the author and the actual function of the text, a text is like Frankenstein's monster: it acquires a life of its own that is, from the standpoint of its creator, both independent and malevolent. . . . Deconstruction has so corrosive a view of language that its own survival is a continual embarrassment.

EDWIN BLACK[1]

A new light seemed to dawn upon my mind; and, bounding with joy, I communicated my discovery to my father. My father . . . said, "Ah, Cornelius Agrippa! My dear Victor, do not waste your time upon this; it is sad trash."

MARY SHELLEY[2]

Even the most dismissive gesture betokens a body. As a craft or producerly art (*tekhnē*), Fredrich Nietzsche taught us that the stuff of rhetoric is gestural and rhythmic, a bodily act, a kind of singing and dancing that is perhaps most familiar to us as music or poesy.[3] But the ancients also taught us that persuasive speech is not only to be understood as bodied forth because it also sends forth bodies, like so many lovely lips setting off a thousand scripts. Or as Steven Conner puts it, "What I say goes."[4] Since the arrival of semiotics and (post) structuralism, Derrida and de Man, and an attitude that displaces the human as "the" center of the wor(l)d, many scholars have argued that rhetoric deconstructs and constitutes bodies,[5] that it has an agency of its own,[6] and that it is even more monstrous (or angelic) than Black bemoaned.

What they said, went: the holy Saint(s) John once evangelized that the ultimate, über-form of rhetoric unleashed is the "word made flesh" (which some pious liberals deign to eat, by the way, perversely perpetuating a predestined reappearance of both).[7] It is tempting to homilize, then, that criticism is "flesh made word," an alchemical transfiguration of bloodletting and sensation into tropes and logic and generic patterns, a persuasion of amputation that inspires the idealism of pragmatic prostheses and the cocky swaggering of high-theory strap-ons. As Roland Barthes once cautioned, however, when attempting to make sense of music we are most often condemned to "the poorest of linguistic categories: the adjective."[8] Perhaps it is because of the adjectival anemia of translation between modes,[9] or what Nietzsche dubbed the forgetful abstractions of sensation in terms of "first" and "second metaphor,"[10] that one mode or another is inevitably deported.[11] As the simultaneous study of feelings and language signified by "speech," at least in its Coca-Cola Classic formulation, rhetoric has typically concerned itself, in one way or another, with the disposal of bodies.

In the twentieth century, one of the more notable dispositions gestures toward a kind of precision regarding body parts, a willful rigor (mortis) toward a corpus that was eventually christened "method." The promise of teaching a method of critical composition is an old one, most familiar to us today in textbooks (which have also been critiqued since the time of Isocrates and Plato).[12] Pace Black, however, by way of a vivi(secte)d analogy I want to begin the discussion of cultural and rhetorical criticism with a decomposing allegory for a disciplined default toward the critical act and its object, albeit in a more patently perverse deportment. Had I the space and patience, I would describe two visual allegories, first from Peter Greenaway's renowned 1996 film, *The Pillow Book*, which depicts an obsession with the painted body and the sensuous pleasures of cross-cultural gestures, aggressive and beautiful. As is typical of a Freudian, though, I prefer to focus on the grotesque counterpoint for em-*fah*-sis: if we've learned anything from Nixon and the dawning of the Age of Aquarius, pathology is the place where the sun shines in (. . . or out of our behinds, as one Morrissey put it).[13]

My interest here is an obdurately offensive and gut-bustingly gruesome autopsy scene in a different Morrissey's infamous 1973 B movie, the 3-D schlockfest *Flesh for Frankenstein*. Whereas *The Pillow Book* explores cross-cultural interpretation through the gentle caress of bodily calligraphy, Paul Morrissey's *Flesh* binds bodies for a master, leaving them like (or for) the living dead. Erroneously marketed as *Andy Warhol's Flesh for Frankenstein* (Warhol had nothing to do with the film except for his imprimatur), Morrissey's comedic take on Shelley's classic is a ham-handed critique of the ideologies of racial purity and eugenics as well as the excesses of commercial romanticism. The film depicts the sexually repressed but ambitious Baron Frankenstein and the hedonistic exploits of his insatiable sister *and* spouse, Baroness Katrin Frankenstein.[14] Driven by a maniacal compulsion to build two "perfect" zombies to breed a superior race in his name, the baron sews together the most attractive body parts of multiple cadavers while, nevertheless, expressing a glassy-eyed detachment from his own compulsions. For the baron, sexual pleasures have nothing to do with the inner life of others. Over the course of the film

FIGURE 3. Baron Frankenstein inspects the organs of a cadaver with his hands as his assistant Otto looks on in jealousy in *Flesh for Frankenstein* (1974).

Frankenstein is obsessed with body parts for the assembly of slaves who never quite unify into whole persons, even after all that needlework. The baron's parade of frustrations serves as an amusing illustration of Hegel's sketch of the control freak: mastery is an administrative achievement that depends on the recognition of slaves who, by condition and definition, cannot give it (Bad infinity! Bad!).[15] And besides, the baron's male monster prefers the stable boy anyway.[16]

In an incisive scene, the baron begins to open the abdomen of a (supposedly dead) nude woman to inspect her internal organs. As the baron is preparing the body and snipping stitches, his assistant Otto looks on in a bemused jealously. Once the viscera are properly ventilated with a crack of the sternum, the baron slips his hands inside, feeling and squeezing and naming the organs:

BARON: Beautiful, we are very fortunate to find such a perfect torso in one piece! . . . Ready?

OTTO: *[nods yes]*

BARON: I go into her digestive parts. *[snips sutures, blood gushes]*

OTTO: *[stares and wipes the baron's forehead with gauze]*

FEMALE CADAVER: *[opens her eyes, revealing she is really not dead]*

BARON: Separate! *[crunchy noise]* Spleen. *[heavy breathing]* Kidneys. *[heavy breathing]* Gall bladder! Liver! *[pulls out the liver and caresses it]* Umm. Umm. Umm.

As the baron plays (with) her organs, he appears to climax in a surprisingly clean head shot (we only see an ecstatic face). Soon thereafter Frankenstein molests his now completely assembled zombie again with his forearm in her chest cavity, and, having climaxed a second time, proclaims triumphantly, "To know death, Otto, you have to fuck life in the gallbladder." Morrissey later admitted that such a shocking line was a critique of Bernardo Bertolucci's *Last Tango in Paris* as a soap opera dressed up in pretentious aesthetic clichés, especially Marlon Brando's notorious line—delivered in histrionic righteousness—that one "won't be able to be free of that feeling of being alone until you look death right in the face. . . . Until you go right up into the ass of death—right up his ass—till you find a womb of fear."[17] At one level, *Flesh for Frankenstein* is intended as an indictment of the patriarchal sex right asserted by Brando in *Last Tango*, or what has come to be known today as "rape culture."[18]

The galling gall bladder scene and statement is pivotal because of a gag at the film's end, in which Otto also assaults the mother—I mean monster— and accidentally kills her, a violation of the baron's paternal authority and the necrophilic primal scene he sought to superintend. As in many of Morrissey's films, this queering of the hetero-Oedipal is quite deliberate, particularly with its critique of straight sexual hypocrisy through grotesque amplification (gore *is* porn *is* gore). In *Flesh*, this critique aims at the perversion of commercialism in respect to the fetishization of parts at the expense of whole persons: in the autopsy scene the exposed breasts of the cadaver are given excessive screen time and squeezed and massaged in blood; less conventionally, so is the liver and gall bladder! Nevertheless, the Other to impress here seems to be Otto, and he, in turn, runs cover for the Other at large.

Because of the baron's fetishization of the cadaver's "parts" (Frankenstein only sees the woman's whole body as a "torso"), as well has his feverish, melodramatic, and humorless dialogue about the beauty of bowels, the autopsy scene in *Flesh* helps to make clearer a structural dynamic long identified as a conceit of literary and rhetorical criticism: not only can a body be read as a text, but also the text or object of analysis is often regarded as a body to be caressed, penetrated, and sometimes violated for another to witness.[19] In other words, conscious or unconscious, for the critic the object of criticism represents another person. And at an ideological remove, the history of criticism suggests that its circulation can be read as a kind of trafficking in the feminine whereby critics communicate *with* each other, and *to* their students or reading publics, with the vehicle of the presumably passive object of discussion (e.g., the maltreated macaroni discussed in the introduction).

At a formal level, suggesting that criticism is a kind of Oedipal relation rests on a "thirdness," or the assumption of some gazing Other (readers, audiences, other critics, the "discipline," and so on) that bisects or mediates the relation between critic and object.[20] Criticism, in other words, is irrevocably a triangular relation of power and usually just as much about the folks writing and reading it as the object studied. As an allegory for the erotics of the critical act, I want to suggest that Baron Frankenstein's disgusting deviance in the filmic diegesis issues an allegorical warning about the excesses of fixation and the violence particular to the critical act: approaching an object or text too surgically, too methodically, eviscerates it, amputates it and disarticulates the whole into something offal. Whenever one is called to precision or "rigor" in analysis, the breaking down of things at their "joints," as Plato explained,[21] we are also enjoined toward a kind of critical listening before disassembly.[22] Only then does one typically resort to the counterpart of writing or the re-membering of criticism ("synthesis") and making of judgments. One of the tasks in this chapter is to describe how a kind of critical cutting has come to cut out listening and tonal affections, or how the Catholic Ear has been replaced by the Surgical Eye as a contemporary analytical protocol for rhetorical studies. Initially, the move toward the burdens of close reading and empirical verification was, more or less, honorable: to avoid hearing what one wants to hear, to keep the projection of interpretation at bay, and to liberate the text or object from critical autobiography or "reporting the state of [the critic's] glands," as Black once put it.[23] Yet moving toward models of empirical verification goes astray when the need for an *appearance* of objective assessment eclipses feelings and aesthetic or ethical judgments or when the literal and figurative counting of words occludes the passions that the ancient pioneers of Western rhetoric were so interested to explain.[24]

I do not mean to critique content or discourse analysis or the methods of social science; a multiplicity of approaches to studying social behaviors, cultural events and things, and speech phenomena helps us to ask a multitude of questions. On one foot, my concern is the deliberate inattention to bodies in feeling and the psyche, particularly in rhetorical criticism since the hegemony of behaviorism (a problem that cultural studies has deftly avoided, perhaps owing to its origins across the pond). Such inattention is why, for example, scholars of political communication and political science alike were at a loss to explain the 2016 presidential election: compulsory behaviorism catalyzed by the fumes of rational choice slowed the refinement of critical vocabularies for thinking and writing about the kinds of feelings that upset the certitude of instruments founded on calculable reason and The Number.[25] Consequently,

I opened this chapter deliberately obliquely to provoke a weird mood, and this to underscore the trouble with reckoning with bodies in feeling in writing; affected bodies inspire an often uncomfortable trouble, which is precisely what makes the appeal to objectivity and the machineries of verification, as well as the demand for a certain, abstinent humorlessness, so powerfully *relieving*.[26]

On the other foot, however, we know that influence or identification among humans (and perhaps other animals and forms of vegetal life) concerns representations or translations between modes of communication and bodies in feeling, and yet the only modes that seem adequate are aesthetic—dance, music, poetics, performance, performative writing, and so on—or crafts that open themselves to expression that seem to gesture beyond representation. We know, in other words, writing about the body and affect unavoidably misses or excludes *in other words*. In the critical humanities we have certainly made much progress in pushing criticism across the threshold of the calculable, especially over the limit of the anagogic appeal of numbers and what a dean or nonacademic public would find as fundable (or fungible) knowledge. For decades scholars have been working to get beyond the empirical imperative of reducing tone to figure, especially with the newer modes of critical insight advanced by cultural and performance studies scholars,[27] the reintroduction affect studies,[28] the poetic modes of working through public feelings,[29] newer materialisms,[30] the queering of rhetorical criticism,[31] and so on. Joining these transrational, body- and feeling-interested perspectives, I am delighted by a renewed interest in returning to one of the earlier approaches to interpretation that took feelings and affect seriously: psychoanalysis.[32] My ultimate goal in this chapter is to suggest that psychoanalytic approaches are more elastic and creative, certainly less systematic, than many less familiar with the perspective have been taught, and that its varied vocabulary and perspectives help to toggle between bodies in feeling and their representation (usually in terms of language). Methodologically speaking, then, the foil here is not method in the general sense, understood as an approach or a scheme, but rather, method as an ossified concept that constrains the critic to a definitive account in the service of some demonstrable mastery. Counterintuitively to some, a psychoanalytic approach to criticism seeks to moderate or challenge the virtuosity and tacit universality that has long been the crux of the critical act.[33]

DE-RIGOROUS DISCIPLINE

Michel Foucault once defined discipline as "a policy of coercions that act upon the body, a calculated manipulation of elements, gestures, and behavior."[34]

Even if we are wary of compulsive or scripted gestures of intellectual propriety, such as the false certitudes ballyhooed as "rigor" or "nuance," I am taxed with rehearsing the discipline of a related but more provincial sort: the schooling, policies, and tribal allegiances of criticism, which I suggest demonstrate how a scientific pretense has led to a fetishization of method, shoring up a sense of disciplinary mastery and the inevitable imposter syndromes that result. Just taking rhetorical studies as a primary example, I have implicitly deployed four objects, four practices that orbit them, and a term for their arrangement. The objects are the ear, the eye, the mouth, and the hand. The practices are listening, watching, speaking, and writing. And I will suggest the particular or unique manner in which these objects and their practices are coordinated is an academic discipline.

Although the techniques of cultural and rhetorical criticism that emerged in the twentieth century owed a debt to formalism and New Criticism, in the postwar period a notable disinterest in affect, bodies, and emotions, pushed in some sense by discoveries of the atrocities and psychological experiments of the Nazis, was notable in a shift toward principles and metaprinciples, rationality, and a generalized outbreak of what I call "model madness."[35] In place of lyrical appreciation and aesthetic rumination, budding critics in US speech or communication studies were taught that a "dispassionate, objective attitude toward the [critical] object" was required, and this was based on "a certain universality of mind."[36] The introduction of a species of humorlessness was the hallmark of the methodizing of criticism, so that "unsupported individual preference moves toward rationally defined and systematically determined choice."[37] Even when the differences between the perspectives and functions of the humanities and sciences were acknowledged, critics were urged to emulate the sober stereotype of the scientist. As Black put it, although "we have not obtained in criticism the exactness of chemistry or physics . . . we seek in criticism to be as exact as our subject will permit, and the highest attainments of science can remain for the critics, if not models to be copied, then at least achievements to be emulated."[38] The image of thought guiding both criticism and pedagogy midcentury was one of efficiency and precision, gradually congealing into a "rhetorical method" that begins with "description," proceeds to "context" (historical or otherwise), then brings a "theory" to bear upon the object and, finally, makes a judgment or evaluation about it.[39] To wit: across the twentieth century rhetorical criticism got anal.

The word "precision" is derived from the Latin *praecīsiō*, "act of cutting off" or of "breaking off (in speech)," and "in post-classical Latin, 'schism.'"[40] Precision is consequently a term of art for *both* surgery and speech, connoting a separation of bodies as with, for example, the slicing off of a mole or the amputation of a redundant paragraph. There is something oxymoronic, or at least at odds, though, in the term "gesture of precision," since it denotes something bodily or embodied on the one hand, but a separation of bodies on the other; depending on one's stance on dualism, something presumed to be whole becomes multiple, or something presumed whole is revealed to have been "always already" multiple.

While contemplating the early modes of cinema, Walter Benjamin addressed the critical gesture of precision in aesthetic technique and cultural critique by contrasting the surgeon with the magician:

> The attitude of the magician, who heals a sick person by a laying-on of hands, differs from that of the surgeon, who makes an intervention in the patient. The magician maintains the natural distance between himself and the person treated; more precisely, he reduces it slightly by laying on his hands, but increases it greatly by his authority. The surgeon does exactly the reverse; he greatly diminishes the distance from the patient by penetrating the patient's body, and increases it only slightly by the caution with which his hand moves among the organs. In short: unlike the magician . . . the surgeon abstains at the decisive moment from confronting his patient person to person; instead, he penetrates the patient by operating.[41]

Such ambivalence addressing bodies is, in the last instance, always about the bodies of an other, often a significant one (an Other with a capital *O*). The critical act, from the ancients to the German Romantics to the New Critics, must contend with bodies, often diagnosing the condition of the corpus as a state of the word or number instead of the world. Bodies are arrayed before the critic on a table that at one end portends a massage and at the other end a dissection. The trick or procedure is somehow to do both (dialectically), but inevitably critics find themselves Rolfing or cutting at one end of the table or the other.

By suggesting that rhetoric is bodily, criticism is sometimes perceived as a kind faith healing in its most laudatory or "appreciation" modes, but today it is most often experienced as variation of amputation and the fashioning of critical prostheses (a genre, a theory, a model, and so on). The critical act disembodies and disfigures, inasmuch as a body of speech has given its vocalization or inscriptions over to the signifier and an encounter with meaning. In this respect, like *Flesh for Frankenstein*, a seemingly random medical image of a child who has inserted a foreign object into their ear is also an overdetermined exemplar of *precision*: the visage of a child with a pencil piercing her ear canal is eerily

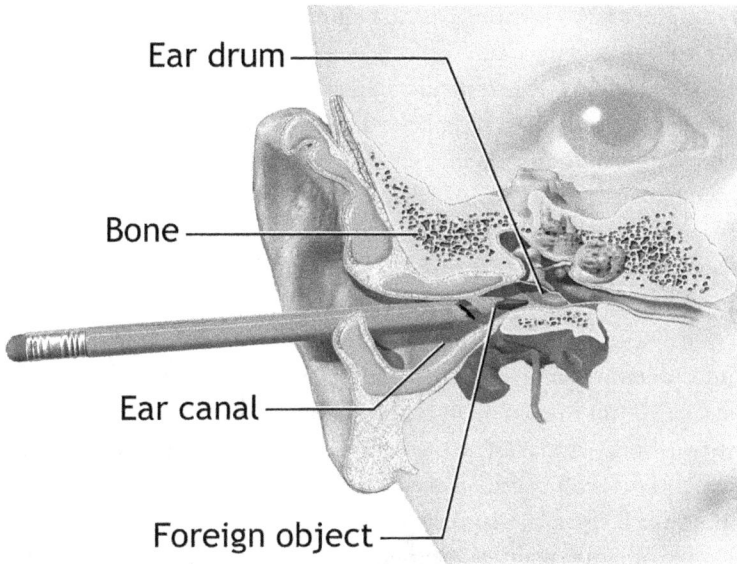

FIGURE 4. Foreign object in child's ear. Medical illustration courtesy of A.D.A.M.

serene. Why is there no crying? Anyone who has spent time with a child knows that such a scene would provoke the tears of trauma. The illustration is for medical education, available to health care professionals for a modest fee, and is the first of a series that instructs professionals how to remove a foreign body from the ear canal. The calm and open face of the babe is strikingly strange, perhaps even a bit painful to look at (How did the pencil get in there? Why did it break off? Why are they so calm?). Reading against the brain, the image stages an amputation not only because it trades out what should be a turbulent toddler with a placid prepubescent; the image also betrays the unwitting conflation of hearing and writing, the fusion of speech and the hand-held implement. The deposit in the ear canal is a leaden body, something like a dead weight, a sharp but nevertheless lifeless point—"What I say, breaks"—which is the fate of a cool and detached criticism, a body lost in translation, "mere rhetoric," an abortion in the ear canal, a published monograph unread and DOA.[42]

As a midcentury advocate of critical precision, the renowned rhetorical theorist and critic with whom I began, Edwin Black, dismissed deconstruction as monstrous, which is odd, at least insofar as many in the theoretical humanities would say that the impossibility of closure or definitive interpretation is part of the reading protocol Jacques Derrida showed us was (always) already at work: the illustration of the child with a pencil in her ear seems dreadful at first glance, but it also denotes the difficulty of distinguishing writing from speech, because these share the traces and marks of inscription, scars of an intercourse between the inside and outside that challenge the discreteness of persons, of subjects and objects, and the kind of mastery that would anchor a critic on *this side* of the subject (where reflection happens in script). In other words, the monster was already loose. The drive to listen, or the invocatory drive, takes "voice" as its object, which, of course, can be written and seen and touched. Still, the weirdness of the medical image is nevertheless the place of criticism, open to interpretation, endless interpretation, and this need not be received as monstrous, an all-too-human habit.[43] My gambit with these creepy cases—the gruesome twosome—is that an incongruity between cinematic sleaze or medical imagery and the craft of criticism condenses the tension many cultural and rhetorical critics face on the contemporary academic scene: making writing about the unavoidably qualitative experience of feelings and culture register in meaning without killing them.

I have been suggesting, then, that if there is a specter haunting the critical craft today, it is (im)precisely the false supposition of an apostolic reversal: that critical reading or analysis is the translation of the flesh into word or, to put this alternatively, to "read" properly a corpus into meaning by identifying a quantifiable body or replicable chalk outline, leaving the organic or original for dead ("Gall bladder!"). Such abstracting is the province of religion too, of course, or at least what happens once this mortal coil is shuffled off on the way back to the dreaded "womb of fear." The body left for dead in our erudite necropolis is more properly the province of scientific knowledge, or what Aristotle termed *epistēmē*, presumably in contrast to the illusionism of storytelling and witnessing, of the sorcery of the arts, and the practical wisdom of a craft.[44]

With the onset of structuralism, phenomenology, post-Freudian psychoanalysis, and other methodologies of systemization in the mid-twentieth century, the humanities trended toward the human sciences in a way that abandoned feelings in favor of an evenhanded, nonpartisan textual flogging (at least death is objective and you can count [on] it).[45] This is to say that much has changed in the critical humanities since Benjamin's day.[46] As Black lamented, at least by the 1960s, "The scientist is one of the cultural heroes of our age," creating a number of problems for the cultural critic. Science has

become, at least to the public at large, the model for intellectual activity, but on the whole the influence of scientific method on criticism has probably been wholesome. If nothing else, this influence has tended to make modern critics especially conscious of their methods. It has encouraged critics to become systematic, to objectify their modes of inquiry, and to restrict themselves to demonstrable, or at least arguable, generalizations. Thus, the modern critic has assumed the burden not only of understanding and evaluating the products of human effort, but also of defining and delimiting the nature of his own criticism.[47]

In retrospect, the charity of describing a wholesome influence is somewhat of a misstep, and the characterization of rhetorical criticism (or cultural criticism) as a "method" requiring justification or readerly replication is a well-intended mistake. Pursued appropriately, with peer review and a transparent use of data, the scientific method is measured in many senses and has unquestionably led to knowledge that has diminished human suffering. But the sciences comprise a number of discrete categories that eschew many of the passionate questions and values rhetorical and cultural critics would like to answer and critique; these cannot be operationalized, and sometimes the answers or evaluations cannot be said. In this context, inducing a yearning for verifiability or objectivity in the cultural critic tempts transforming her into a critical Dr. Frankenstein, the consequence of an intercourse between Cornelius Agrippa and Luigi Galvani that doesn't end particularly well. But Freud argued that there is another way, and it finds inspiration in the interpretation of dreams.

WHENCE PSYCHOANALYSIS?

There is no question Sigmund Freud originally advanced psychoanalysis as a scientific pursuit, and the "science" of psychoanalysis remains a contentious topic.[48] Yet in the September of his years, Freud turned to the analysis of culture in a way that is much closer to literary and cultural criticism than his earliest work, and by most accounts, it is in this spirit that psychoanalysis entered the humanities. In the United States, psychoanalysis was incorporated into the criticism of the (supposedly) best aesthetic expression a given culture had to offer: literature. Freud himself was fond of literary examples in his own work; however, psychoanalytic criticism first got its start with critical readings of Henry James's masterfully convoluted ghost story, *The Turn of the Screw*.[49] Although Freud-ish readings of the novel appeared as early as 1924,[50] Edmund Wilson is credited with popularizing psychoanalytic criticism in his 1934 essay "The Ambiguity of Henry James."[51] Wilson dared to suggest that the protagonist of James's story was neurotic and that the ghosts she experienced were in fact stirrings of the unconscious. While controversy over Wilson's Freud-filled interpretation has raged for decades, the essay's publication marked the moment when psychoanalysis became a perspective or way of "reading culture" in the academic humanities.

So why was psychoanalysis taken up? For some, the appeal was its early scientism (what is called "ego psychology"), which fed into therapeutic impulses and a general push toward "adjustment."[52] In the humanities, however, the motive has more to do with Freud's reading protocols, which he introduced in his massive, continuously revised dream book first published in 1900. In *The Interpretation of Dreams* Freud argued that dreams were akin to a rebus or picture puzzle that should be analyzed as a kind of evasion, or more specifically, dreams were code for condensations and displacements of wishes in disguise.[53] In waking life such wishes are repressed, but in dreams they find temporary expression in oblique representations unique to a dreamer's culture and experiences. Freud argued that the dream encyclopedias and dictionaries popular in his time and ours—that perennial pulp on "sale" tables in bookstore chains—are compendiums of misleading correspondences that fail to take into account the role of the dynamic unconscious;[54] only sustained and time-consuming analyses of one's dreams with a therapist can begin to reveal the contours of unconscious wishes. What is at stake in Freud's analytical protocol is actually not the dream itself but how one describes and redescribes it; Freud is after what a description of a dream—or art, or other kinds of imagery—says about one's unconscious investments. This analytic protocol is consequently doubtful and cautious, participating in what philosopher Paul Ricoeur termed a "hermeneutics of suspicion."[55]

Ever since Wilson published his suspicions about James's ghost story, many scholars in the humanities have found Freud's method of analysis useful for reading culture. Many principles and concepts from psychoanalysis have subsequently been taken up in the humanities (the unconscious, defense mechanisms, the Oedipal complex, and so on), but perhaps none more deeply than suspicious reading, especially in cultural, literary, media, and rhetorical criticism. For example, few of us are free from cultural commentators who claim we should not be worried about violence in Hollywood films: after all, it's just entertainment! Freud had a profound effect on the academy if only because those of us who study popular culture begin with the commonplace of suspicion: no, it's *never* just entertainment. We don't care what Freud once said, a cigar is *never* just a cigar! If all structural or formal characteristics of a "text," be it a dream or a film or a tweet, were wholly conscious, there would be no role for criticism in the first place.

Still, as with any figure who has inspired powerful protocols of interpretation—from Kenneth Burke to B. F. Skinner—psychoanalysis has taken
on the trappings of a cult for many.[56] No doubt the perception of a Freudian
cultism is partly to blame for the dismissal of psychoanalysis; however, there
are other common arguments:

- Psychoanalysis is fundamentally Freudian, and Freud has been discredited
  by the scientific community; because his ideas have been disproven, psychoanalytic criticism is without value.
- Freud was a sexist, and therefore psychoanalytic criticism is sexist.
- Criticism is a political endeavor, and psychoanalysis is apolitical.
- Psychoanalysis is practiced with individuals in a clinical setting, but criticism is a cultural endeavor. Psychoanalysis fails to address the social or the
  group.

There are, of course, other arguments against the use of psychoanalysis in
criticism; the above have come, more or less, directly from blind reviews of
psychoanalytically themed essays I have tried to publish. I suspect most readers are familiar with these objections and can anticipate responses, so I won't
belabor them except for the last: that psychoanalysis is keyed to the individual
psyche, while literary, cultural, or rhetorical criticism is keyed to the social or
the group.

Not surprisingly, Freud recognized this problem too, which is why he
published his study *Group Psychology and the Analysis of the Ego* in 1922[57]
and subsequently a number of theoretical studies, such as *The Future of an
Illusion* in 1927 and *Civilization and Its Discontents* in 1930.[58] In the 1920s,
Freud gradually turned his thinking toward what I would term cultural studies, suggesting that one could analyze the group and social trends much as
one would an individual. In the growing shadow of a mounting Nazism, by
the 1930s Freud would have argued that individuals could function as cultural
superegos, temporarily suspending inhibitions with the will of a master.[59] It is
difficult to engage Freud's later writings and conclude that the psychoanalytic
enterprise is apolitical.

Nevertheless, my point here is that psychoanalysis did hit something of a
snag among cultural critics, especially in the fields of communication and cultural studies, because many could not envision how the clinical experience of
an individual in therapy translates to social movements and cultural events.
How do the dynamics of individual therapy translate to the group—to auditors
or readers or audiences? And the question is profitably asked the other way

too: How does the individual psyche reckon with the political? It is at the juncture of these kinds of questions that the thought of a number of post-Freudian scholars—Melanie Klein, Jacques Lacan, and D. W. Winnicott especially—was taken up in the academic humanities. It was also at the meeting place of these types of questions that a profoundly influential group of thinkers emerged who sought to wed philosophy, psychoanalytic interpretation, and political science into a critique of authoritarianism and popular culture: the Frankfurt School.

FRANKFURTERING THE SYMPTOM

One of the primary reasons Freud's work was taken up in the humanities is because of his elegant approaches to interpretation, which suggest, like a dream, that a cultural object such as literature should not be "read" at face value but rather "translated" in respect to a variety of contexts (individual, historic, linguistic, and so on). So far, my example analyses of the Devour commercial in the introduction and *Flesh for Frankenstein* and medical imagery here are commonly perverse, in part because the readings are "oppositional" to dominant frames and in part because this style of writing is meant to challenge common assumptions—or make conscious the unconscious ones—with a humor of associative excess. This way of reading and writing culture is anticipated somewhat by Kenneth Burke's conception of a "perspective by incongruity," an iteration of dialectical thinking that mines apposition for insight.[60] The critical approach I adopt for reading culture attempts to preserve something puzzling or elusive about the critical object, while also working against enchantment or fetishization, refusing to yield the object of scrutiny anything like autonomy or an "aura" that would foreclose critique in a kind of common, comedic, or ritual reverence.[61] My perspective on cultural criticism owes a debt to Freud and Marx, even to the New Historicism pioneered by Peter Greenblatt, but perhaps most directly to the thinkers of the Frankfurt School, who were doggedly skeptical of apprehending any popular object at face value, and who had an insightful and jarring habit of juxtaposing presumably dissimilar objects to discern the cultural structures and (bourgeois) dreams these both promote and mystify. For the Frankfurters, reading suspiciously for semiconscious and unconscious dynamics was incorporated into Marxist critique as a supplemental explanation for the role of desire and aggressivity in class struggle and institutional domination. In a qualified sense, their collective aim was a kind of materialist psychosurgery of mass culture.

As prominent figures associated with the Frankfurt School, Theodor Adorno and Walter Benjamin took to analyzing cultural objects—or rather, their representation—as indirect symptoms or distorted expressions or re-creations of the society that reared them. Adorno's criticism evolved into a ruthless critique of mass culture and Western thought through a rigorous method of analysis that he termed "negative dialectics."[62] Somewhat gentler on the reader than his friend and colleague, Benjamin conceived of criticism as a necessary "mortification of the text" or even the destruction of a work of art in the act of criticism.[63] Although not discussed in such terms, Benjamin's deconstructive approach to objects of culture intentionally perverts (as opposed to abandons) the ideology of Romantic idealism underwriting cultural criticism in Europe and the United States in the interwar period. Such idealism persists, albeit much more dimly, in contemporary scholarship and even in popular conceptions of critique (e.g., critics on popular competition shows about dancing or singing or, of course, cooking and even plastic surgery).

An admittedly crude gist of the critical approach of the Romantics was for the critic to merge with or "complete" a work of art in the sensual act of "poetic criticism" and thereby experience something like freedom or emotional transcendence.[64] In the United States, the practice of "close reading" common to many forms of criticism continues to harbor related Romantic aspirations, as the critic is envisioned as a cocreator of a "text," or at least a prophet of the contextual horizons of a reader's experience. Such an intimate reading protocol is reflected in the New Criticism movement in US literary studies, which isolates texts in their presumed aesthetic autonomy, as well as the reading codes of many rhetoricians. As the late, great maestro of close reading, Michael C. Leff, put it, "The act of interpretation mediates between the experience of the critic and the forms of experience expressed in the text. To perform this act successfully, critics must vibrate what they see in the text against their own expectations and predilections. What [rhetorical] critics are trained to look for and what they see interact in creative tension; the two elements blend and separate, progressively changing as altered conceptions of one shape the configuration of the other."[65] The erotic connotations of interpretation described here recalls a bedroom scene; rather than disavow one's prejudices, for Leff the critic attempts to merge or fuse their understanding with the text such that the horizons of experience in each open up into a new experience or event of insight, transforming the text and critic alike. Such a self-surrendering view succumbs to the "text" and the text to the critic. Of course, in the middle of all of this the reader gets lost as a voyeur watching the expenditure of critical genius.[66]

Unfortunately for humanists in the United States intrigued by Freud's interpretive innovations, an analogous Romantic idealism also held fast in the clinic and critical essay. "American psychoanalysts," explains Bruce Fink, "many of whom were trained in Europe," found themselves in the United States, having fled fascism in Europe, thus emphasizing

> the adaptation of the human subject to the prevailing social, economic, and political environment; seeking recognition by the American medical establishment, they diligently excluded all those who might potentially jeopardize their good reputation in the public's mind. . . . These American psychoanalysts came to see it as part of analytic therapy to teach their [clients] how to adapt to their own environments. . . . The [client's] ego was too weak for the task of adaptation, and had to be encouraged to identify with the analyst's supposedly strong ego.[67]

In other words, the idiom of psychoanalysis was taken up in the United States with a particular focus on the adjustment of an individual to their environment by emulating the analyst (or critic). This post-Freudian approach has the net effect of setting up the psychoanalytic therapist, teacher, or critic as an expert to *emulate* for a client, student, or reader. Lacan termed this US approach to psychoanalysis "ego psychology" and spent a good many pages over many decades critiquing it.[68]

The problem with ego psychology is that it rehearses the idealistic and often projective conceits of virtuoso modes of interpretation, and in criticism "frequently deserves the scorn with which it is repudiated." Maud Ellmann continues that the reason is because it is not possible to "understand" a text or cultural object without "participating in their dreams or illusions," as Benjamin argued decades earlier. She elaborates:

> The critic necessarily conspires in the text's imaginings: the act of reading is a process of mutual seduction, whereby the reader and the read arouse each other's fantasies, expose each other's dreams. It is when we think we penetrate the text's disguises that we are usually most deluded and most ignorant, for what we see is nothing but our own unknown selves. Traditional psychoanalytic critics . . . fall into this trap precisely by asserting their authority over the literary text, and by claiming that they can see through *it* better than it sees through *them*.[69]

Such is the problem of mastery, succinctly stated. Close reading in rhetorical criticism tempts a similar sensibility, a pouring of a critical crackerjack's special sauce onto the object of interpretation. This scene of reading is particularly demonstrative of what Lacan dubbed the "Master's discourse," a language game in which a subject (or person) asserts authority over others, as with primary relationships with one's parents or an institution, like a church.

An awareness of the critic's own projective tendencies suggests an ethic for criticism that is intoned (but not always followed) by Freud, originally in the *Interpretation of Dreams*, but throughout his work. The key concepts that undermine the totalizing pursuits of mastery are the same concepts frequently deployed in psychoanalytic criticism: the unconscious and the drives. For Freud, these introduce a sort of humility-by-necessity: "These two discoveries—that the life of our sexual . . . [drives] cannot be wholly tamed, and that mental processes are in themselves unconscious and only reach the ego and come under its control through incomplete and untrustworthy perceptions—these two discoveries amount to a statement that *the ego is not master in its own house*."[70] The unconscious makes room for influence, for ideologies, that will elude our notice. And an inability to completely master the drives implicates the magisterial, virtuoso critic—"Would you like some Fryes with that Black?"—as something of an accidental comedian.[71]

Even so, isn't criticism a demonstration of mastery? After all, if one is to critique a text or culture or event or figure, does this not assert some sort of epistemological privilege, that one can communicate the logics or structures of an object better than the object itself? Of course! The most stereotypical figure of the critic—like that of the college professor—is one of (sometimes arrogant) mastery. Perhaps this figure is part of the appeal of an academic career in the first place. Now, one might argue that scholars should strive for what Lacan termed the "university discourse," whereby "knowledge" takes the place of the master and one is led to accept their ignorance. Yet as Bert Oliver observes, following Lacan, "The university discourse is that of a slave to the master, insofar as the university (and the sciences represented there) more often than not serve the master's discourse of the day"—at the time of my writing, neoliberal wrangling over outcomes-based education, critiques of left-leaning bias, and the veneration of science, technology, engineering, and mathematics.[72] Other discourses are possible too—the hysteric's or the analyst's or even global capitalism—but the point of each is a rearrangement of the rhetorical furniture. There is no metalanguage or epistemological point of privilege from which to except oneself from discourse, only different positions in our cultural living room.[73]

Despite its ubiquity, the problem with "mastery" is that it implies an impossible equilibrium or definitive lock on meaning, a certitude that is paradoxically betrayed by the need to declare mastery (e.g., Baron Frankenstein's quest for a master race). Reckoning with the mastery of the critical act does not imply that one can somehow transcend the horizon of one's preunderstanding (we can't, and at least on this point Freud and Gadamer shake hands). Relatedly, the universality that undergirds any interpretive claim is unavoidable; the key to moderation is never believing interpretation is exhausted and maintaining a cultivated uncertainty, in spite of the job description of "scholar" or "critic."[74] The appeal of the Frankfurt School's approach to cultural criticism is its attempt to resist—as opposed to overcome—the temptations of mastery at the inevitable moment of its assertion, seeking instead to deconstruct or disfigure the mystifications of culture while undermining its own tools for doing so, by suggesting that the tools for critique come from the same house of culture, and by pointing out the contradictions or paradoxes in its own observations. Critical rhythm is achieved not by the frame of pages or time but rather by ceaseless and never-ending critique, playfulness, and (good) humor.

I am particularly attracted to Benjamin's brand of Marxist symptomology, which sought to disfigure or embarrass an object or text—perversely counter to common receptions—to get at what Fredric Jameson has termed the "political unconscious" of a given community (Benjamin's unfinished *The Arcades Project* is a particularly enormous exemplar).[75] Benjamin's paradoxical notion of immanent critique simultaneously completes an aesthetic object at the moment of its destruction,[76] a kind of tempering of mastery with the biting questioning of the hysteric: to claim to have something to say about an object of criticism is to assert that the object is incapable of bodying forth its own sensuous meaning; pointing this out may yield a more robust impression, fulfilling its presumed promise, but in so saying its coherence as an autonomous object is obliterated or made strange. A familiar analogy for us today, particularly for critical "appreciation" approaches, is the oft said adage "Never meet your heroes."

While unquestionably Benjamin opted to leave the world as a materialist interested in the possibility of revolutionary shocks of illumination, among other adjectives I would argue that Benjamin's approach to criticism is *psychoanalytic* in practice. In part, Benjamin's mode of criticism is psychoanalytic because of the critical "abstinence" he adopts toward objects of critique in order to avoid "rhapsodic," private pronouncements as gospel; displays of a critic's mastery upset the dialectic between subject and object on the subject's side, making the audience or readers of criticism either uncomfortable or admiring voyeurs.[77] I also describe his approach to criticism as psychoanalytic because of the role Benjamin afforded to the unconscious, both as an adjective and noun; his reliance on dreamlike, "dialectical images"; and the way in which he coaxed unnoticed norms of culture from the analysis of material events, experiences, and things.[78]

Benjamin's dialectical approach was, in some sense, a more reflexive cultural or media studies parallel to the formal, self-proclaimed "psychoanalytic" criticism that arose in literary studies during his time, which became an "embarrassment" in the United States.[79] Despite the appeal of Freud's suspicious hermeneutics, early attempts to use psychoanalytic theory in literary criticism betrayed the approach by retrofitting analysis to a dominant critical gesture of mastery, whereby critics shored up their authority by slapping psychoanalytic concepts on a text, producing a crude psychobiography of an author or (fictional) characters.[80] Worse, as rhetorical theorist Edwin Black put it in 1965, "Just as Freud discovered a person who has mastered ordinary language can use it to conceal his motives, so a person who has mastered Freudian vocabulary can use it too to conceal his motives. The possibilities of deception, deliberate or unconscious, seem endless, and consequently the problems presented the psychological critic seem insoluble. . . . There is clearly no system of analysis or body of techniques available to the critic for the reliable psychological examination of argumentative strategies or discursive texture."[81] Compared to many scholars in rhetorical and cultural studies, Black's views on psychoanalytic criticism here are quite restrained. Thanks to new and better English translations of scholarship from the continent, this attitude would change with the arrival of structuralism and poststructuralism (if the two are assumed to be distinct) and a renewed interest in the work of Frankfurt School figures in the last quarter of the twentieth century.

Since the Frankfurters,[82] the figure most identified in the West as defending psychoanalytic approaches from puerile psychobiography and cookie-cutter critiques is the Lacanian psychoanalyst and philosopher Slavoj Žižek. Žižek helped to revive and return psychoanalysis to the symptomatic reading of cultural objects pioneered by Adorno and Benjamin, reviving the dream of mediating psychoanalysis and Marxism.[83] Tracing the tremendous influence of Žižek in the theoretical humanities, Tim Dean argues that "whether or not one employs the vocabulary and methods of psychoanalysis . . . this approach to aesthetics has become so widespread in the humanities that it qualifies as a contemporary critical norm."[84] This norm is "the tendency to treat aesthetic artifacts as symptoms of the culture in which they were produced," much like an analyst might interpret a dream, or much like Benjamin might interpret the wares and waste of a Parisian shopping mall. Arguably, the now common attitude of suspicion shared by critics—cultural, literary, rhetorical, or otherwise—is a perversion of the more faithful reading practices prior to

Romanticism, tracing back to the norms of scriptural exegesis. But I mean perversion only in a more common sense of deliberately violating norms because,
as I shall argue in the next chapter, criticism as such is a characteristically neurotic notion and hysterical hustle.

CONCLUSION: PSYCHOANALYTIC CRITICISM AND/AS THE CONTINUAL UNDOING OF MASTERY

In one way or another, humanists who continue to work with psychoanalysis
bemoan a general retreat from the linguistic character of culture in the earliest critical uses. "In literary studies," says Ellmann, "psychoanalytic criticism
often disregards the textuality of texts . . . in favour of the Freudian motifs supposedly encrypted in their depths."[85] Together with scholars such as Shoshana
Felman, Christian Lundberg, Elizabeth Wright, and others, Ellmann argues
that the psychoanalytic critic should attend "to the rhetoric of texts, the echoes and recesses of the words themselves" lest the perspective be "doomed
to rediscover its own myths."[86] Although there is some disagreement about
the verbal character of the unconscious,[87] the push to *rhetorically* analyze objects in psychoanalytic modes in terms of tropes, psychical structures, semiotics, and so on draws direct inspiration from Lacan, who insisted in his 1950s
seminars that the unconscious, "in symptoms and neurosis, is structured *like*
a language" (my emphasis).[88] Indeed, as Gilbert D. Chaitin suggests, Lacan's
theory of the subject is rhetorical because his theory of culture also "arises
through the process of symbolization."[89] For this reason, Lundberg argues that
"Lacan's psychoanalysis requires an ontology of rhetoric because it relies on
an account of the trans-subjective formal properties of the Symbolic to render
analytic discourse interpretable."[90] In other words, to propose something like
a psychoanalytic rhetorical criticism is redundant: ever since Freud elaborated
his analytical protocol as the deciphering of the "dream-work" as an expression of subjectivity *and* culture in 1900, analysis could easily be described as a
variety of criticism.[91]

What distinguishes forms of psychoanalytic criticism are its various schools,
which have proliferated since the 1920s. Those inspired by Freud and Lacan's
"return to Freud" are much more invested in characteristically rhetorical stuff.
In general, what is termed *classical psychoanalysis* references both early and
late Freudian theories, including his initial "topography" of the unconscious,
preconscious, and consciousness, and the later, secondary topography of the
id, the ego, and the superego. One element of classical psychoanalysis that is
downplayed or missing in post-Freudian modes is *drive theory*, the notion that

humans are born with what one could describe as half-baked instincts that require interpersonal interaction and encounters with culture to realize their aims. Unlike instincts, which appear in some animals as "hardwired" (such as an infant kangaroo migrating to its mama's pouch), human drives require the supplication for, and provision of, objects for them to continue working. For example, the oral drive requires *another human* to supply a breast or a bottle or an infant would starve and sucking would cease. In a qualified sense, then, classical psychoanalysis requires rhetoric as the logic of demands and object influence.

Unfortunately, the uptake of psychoanalysis as ego psychology in the United States imported Anna Freud's outspoken emphasis on Freud's secondary topography and defense mechanisms.[92] Tending to her ailing father in London, the junior Freud was a proponent of psychoanalyzing children, as was her emergent rival Melanie Klein, an Austrian figure who challenged the classical focus on paternal relations in favor of an interest in mother-child dynamics. Klein's influence in the international scene would become so profound that in the 1940s the British Psychoanalytic Society split into three groups: the Anna Freud group; the Klein group; and the so-called independents, the latter including D. W. Winnicott, a figure who has become increasingly important to the social sciences and humanities because of his theories of play and transitional objects (e.g., Linus's blanket). A number of analysts would eventually develop what came to be known as the "object relations" approach to psychoanalysis, substituting drive theory with a relational or interpersonal model focused on connections to others ("objects") instead of language and culture. Although leaders like Klein, Winnicott, and Heinz Hartmann never formally broke with drive theory, in general object relations have taken on an essentialist connotation such that objects are understood as more or less "hardwired" or the product of evolutionary adaptation. Consequently, post-Freudian, antidrive approaches appear to minimize the role of discourse and rhetorical mediation.

Owing to its overlaps with rhetorical theory, most of the chapters that follow will proceed more or less—although not exclusively—from a Lacanian perspective. In general, we can characterize psychoanalytic criticism as a perspective that takes off from a series of concepts that, as Black once put it, "instruct [us] where to look, but not in what to see."[93] Retaining some respect for the elusive and ineffable while nevertheless resisting the mystifications of political culture is my guiding principle, along with the understanding that my critical interventions are unavoidably self-deceptive and, by definition, participate in the aggressivity of a master's discourse (of rhetorical or cultural criticism, of high theory, and so on). The critical ethic here is to ceaselessly insist there is no definitive "reading" of any cultural object, that criticism is *not* a method but rather a craft, and to recognize that criticism is a form of violence—or at the very least, a kind of pastoral or surgical aggressivity. The labor of criticism is never finished or complete and always partial. And because of its amputations, criticism is inevitably mistaken. To this end, I elaborate my approach inductively as I work though each case study, deploying only those concepts that are relevant and useful for the criticism at hand. As I see and hear it, the ultimate task of the cultural or rhetorical critic is to interrogate a given corpus without leaving it for dead. To deity or science we leave cadavers. To crafts like criticism we leave something to be desired.

CHAPTER 2

The Psychoses of Speed, with the Example of Social Networking

But time to think [in off-hours]? If you're not driving a hundred miles an hour, at a clip where you can't think of anything else but the danger, then you're playing some game or sitting in some room where you can't argue with the four-wall televisor. Why? The televisor is "real." It is immediate, it has dimension. It tells you what to think and blasts it in. It *must* be right. It *seems* so right. It rushes you on so quickly to its own conclusions your mind hasn't time to protest, "What nonsense!"

RAY BRADBURY, *Fahrenheit 451*[1]

Time to burn for America again!

CROWD CHANTING IN RAMIN BAHRANI'S FILM, *Fahrenheit 451*[2]

After it debuted in the spring of 2018, Ramin Bahrani's HBO film, *Fahrenheit 451*, was widely fanned as a lot of smoke without a discernable spark.[3] Although his adaptation of Ray Bradbury's dystopian novel replaces the ubiquitous "televisor" with the addictive screens of contemporary social media, Bradbury's 1953 warning about the impressionable affects and effects of tele-life only shines through darkly, despite bright-light intentions. In both the novel and the film, books have become obsolete and regarded as a threat to the merchandizing state; roving bands of "firemen" are charged with flame-throwing unapproved "books" wherever they are found, incarcerating or exiling their clandestine readers as traitors to the cause of consuming an unremitting rush of state-sponsored ephemera. Both sorts of storytelling are about the state's demands for docile digestion, the desuetude of speech, and the supreme sovereignty of the screen.

But the HBO version sucks.

The incongruity between Bradbury's dystopian destiny and Bahrani's fascist fantasy is the film's failure to address the social and cognitive functions of what Paul Virilio terms the "phatic image." For Virilio, the phatic image is "a targeted image that forces you to look and holds your attention" instead of reflecting on its meaning, constituting a kind of community as reflex. The phatic image is "the result of an ever-brighter illumination, of the intensity of its definition, singling out only specific areas, the context mostly disappearing into a blur"—like the darkened, warehoused background of a fore-grounded, book-burning bonanza.[4] The irony of Bahrani's use of the same medium scorched by the story is somewhat on the side: the prophecy is about the effects and affects of *the blur*, the ever-shifting flash of an inferno, not so much the heat itself. It is the movement and not the medium that is the message.[5] The burning of books heralds the ascent of the phatic *object*, which directs attention to the frequency of its repetition and the acceleration of its circulation as the self-sealing inertia of culture: "Picture it," explains Bradbury's antihero Captain Beatty. "Nineteenth-century man with his horses, dogs, carts, slow motion. Then, in the Twentieth Century, speed up your camera. Books cut shorter. Condensations. Digests. Tabloids. Everything boils down to the gag, the snap ending."[6] Or as we might quip today, the Snap*chat*.[7]

In our time, "The Snap" sounds the punchline of our predicament, a *flare* apprehended as both an arresting image and a sharp tongue, except the ending never ends in a kind of parallel, phatic *temporality* of the "now this, now this." Bradbury's prognostication of The Age of the Befogging Blur has come to pass for those of us on *this* side of the digital divide and who subsist in a world largely without (the recalcitrance of) geography.[8] Bradbury's dystopian dream resonates today because of its critique of the hegemony of the phatic, or of the reduction of discourse to the *relation* or reaction—to affect—not the dominance of the screen or the salacious snippet per se. What is at stake in this chapter, then, is the general *coherence* of our contemporary social and political conversations in a high-speed, hypermediated world. My argument is that our mainstream politico-cultural situation is accelerating toward the *psychotic*, but in a qualified, nonmoral sense animated by a number of aftermarket modifications to Lacanian locutions. I am concerned primarily with what is made possible in publics because of a growing addiction to affective reflexes, or more directly, what happens when our sociopolitical environment is accelerated to a point beyond reflection.[9]

To this end, in this chapter I explain the relationship between social networking and what is termed the "decline of symbolic efficiency,"[10] working toward the conclusion that such a decline can be described as increasingly psychotic. Along the way it will be helpful to define key concepts, distinguish between psychosis as a clinical diagnosis and psychosis as a psychical structure, and explain how cultural psychosis is facilitated by technological and social acceleration. It is for the ferment of reflection, however, that I begin inductively, baking a case for a general decline of symbolic coherence with everyday exemplars that are, without fail, a leavening faster than fiction.

DIODE DEMOCRACY, OR, THE COMMUNISM OF AFFECTS[11]

Example the first: student sexting. In our so-called screened life, many of us have become accustomed to a routine stream of salacious stories in (the) news media. In both national and local news programs, an increasingly familiar narrative recounts youths circulating smartphone snapshots of their "junk." The following lead-in for a 2015 *Nightline* episode previews what has become a fairly predictable "youth news" subgenre: "[Tonight] a story involving nudity, technology, and adolescence. A small town in Colorado finds itself in the white-hot glare of the national media spotlight because of a so-called sexting scandal. Scores of students, some of them only in middle school, suspected of trading naked pictures on their phones using secret apps to hide it from their parents and teachers."[12] Such stories are typically packaged with evocative language ("white-hot glare"); a blurred, (juvene)scence of texting teens; interviews with outraged officials and (presumably) profaned parents; depositions of striplings censuring "sexting" obsessions in answer to (mis)leading questions; and more blurred shots of young people, many "suggestive" and consequentially journalistically perverse. In recent years such stories also tend to call attention to overly harsh child-pornography laws that, in some states, can class a concupiscent kid as a lifelong sex offender.[13]

In addition to dealing with fights, bullying, and all kinds of physically abusive behavior, then, teachers and administrators in secondary education now have to deal with the dreaded advent of sexting, a technological mainstay that news journalists and concerned parents will only continue to hype in a phatic form of panicked perseveration.[14] Of course, such raunchy reportage rides atop a larger, Western fantasy of "youth in crisis" that bemoans the teenage libido run amok.[15] For example: *Don't text and drive.* Although the admonition that we should not text and drive is an important message with a lot of empirical evidence to support its prevalence and harm,[16] the warning nevertheless has echoes of that familiar adolescent prohibition, "Don't touch that or you will go blind!"[17]

All too often commentators and journalists are ready to indict the compulsions of youth—what with their undeveloped prefrontal lobes!—however, it only takes a moment to recall any number of so-called grown-ups who are or have been similarly compelled: surely readers (re)member former New York state representative Anthony Weiner's popping pectorals, which he tele-brandished as "Carlos Danger" to a twenty-two-year-old woman, thereby effectively ending his mayoral ambitions in 2013—but this only after an earlier, forced resignation from Congress for dispatching a "dick pic" to another person in 2011.[18] Whether sexting scandals concern younger or older persons, they nevertheless seem compulsive and presume the absence of a kind of symbolic authority or internalized limit.

Adults behaving badly bring us to a second example that hits, uncomfortably, closer to home. It is tempting to discuss the middle school teacher who allegedly Snapchatted nudes to a student[19] or to discuss the many teachers who have been fired for racist remarks (particularly against Muslims).[20] One of the earliest cases of socially networked outrage, however, concerned Christine Rubino, a fifth-grade teacher from Brooklyn who was fired some years ago because of insensitive comments she made on "The Facebook." In June 2010, a twelve-year-old girl from Harlem drowned during a school trip to Long Beach on Long Island. Rubino posted the following status to her "wall": "After today, I'm thinking the beach sounds like a wonderful idea for my 5th graders. I HATE THEIR GUTS! They are all the devil's spawn!" She was, of course, eventually fired.[21] My point here is *not* to assess if such a post is morally wrong—it is, of course—but rather to underscore the fact that this teacher believed that her remarks *were safe to say in public*.

Finally, example the third: presidential campaign rhetoric. Much has been said about how political rhetoric in our time appears to have devolved into the creation of "gotcha" moments and vulgar melees of bombastic braggadocio,[22] particularly in the wake of Donald Trump's 2016 presidential campaign.[23] Aside from a bemoaned change in tone, contemporary political rhetoric is also frequently critiqued for its inconsistencies with science, especially that concerning climate change. Consider, for example, an early exchange between then presidential hopeful Donald Trump and CNN reporter Jake Tapper from 2015:

TAPPER: Um, back in 2012 you tweeted, quote, "The concept of global warming was created by and for the Chinese in order to make US manufacturing noncompetitive."

TRUMP: Well, of course I'm being sarcastic. You know, I mean, I love—

TAPPER:—That's not to be taken seriously?

TRUMP: No, it's a little bit serious, there's a little bit of serious there. Look, we are restricting our factories much more than China. . . . I'm not a huge believer in the global warming phenomenon.

TAPPER: But the overwhelming majority of scientists say it's real, it's man-made, and things are happening—

TRUMP:—That could be, there can be some man-made too, I mean, I'm not saying [unclear word] zero, but not nearly to the extent. When Obama gets up and says it's the number one problem of our country, and if it is, why is it that we have to do our [*sic*], and clean up our factories now, and China doesn't have to do it for another 30 or 35 years . . . ?[24]

Trump's competition for the Republican ticket, Senator Marco Rubio, similarly dismissed global warming in a number of primary debates,[25] echoing an increasingly unpopular public sentiment: that global warming is not an established, scientific fact[26] but rather a conspiracy fabricated to impede free-market capitalism.[27] Long before becoming the US president, Trump and his followers repeatedly asserted that facts are either malleable or simply do not exist,[28] impugning the authority of respected experts, scholars, researchers, and scientists.

Other than their forgotten feeling, these three examples of discourse may not initially seem related: the advent of sexting and the publicity of hateful feelings toward children—both technologically catalyzed libidinal compulsions—and the well-known and discredited claim that global warming is a myth. Certainly their relationship has to do with their phatic, now-this-now-this character, but more importantly for what follows, their relationship has to do with *authority*, and more specifically, with the *perception of an absence of authority* or a kind of contextual clout. In each example the texter, writer, or speaker appears to operate impulsively under the assumption, conscious or unconscious, that there is no oversight, that there are no anchoring facts, or that there is no almighty truth.

SOCIAL NETWORKING AND THE THIRD THING

Before diving headlong into the digital marsh, I should note that by "social network" I mean to reference a broader "system of social interactions and relationships" or plexus of "people bound by similar interests,"[29] not simply or only interfaces such as Facebook or Twitter (or whatever "new media" fetish higher education administrators seem interested in funding for research), but also emergent circuits that we do not yet know. The term "social networking" is frequently conflated with "social media" in both scholarly and popular discussion; however, for our purposes "social networking" connotes relational connections and structures, while "social media" references modes of publicity and distribution that may or may not have networking characteristics.[30] Put alternately, social media consist of various representations that we can analyze to discern networking infrastructures: a YouTube video or a story from BuzzFeed are objects of social media; however, the interaction among people in the comments section, or discussion about a video or story on Facebook, indexes a social network. Social networking references the relational dimensions of social media rhetoric.

Of course, social networking is typically associated with "social networking sites," which include "web-based services that allow individuals" to create profiles and share information,[31] or microblogging services like Mastodon or Sina Weibo, but the parade of new interfaces is only going to change in ways that are hard to predict. Although scholars and commentators are usually limited to analyzing the dominant social networking interfaces of the moment, I side with those who reference social networking somewhat more loosely and abstractly as a *social structure*, appealing to the theories pioneered by Georg Simmel, Friedrich Kittler, and others who might describe social networks as clusters, "nodes," or congeries or social affiliations enabled and constrained by communication technologies.[32] At one time, for example, a perceived dominant social network might have been a social club—like the Freemasons or Kiwanis— while today it's a snapshot that someone shares with friends on a smartphone before it disappears in ten seconds.[33] Such a perspective on social networks has some common cause with Jacques Lacan's perspective on communication, implying a network of relations that I think recommends his insights.[34]

My interest is in the discernment of psychical structures that enable forms of public address, even though these forms may masquerade as private or semipublic communications. I say "masquerade" because, for Lacan, the individual psyche is an expression of structural positions that are part of a larger communicative network; the implication, as Christian Lundberg notes, "is that the primary site where the subject is articulated is not in relation to the family but in relation to the whole economy of discourse that determines *even the character of the family*."[35] So although news media (both on the Internet and television), Facebook, and Twitter may still provide the dominant examples for discerning psychical structures beyond 2020, I also mean to refer to other modes of publicity or being in publics that encourage or discourage relationships within a larger, communicative network—"the Symbolic" writ large. Rather than ground social networking in branded interfaces, then, I propose to locate the structure of social networking dialectically between communication technologies and subjectivity. It is not simply that the human psyche—individual or collective—is the ground of social networking, but also

THE THIRD THING

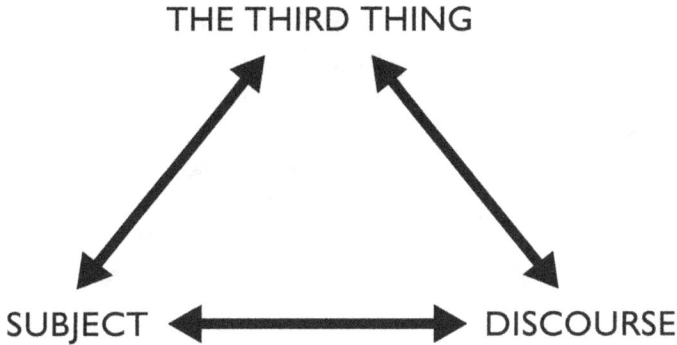

SUBJECT ⟷ DISCOURSE

FIGURE 5. The Third Thing.

that networking technology in some sense is productive of the psyche as well. There is, in other words, no "first" or "ground" because the chicken and the egg are mutually constitutive, which calls into question any hard line on technological determinism. Pragmatically, however, we must posit a place to begin thinking, and I do so with the chicken of psychical structure because networking technologies change so quickly. In short: let's start with Freud before we get to Facebook and see where that gets us.

I have already suggested that three examples—sexting, hateful posts, and the myth of global warming—concern the perception of the lack of authority. Such a perception is more easily grasped as formal: there is the disappearance, erasure, or erosion of a *Third Thing*. In each case we can image a paradigm person or "subject" set in relationship to a meaningful object, which I will designate as "discourse" (see figure 5): a student is set into a relation with revealing photographs; a teacher is set in relation to her Facebook status updates; and a politician is set in relation to climate science. In a world in which sending nude photos of yourself or speaking ill of children is naughty, that Third Thing might be something like morality, a government official, or God. In a world of scientific belief, that Third Thing might be natural law or the expertise of trained scientists. Yet in each case, this Third Thing is perceived to be absent or inconsequential: state authorities are merely kids with experience and power; God is a fiction; and scientists are merely pundits in disguise.

Žižek describes the disappearance or erosion of the Third Thing as the demise or decline of "symbolic efficiency,"[36] which is a term modified from the work of anthropologist Claude Lévi-Strauss.[37] Symbolic efficiency refers to the ways in which a given community can communicate quickly and effectively with reference to something most members hold as true, certain, or likely. As

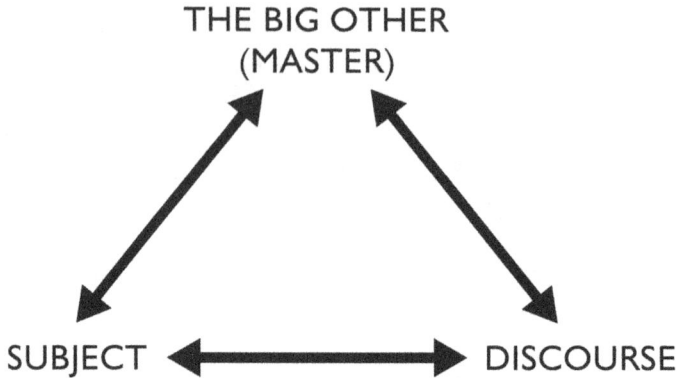

FIGURE 6. The big Other.

Jodi Dean puts it, symbolic efficiency is a consequence of "what everybody knows."[38] At the most basic level, symbolic efficiency is made possible by sharing a language, and in speaking or writing a community references a shared semantic and affective Rosetta Stone—a Third Thing—to traffic in meaning and coordinate behavior. For Dean, Žižek, and others who employ the concept,[39] however, symbolic efficiency means much more than a shared language because it also connotes a shared (sense of) authority. For these thinkers, symbolic efficiency also references a kind of deference to something larger—a sort of humility toward something or someone greater than ourselves. This larger, outside something is first experienced in childhood, of course, as the disciplining parent. Abstracted to a more formal level, the Third Thing that enables symbolic efficiency is described as the "big Other" by Jacques Lacan (an English port of the French *Autre*) but is perhaps more familiar to us in public discourse as an iteration of "the Master," such as in the philosophy of G. W. F. Hegel,[40] or in certain religious or spiritual traditions in which the master doubles as a teacher and kind of internalized authority (see figure 6).

For Lacan, however, the master is just one figural proxy for the big Other, which is also the symbolic register of human experience in general.[41] This is to say that the big Other refers primarily to the symbolic order, but we tend to reckon with it as an external authority that or who establishes limits for our enjoyments. The big Other is the Third Thing that we often mistake as a person (or leader or deity) with the power to punish or, more to the point, an authority with the power to say "No!" The decline of symbolic efficiency is thus an erosion or disappearance of the big Other, which is perhaps most easily recognized as an inability to distinguish between facts and opinions, or "a mistrust of what is said in favor of what can be detected."[42] Dean elaborates:

> The decline in symbolic efficiency refers . . . to a fundamental uncertainty in our relation to the world. We aren't sure what will happen, we can only speak about probabilities, about how good or bad our chances are. Likewise, we aren't sure whom to rely on, who has the best data or the most impressive credentials. Arguments or authorities persuasive in one context can have no weight in another one. . . . Most people in wired cultures experience this uncanny excess and lack of meaning with ever-increasing frequency: we get conflicting information from nonstop multiple media . . . we don't know what to believe, whom to trust, or what criteria with which to decide questions of trust and belief.[43]

Such a decline is not total—yet. But the argument here is that as the big Other continues to erode, people clamor for authority in smaller contexts—enclaves, perhaps fashioning a temporary mini-master in a community of political allegiance or in the assemblage of a social movement.[44]

ENTER THE DRAGON: LACAN AND PSYCHICAL STRUCTURES

So far I have argued that popular public discourse enabled and constrained by networking technologies is demonstrative of a decline in symbolic efficiency. To explain what this decline re-presents and how it has been catalyzed by contemporary, communicative technologies, I return to psychoanalytic theory and take up a pickle left languishing at the bottom of chapter 1: that the enterprise of psychoanalytic criticism is founded upon the analysis of particular individuals and specific case studies. How can the clinical experience of an individual in therapy—even an aggregate of clinical experiences that suggest larger, transpersonal patterns—lead to insights about publics? About social movements and cultural events?

As I noted in chapter 1, an initial answer was the critique of "mass culture" and communicative technologies pioneered by figures of the Frankfurt School, which further entrenched the unconscious and a suspicious or symptomatic reading protocol in the critical humanities. Another answer to these kinds of questions is found in the work of Jacques Lacan, whose characterization of the individual or subject as a sort of enfoldment of cultural structures became attractive in the humanities midcentury, largely as a result of English translations.

Although Lacan's theories were applied in literary criticism by the 1970s (rhetorical criticism was very late to this house-call party),[45] they initially made the strongest impact among film scholars and feminist thinkers who read Lacan as a diagnostic and corrective to Freud's perceived patriarchal proclivities.[46]

Lacan was a student of both psychology and philosophy, and his writing and teaching weds both. Powerfully influenced by the complex theories of structuralism in anthropology and linguistics, as well as Alexandre Kojève's readings of Hegel,[47] Lacan's work is deliberately and notoriously difficult. Nevertheless, Lacan's appeal is *critical* in many senses. US academics started reading his work in the 1970s because the theoretical humanities had folded philosophy and psychology into its own reading protocols. Lacan's theories translate well to critical approaches to culture in part because the distinction between philosophy and psychology was already blurred in the French intellectual scene.[48] Lacan's theories also translate well because of his views on language and meaning, because of his interest in the arts and culture, and because of his novel approach to the relationship between speech and feelings. Whatever utility Lacan's theories have for the clinical setting,[49] there's no denying that Lacan was a keen cultural critic; analyses of literature and art figure prominently in his work (e.g., see his reading of Poe).[50] Regardless, although there is lot to say about Lacan's appeal to North American academics, let's confine the rehearsal of Lacan's relevance and utility to criticism with a return the thesis that US public discourse is veering toward psychosis. With this claim I do not mean to reference the popular understanding of psychosis as insanity or psychopathology but, rather, Lacan's many elaborations of psychosis, which are at once both individual and social.

In North America and especially in the United States, our psychological health care system is bound, for good or ill, to *The Diagnostic and Statistical Manual of Mental Disorders*, currently in its fifth edition (*DSM*-V).[51] Diagnosis is behaviorally based on *symptoms*, and the *DSM*-V locates the symptoms of psychosis on a "schizophrenia spectrum" with a host of definitions that are continuously debated. It is difficult to assert a general definition of psychosis, but the *DSM*-V does note that the spectrum includes "delusions, hallucinations, disorganized thinking (speech), grossly disorganized or abnormal motor behavior . . . and negative symptoms."[52] Lacan thinks about psychosis differently: all symptoms of so-called psychological disturbance can be better described in reference to *psychical structures* or "*structural positions* that indicate particular ways of moving about in the languaged world with others."[53] For Lacan, people evince one of three psychical structures: neurosis, psychosis, or perversion. Everyone can exhibit symptoms of all three in our behavior or discourse; however, for Lacan one tends to be structurally disposed as a neurotic, psychotic, or pervert independent of observable symptoms. Symptoms do not make the structure; they can only gesture toward where a structure might be.

Lacan's refinements and elaborations of his nosology are many and complicated, but for brevity we should note that a Lacanian perspective does not truck in biology but rather with the domain of language, meaning, and representation. This is to say that a Lacanian approach to psychical phenomena is concerned with labels and the underlying patterns or structures these betoken, which can be culturally relative. Of course, one should not discount biological causation when reckoning with psychological disturbances (e.g., chemical imbalances and so on); a Lacanian perspective, however, is concerned with how a presumably physiological "disorder," whatever it may be, is delivered to meaning in a culture's given language games. Lacan is fairly strict in drawing a boundary between psychoanalysis at the horizon of meaning and psychical structures, which are cultural. Lacan located Freud's conception of fantasy as one discernable horizon of psychoanalytic inquiry.

Fantasy, Psychical Structure, and the Neurotic Default

Since its inception as a clinical practice, psychoanalysis has wrestled with the ontological status of the subject in the treatment of psychological disturbances, straddling the singularity of an individual's experience and physiology with meaningful patterns that inhere in culture; this is why psychotherapists often discuss pseudonymous "cases" in general discussion, because the focus is on the pattern and not a person. In this respect, to help provide an account of the foundational role of language and culture to subjectivity, Freud was among the first to suggest that a given subject is animated or structured around *phantasy*, an unconscious scene or scenario that stages a relation to the Other, running interference for some original trauma or primal pain.[54] Written with the now silent but implied "ph," fantasies help us coordinate meaning by providing scripts for understanding what we want from others and what others want from us.[55] Paul Verhaeghe elegantly explains that, for Freud, "the starting point for human development is an original experience of unpleasure . . . which is the consequence of an internal need whose prototypes are hunger and thirst. . . . Because the stimuli are internal, defense is virtually impossible; running away won't help. The child's reaction to this unpleasurable situation is prototypical and provides the foundation for all subsequent intersubjective relationships. The helpless baby turns to the other by crying."[56] As a child matures the character of her cry begins to utilize the "images and words for its internal experience from the other," which is to say meaningful selfhood is a "prototypical" articulation of a script from an external culture.[57] Such images and words eventually cohere into an imaginary scene or scenario that Jacques Lacan dubs a "fundamental fantasy," which is a somewhat retrogenerative, unconscious movie about one's psychical reality. Taking cues from the structuralist insistence that the foundational unit of human culture is the *relation* (not any one thing, person, or object, but rather their connections), Lacan stressed that psychical reality constitutes the subject as such in terms of (eventually) habituated behaviors toward others, which coalesce as a psychical structure. The fundamental fantasy is in some sense the primary, unconscious scene of a psychical structure, and fantasies are more or less conscious "image sets" that run cover for this ur scene and the original traumatic pain of being.[58] For Lacan, the direction for treatment is the discernment, elaboration, and eventually "traversal" or alteration of a patient's heretofore unconscious home movie.[59] The result of this traversal depends on the individual in analysis, and Lacan was quick to observe that "this is the beyond" of therapy as such.[60] Even so, Bruce Fink observes that traversal in general better enables a subject to stop "blaming the Other for one's problems or one's fate," while nevertheless accepting the perpetually unresolved demand for recognition or love represented by the original, infantile cry.[61]

Whether an analyst is dealing with conscious or quasi-conscious fantasies or the more fundamental, unconscious fantasy that these collectively betoken, the symbolic netting that predisposes (as opposed to predetermines) a person toward particular kinds of relations with others is a *psychical structure*. Unlike the dominant, behavioral approach to psychology based on symptoms, which is so aptly demonstrated by the *DSM*-V,[62] Lacan elegantly grounds his nosology in symbolic structures that may or may not express discernable symptoms indexing an accrual of a set of dispositive reactions (or defenses) toward primary others that compulsively recur. Lacanians often describe psychical structures in terms of the Oedipal allegory that Freud made so familiar, but only formally and stripped of "real" body parts: psychical structures concern a given subject's relation to the presence (or absence) of early parental figures, conceived as maternal and paternal roles that have only a contingent relationship to biological sex.[63]

Lacanians and post-Lacanians maintain that the paradigm person is *neurotic*, and the story of that subject's formation goes something like this: the classical or paradigm neurotic comes into the world with a primary bond or identification with one parent (usually the "mother"), but when confronted with the presence of a second parent (historically the "father"), they are caused to give up this primary bond through a kind of sharing, initiated by the "No!" or law of the second parent ("No! You cannot have mommy all to yourself!"). As young people we learn that we can substitute the original (maternal) bond with other bonds, *initially* with "transitional objects" (such as a stuffed animal or blanket),[64] but *eventually* other people, such as the second parent, the family pet, an aunt or uncle, a sibling, and so on, all of whom collectively represent the "social" broadly construed.

The establishment of the default neurotic structure entails, then, two moves: first, an *alienation* from the primary parent with the introduction of a second parent who embodies limitation or, simply, "No!" Second, a resulting *separation* from the primary parent, leading to the "ego" or self-conscious "I" ("I am Josh, I am not my mother"). This dance of relations, resulting in (metaphorical) "castration," inculcates the neurotic into culture because the initial, second figure or "paternal metaphor" represents society and social order (the name/no/law of the father), replete with rules on how to behave, what is appropriate and inappropriate, what to feel guilty about, and so on.

The achievement of neurosis depends primarily on the mechanism of repression, whereby affects are detached from their representation in thought and displaced from consciousness, their residue—usually as a symptom—indexing the emergence of the unconscious. Affects are *not* repressed, but the thought or representations articulated to them is repressed and forgotten (this is why one can feel sad without explanation).[65] The processes of alienation and separation are not fun for the young neurotic, but whatever affects linger for the emergent subject have long been detached from conscious memory. In other words, when we are confronted with the fact that there are more folks to love and love us than the primary parent, we become social creatures by learning the techniques of substitution, collectively an art of forgetting by diversion that is achieved—at least initially—through speech. Empirically, most of us are neurotics, alienated and separated from a primary relation to the maternal body; we fumble about in life forging various substitute bonds with others (such as, say, with rhetorical criticism). Consequently, neurotics have a kind of inner sense that something is incomplete or missing, but such doubts are begrudgingly accepted and managed through repression and sleep.

Of course, Freud's theory of developmental identity has received sharp critiques for its heterosexist assumptions and masculine (or phallocentric) biases.[66] Part of the appeal of Lacanian theory is thus the analyst's insistence that we are not to read Freud's Oedipal scheme literally but figuratively.[67] It's not that we actually have a father forbid a relationship to our mother under

PARENT II
(PATERNAL METAPHOR)

PARENT I ←——————→ SUBJECT

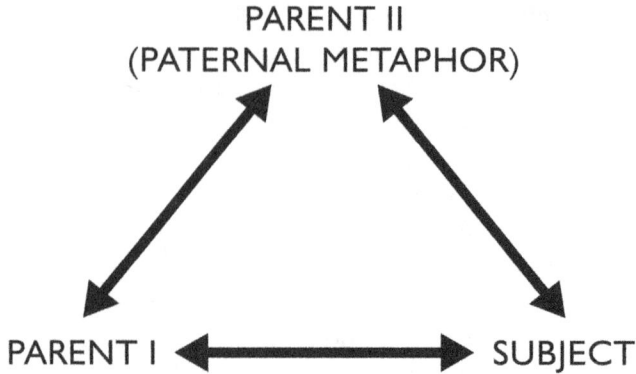

FIGURE 7. The Oedipal triangle.

the threat of castration (which, of course, excludes those without a penis) but, rather, that the introduction of a *second parent* encourages the realization of two things: first, that there is a limit to our enjoyment, that there is something called "No!" that curbs any delusions of omnipotence; and second, that the arrival or "insertion" of a second parent means that there are more objects in the outside world to love in addition to the primary parent (or mother). In other words, with the introduction of a third figure—a Third Thing—we become social animals.

This third figure, which Lacan dubs the "paternal metaphor,"[68] is the nascent Third Thing with which I began the chapter; it introduces the subject to the *idea* of the Other and hence the world of others, as well as the notion that there is some external authority that places limits on what is possible to enjoy or know (see figure 7). For Lacan, the arrival of the paternal metaphor heralds a substitution or exchange: *we give up a primary and primal relation to the maternal in exchange for the symbolic; we relinquish an original plenitude in exchange for meaning.* Or, to put this deliciously and admittedly sloppily: *rhetoric is a substitute for your mother.* Or perhaps more soberly said, from a Lacanian perspective rhetoric is the influential discourse, force, or movement of substitution (e.g., tropes) and a variation of identification.[69]

Flatline (to the) Mother, or, the Psychotic Structure

While the neurotic subject and its repressive maneuvers should be most familiar to readers (certainly to academics), insofar as psychical structures are repetitive sets of relational habits, neurosis is more recognizable as the cultural default when contrasted with psychosis—and of course vice versa. Simply stated, the psychotic forecloses "castration," which is to say they never recognize the second parental figure, never experience alienation and separation, and thus are immune to the conception of authority or law. There is no "No!" for the psychotic; "His or her unconscious is exposed for all the world to see" because repression simply doesn't work.[70] Instead of the two-step dance of repression, whereby thoughts are detached from affects and then subdued, *the psychotic simply can't dance*. The psychotic is the subject who has never endured the "cut" of the Third Thing, or to put it somewhat allegorically, the psychotic is the one who neither heard nor accepted the "No!" from the second parent and thus lacks the sense of an authority that anchors meaning. Instead of undergoing a triangulation of the first dyad (or "primary identification"), the psychotic gets an antisocial flatline to the maternal bosom. In this respect, the contemporary crisis of paternity—the much-discussed popular discourse of the "absent father"—registers a tacit fear of psychosis.[71]

The psychotic is the person who "acts out" or is prone to aggression,[72] who does not understand limit and who fails to internalize or recognize boundaries because of a "foreclosure" of the law of the symbolic. Consequently, psychosis is the position of someone set adrift in the sea of discourse, and for this reason, the psychotic has an unusual relationship to language that is "thrust into the foreground, that speaks all by itself, out loud, in its noise and furor," but in a way that seems to him, her, or them as objective and certain.[73] Most of us lodge in language, but the psychotic is "possessed, by language" in ways that seem somewhat counterintuitive: the psychotic asserts absolutes, parading truths with a righteous certitude.[74] "*Certainty is characteristic of psychosis, where doubt is not,*" explains Bruce Fink, because the "psychotic is convinced not of the 'reality' of what he or she sees or hears, but of the fact that it means something, and that this meaning involves him or her. While the psychotic may agree that what he or she heard or saw was not audible or visible to others . . . in other words, that it was not part of socially shared reality—this may make it all the more special to him or her: he or she has been *chosen* among all others to hear or see it, or it concerns only him or her."[75] Most people are neurotic and so do not evince a psychotic structure. Reckoning with the decline of symbolic efficiency, neurotics don't know who or what to believe; we doubt. The neurotic accepts uncertainty as a part of life because we have internalized the "No!" in childhood, a variation of the truth that we are limited in what we can do or comprehend. The psychotic, however, never heard the "No!" to begin with, so there is no prohibition with which to comply. Consequently, the psychotic's response to the demise of symbolic efficiency is to cling with certainty to even the most patent absurdities—conspiracy theories, religious fanaticism, political extremism—because this is a way to anchor social being.

As with the neurotic, it is important to underscore that for Lacan all psychical structures are descriptive and should not be conflated with the ethical or juridical subject or measured by ever-changing norms of cultural propriety. One might find trouble or fault with psychotic behavior or traits, a temper tantrum or drug-fueled "psyche-out," for instance, yet such judgments are inappropriate in respect to psychical structures: structures simply are that they are; symptoms can tell us where to look for them, but symptoms are frequently misleading too. A person's psychical reality may be structurally psychotic, but they may never experience the kind of crisis that results in hallmark delusions, hallucinations, or "breaks," and it certainly goes without saying that neurotics are capable of extreme acts of idiocy or cruelty. Neurotic and psychotic structures are typified by the mechanisms of repression and foreclosure and their signature traits respectively (e.g., malapropisms and delusions), but moral or ethical censure has no mooring in structures—that comes with consequences that are, in the last instance, cultural.

Of course, the nonmoralistic, Lacanian understanding of the psychotic structure does not square with the more commonplace connotations of violence or any well-established definitions of psychosis in the United States. This is why we should make a distinction between *psychotic beliefs and behaviors*—which *do* overlap with commonly understood symptoms—from a person who exhibits a *psychotic structure*, which is, again, very rare. That said, used as an adjective for behavior, and more narrowly for speech, I want to suggest popular, public discourse has started to exhibit its own psychotic structure, akin to a genre, discernable in public refusals or failures to acknowledge doubt and a symbolic authority that or who establishes and polices limits. Žižek explains that this emergent, psychotic discourse advances its own figure or paradigm person in postmodernity: "The typical subject today is one who, while displaying cynical distrust of any public ideology, indulges without restraint in paranoiac fantasies about conspiracies, threats, and excessive forms of enjoyment of the Other."[76] For the psychotic, this Other who enjoys is not the big Other of the symbolic, but rather an "Other to the Other," some "all powerful agent" who is external to the order of the symbolic, an agent who or that "actually 'pulls the strings' and runs the show . . . an obscene, invisible power structure."[77] Psychotic discourse often advances a kind of "compensatory delusion" for the eroded symbolic, sometimes "a world conspiracy" or a "new messiah or alien invasion,"[78] but it also issues righteous, narcissistic assertions of prophecy—cultural, political, and religious.

To characterize discourse as psychotic is not, of course, to diagnose any one person as exhibiting an individual, psychotic structure—which cannot and should not be done without extensive training and in the context of the clinic. Even so, from a critical perspective *a focus on the individual is somewhat beside the point.* From a Lacanian perspective, that psychical structures reside in culture provides for making sense of public discourse by locating and naming the structures productive of it—in this case, networked communication marked by the perception of an absence of authority and righteously aggressive, violent, or otherwise inappropriate speech that is palpably narcissistic. The absence of this Third Thing with which I began bespeaks a failure of the symbolic formally figured with the (allegorical) absence of a second parent but, by extension, the foreclosure of a symbolic authority that or who guarantees truth and reminds one of fallibility and a dependency on others.

CAN'T GET OFF (ON) THE BUS: FAST NEWS AND THE CULT OF SPEED

Time is the essence
Time is the season
Time ain't no reason
Got no time to slow.

BLUE OYSTER CULT, "Burnin' for You"[79]

I have been arguing that the kinds of discourse we are increasingly experiencing in our dominant social scenes and networked screens—in the news, on Twitter, and on Facebook especially—are trending toward the collapse of a traditional, symbolic authority or the "big Other." By explaining Lacan's conception of psychosis as a psychical structure or patterned relation to others, the suggestion is *not* that public culture *is* psychotic but, rather, that psychotic episodes of popular or public life—cultural psychoses—seem increasingly sustained, or that US culture at least appears to be heading in this direction for longer and longer terms. The utility of thinking about psychical structures is that these inhere in culture, not any one individual, and consequently one can speak about psychosis as a social or cultural disposition of a given public. For a paradigm person, Lacan maintains that once the subject is brought into being with a structure, it will not change because the structure is a scaffolding of selfhood itself (there are affinities here with Althusser's elaboration of interpellation, a concept inspired by his reading of Lacan).[80] Despite Lacan's insistence that structures of subjectivity are cultural, for many his approach in regard to specific individuals in a clinical setting appears totalizing or essentialist, as it seems an intractable stance closed to futurity. Although I share this worry, our focus is on the group, community, or public level, which is less "Lacan to the letter" than it is using Lacan to think through sociocultural problems. Whether or not an increasingly psychotic public or community is permanently so remains an open question, and I think it is a question that should remain open for many reasons, including the fact that groups act out differently than individuals, but most important among them brute contingency, political possibility, and ethical responsibility (understood as a never-ending, always revised relationality).

Upon my sharing this argument across the country for some years with friends, students, scholars, and psychotherapists, one question that always arises in various guises is this: What accounts for a larger, cultural erosion of neurosis and the trending toward psychosis? Or as it was put to me more recently,[81] how do we explain the perceived pendulum swing from the slow or deliberative civility of the "Obama era" to the impulsive, irascible outrage of "Trump's America"? How is it that people come to reactively accept "fake" or "junk news" as dogma? Why are people denying the possible consequences of sending "dick pics" or the unregulated and continuous ejaculation of greenhouse gasses? Whence these cultural breakouts?

As is typical of an academic, the first answer is that some of the common assumptions behind these and similar questions, reasonably prompted by a widely shared frustration with our recent political predicaments, are mistaken: the idealism of "civility" relies on a conception of the public sphere or civil society that never actually existed; the claim that "fake news" is new is false, and the argument that we now live in a posttruth era forgets a litany of precursors, such as the midcentury denial about the harms of smoking.[82] A psychotic public has always been with us insofar as publics sometimes resemble one of the basic psychical structures Lacan elaborates given the sufficient contextual constraints. And as Benjamin elegantly observed, the materialist—as opposed to idealist—history of humankind is a chronicle of barbarism, denial, and mistake (to which we add, of course, repression and foreclosure).[83] The argument that culture is increasingly psychotic does not presume an Edenic past, only renewed emphases of recognized patterns in the context of the present.

The second answer is the most honest one: *I'm not sure.* Lacan certainly does not offer an explanation, only a compelling description of the structures involved, which, to be sure, express themselves differently in our time. I am persuaded that Lacan's description of psychosis as a psychical structure *names and explains a pattern* and consequently has some predictive value, helping us to think about the dynamics of contemporary popular/political culture. Beyond the utility of an argument of definition, however, the third, related, and predictable answer is unavoidably speculative: like you, dear reader, *I have a hunch*. Whatever the precursors and regardless of similar dynamics in the past, many of us nevertheless *experience* our popular political reality as having changed—*and thus it has*, which is the only reason why a claim that Western culture is moving toward psychosis is persuasive at all. Even so, thinking dialectically—that in the totality there is only antagonism or movement— suggests that locating any one causal factor is too easy, if only because we are sitting in the moving (city) bus of culture while trying to get a sense of what it looks like from the side of a road that we (mis)take to be history.

I have borrowed and revised the metaphor of culture as a moving motor from the Marxist theorist Bertell Ollman.[84] Whether or not one shares Ollman's dialectical approach, his metaphor for the totality is one few in the (post) modernized West can deny. I'm revising the metaphor with the plot of Jan de Bont's 1994 feature film *Speed* in mind (featuring, I must note, the ironically slow-to-act Keanu Reeves): we're in it, we long to get a sense of what it looks like and where the bus is going, but we can't slow down. The metaphor also echoes a pervasive scholarly party line that, outside of a strategic essentialism or polemic, there is no metalanguage or privileged epistemological vantage for ultimate adjudication.[85] Intriguingly, the increasingly widespread recognition of the dynamism and complexity of a shared reality, so well signified by the "city," as well as the inability to comprehend it (at) all because it is constantly on the move (hence the speeding bus), also reflects our experiences and feelings about the temporality of communicative exchange in our time, the *rush*—in many senses—of an ever-accelerating, real-time world of immediacy.

A focus on the anxiety or the high of not having or getting brakes or breaks— of driving, in many senses, toward death—suggests at least a partial explanation for why a neurotic default is on the decline: *we seem to have a cultural addiction to speed*.[86] Such a dependency is easily referenced by aerial expressions of white-line omnipotence, "life in the fast lane,"[87] or oft heard expressions like "Where did the time go?" or "I don't have enough time to get it all done!" all of which Mark C. Taylor would describe as the phatic chants of a modern "cult of speed."[88] This is to say the cultural bus seems to be accelerating, except that the bus has become a camera and the windscreen a widescreen; the shift from one cultural-psychical structure to another tracks the compression of time and geography and an undeniable technological transformation capable of moving minds and the sites of sensory perception while seat-belting bodies in place. Many assume that an experience of "virtual reality" entails wearing a rather bulky set of goggles and staring into stereoscopic screens; however, the amputations of telepresence have been part of human experience since the advent of aerial reconnaissance, the motor, and the moving image.[89] Virtual reality goggles or immersive screen rooms are accelerated iterations of the same logic; so, too, is social networking.

A larger, cultural equivalence of speed with power—a modernist ideology of efficiency and "faster is better"—helps to explain how a default neurotic psychical structure, dependent on *reflection* for a recognition of authority and limit, begins to efface the anchoring function of the Third Thing. Presently there is a robust body of research, especially among social theorists and cultural studies scholars, examining speed, mobility, and the logics of acceleration as hallmarks of (post)modernity.[90] As Nigel Dodd and Judy Wajcman have argued, speed studies is rooted in the early work of Georg Simmel on the "philosophy of money" and the logics of circulation and city life, as well as Benjamin's examination of the pace of urban living and the speed of mechanical reproduction (to which I would add Adorno's strident critiques of the culture industry and the speed of standardization).[91] German sociologist Hartmut Rosa also finds the scaffolding of speed studies in the work of Durkheim, Weber, and of course Marx, because of their attention to the emergent "temporal texture of modernity."[92] Rosa's work has been particularly helpful for organizing and theorizing speed studies in relation to three emerging modes of acceleration and globalization: that of technology, that of social change, and that of "the pace of life."[93] In the critical humanities, however, the scholar most identified with theorizing the social, cultural, and political dynamics of speed remains the late Paul Virilio.[94]

Published over forty years ago, Virilio's first book, *Speed and Politics*, advanced "dromology" as a dialectical methodology for studying how speed alters and changes our experience of the world, particularly in respect to militaristic mobilization, geographical conquest, and various innovations in communication technology—much of which he describes as "logistics."[95] Taken from the Greek term for "race" (*dromos*), Virilio's various dromological projects refigure warfare and politics, not as the "art of the possible" but as the power to move faster and surveil faster than others and to make bodies (through prosthetics) and geographies (through telepresence) obsolete; the consequence of either is the equivocation of speed and violence and the characterization of the modern state as a "dromocracy." With what reads to many like hyperbolic aplomb or technological pessimism, Virilio has long argued that an addiction to speed for its own sake obliterates difference; the space and time for reflection; the establishment and maintenance of interpersonal, intimate connections; and even the utility of speech itself: "With the realization of dromocratic type progress, humanity will stop being diverse. It will tend to divided only into *hopeful populations* (who are allowed the hope they will reach, in the future, someday, the speed that they are accumulating, which will give them access to the possible—that is, to the project, the decision, the infinite: *speed is the hope of the West*) and *despairing populations*, blocked by the inferiority of their technological vehicles, living and subsisting in the finite world."[96] Virilio redescribes here what we know today as the "digital divide," and for decades he has elaborated in various ways how the ideology of acceleration manifests in myriad dialectical pivots between human perception and technology—the advent of the motor and its eradication of the city, cinema as war by other means, and live cams and reality television as a universalized (and seemingly bodiless) voyeurism.

It is at this juncture that I return to where we began, *Fahrenheit 451*, Bradbury's critique of the speeding clip, and Virilio's description of the gravity of the phatic object. Virilio would describe our addiction to clips, blurs, and flares as the "latest electronic illuminism" that is "metamorphosing" humanity

> into hybrids of the plant species as they in turn become HELIOTROPICAL and photosensitive, "object-oriented" through the framing point of view, and captured by the interface-to-face confrontation of the multiple screens of an environment that's suddenly gone interactive. . . . Surely we can't fail to see the enormous time difference that exists, today, between our at once untimely and interactive practices—practices involved in supersonic transport and instantaneous transmission—and our daily life, now so exhausted, so deprived of the intervals of time needed for reflection and responsible action.[97]

Which is to say that our contemporary, sedentary life of the screen emplaces us for hours on end in war rooms and living rooms—which are of the same logistical form with the advent of the Nintendo war of Desert Storm and the "interactive sport" of the video game—as the place of political business in our culture. Virilio argues that "peace," consequently, is simply the word for exhaustion.

Virilio's prognostications may be bleak, but those of us presently wired into a sociopolitical public of the speaker and screen should at least resonate affectively with the truth of caricature. I tend to agree with Jason Michael Adams's warning to those who dismiss Virilio's analyses as too pessimistic or deterministic or too dismissive of people and publics who are invigorated and goaded to the novel possibilities an accelerated reality. "While one might not agree with every element of the argument," writes Adams, "the assertion of a centrifugal rather than centripetal sensibility is one that we should take seriously, for, as Virilio has lamented, an uncritical affirmation" of the glories of speed is its own kind of despondency.[98] That we might describe public address in our time as increasingly psychotic and lacking a general sense of reflection, that everything is reactive and phatic, indexes the "obsolescence of intervals by the interface," as Peter Zhang puts it, threatening democracy as the sharing of power with a dromocracy of instantaneous temporality or "real time."[99] "When there is not time to share," warns Virilio, "what will be shared? Emotions."[100]

Acknowledging the now well-worn (and often challenged) distinction between *affect* as an atemporal intensity of a body in feeling and emotion as translation of such an intensity into language, meaning, and the temporality of the past or just now, Virilio's warning about a democracy of real-time emotion is perhaps better put as a looming dromocracy of pure *affect*.[101] It perhaps comes as no surprise, then, that in studies keyed specifically to the clinic, as Marina Denischik explains, an experience of psychosis entails a temporality that "ceases to exist as a continuous, meaningful, lived time," a kind of short-circuiting of the sensibility of duration.[102] In this respect I would suggest that the coming dromocracy, fleetingly realized but not yet pure, is characteristically psychotic and thus also typified by the decline of symbolic efficiency or a shared sense of authority that similarly stabilizes affect *as emotion*. In this modified sense, then, a "democracy of emotion" allows room for a sense of continuous time and reflection, whereas a "dromocracy of affect" does not.

I would argue, then, that the dromocratic addiction to speed and phatic objects prized for their affective social character and episodes of cultural psychosis are part of the same dynamic (or if you want, *logistic*). Insofar as a psychical structure entails a patterned series of *relations* or *strategies* toward others to manage affective intensities that, in turn, ultimately reflect a formal (dis)connection to the Other, a shift in how those relations are enabled or prevented contorts the character of the "logistical" structure. The suggestion here is that technological acceleration and an addiction to speed have militated *against* the acceptance of a shared symbolic by eroding the possibilities for reflection. Cultural psychosis is a (pre)condition of speed.

I should underscore that for Lacan the condition of psychosis is *not a denial* of the big Other (that would be perversion, about which next); it is the *foreclosure* of any relation to one at all, any possibility of a relation. I'm suggesting, then, that one of the reasons for a decline in symbolic efficiency is, paradoxically, simply our *not having time for it*. Cultural psychoses, however momentary, are not the consequence of some moral shortcoming or a failure to slow down the rapid pace of social being, which is precisely what so many "slow" movements (e.g., "slow food") seem to suggest ("Slow time so that the roses can be smelt and pressed into coins!").[103] The sin or annoying sense of guilt cultivated by slow movements is a consequence of a choice between the promise of futurity entailed by public engagement, now a frenzy of a paradoxically steely (or "space gray") futurism, and the despair of a counterpublic resigned to the Land of (the) Lost Finitude. From this perspective, psychosis, or a kind of psychotic *break* (in both senses) becomes a somewhat predictable, collective strategy for contending with a world in which the very conception of *limit* has been ideologically recast as something to be (inevitably, fatalistically) overtaken in the name of "hope."[104]

Lacan's nonmoral take on psychical structures is helpful as a description because the condition of ethical responsibility is not volitional; it is reflection, and consequently, ethical judgment is temporal. One does not *will* a psychical structure into being for a self-sensory life any more than one can choose a skeletal structure for one's body. The analogy here is that, among other things, cultural psychosis is the consequence of technological innovations and an ideology of acceleration that incessantly erodes neurosis as a strategy of relating to others. As a strategy for contending with a hypermediated and accelerated world, neurosis—like cultural criticism—*can't keep up*. Insofar as a psychotic strategy cannot be sustained, at least collectively, we can begin to make the case for why perversion has become an increasingly popular alternative.

CONCLUSION: FROM PSYCHOSIS TO PERVERSION

In this chapter I have argued that contemporary public discourse evinces the decline of symbolic efficiency, which leads to increasingly psychotic discourse. I have suggested that Lacan's preference for structures over symptoms led him to specify three basic subject positions—neurosis, psychosis, and perversion—which concern whether and how a subject reckons with the big Other vis-à-vis the paternal metaphor. Psychosis is characterized by an inability to acknowledge a more commonly accepted big Other of social consensus, leading to absolute, even righteous, certitudes about the illusory and absurd. Because psychical structures articulate individuals and inhere in culture, I have also argued that one can describe a public or culture as characteristically neurotic, psychotic, or perverse, either episodically or long term depending on the context. Drawing on the work of Paul Virilio, I then argued that episodes of cultural psychosis are enabled by a widespread addiction to speed, tracking a transition from a democracy in which power is shared to a "dromocracy" in which affects are shared in a "real-time" politics without interval. Public address characterized as reactive, affectively saturated, and phatically focused consequently reflects what I'm calling *the psychoses of speed.*

Even if readers agree that Lacan's notion of psychosis and Virilio's understanding of speed help to characterize and make sense of a lot of the public discourse that circulates in our time, the question raised is still whether our ever-expanding, networked frontier contributes to a shift from the paradigm or default subject structure of neurosis toward psychosis. I opened with a few examples suggestive of a "yes"—sexting, online hate speech, and climate change conspiracy—but since I first started composing this book many years ago the examples have become increasingly extreme. At the moment of my writing, presidential discourse is the most conspicuous—and I'll turn to that next, as promised—but I want to stress that an emergent, psychotic structure travels all the way down (or up) from culture to the interpersonal level in alarming ways. For example, in April 2016, an eighteen-year-old Ohio teen pleaded guilty to charges of kidnapping, rape, and the distribution of child pornography because of her use of a Twitter "app" named "Periscope": Marina Lonina filmed and "live streamed" the raping of her seventeen-year-old friend.[105] Lonina claimed that she live-streamed the assault in an attempt to help the victim; however, analysis of the video by authorities reveals Lonina giggles throughout while the victim pleads for the rapist to stop. The prosecutor argued Lonina enjoyed the attention and that "she got caught up in the 'likes,'" or the expressed approval of the stream from online onlookers.[106] Whether or not Lonina understood the consequences of her alarming behavior might suggest that her disposition is *clinically* psychotic (she did not understand) or perverse (she understood and did it anyway), but such a conclusion is not up to us. As a form of quasi-public discourse, at least in the moment, such *behavior* is psychotic and certainly bespeaks an erosion of the big Other, a failure to acknowledge the social and moral codes to which *most* people assent.

What these kinds of examples demonstrate is that what we used to count on as a governing authority no longer anchors a shared (rule of) law or meaning, and I've suggested that social and political acceleration, hastened by technological innovations of speed, provide at least a partial explanation. From a Lacanian perspective, we might say such examples represent a society and culture that no longer experiences an efficient symbolic of hypotaxic arrangement; we seem, increasingly, returning to a parataxic and clunky symbolic, a public set adrift in the sea of discourse—of imagery, of status updates, of live streams and "BREAKING NEWS!" News stories or events are valued not for their truth but for their affective inducements and feelings in the ever-present now of the "live." In our political discourse, especially, we find ourselves immersed in the melee between those who argue for truth and those who insist that "there's no such thing . . . as facts."[107] If my argument has purchase, however, the increasing frenzy of fact-checking in news media is itself a kind of fetishization or mystification, obscuring the real crisis of power it confronts: the decline of symbolic efficiency and the growing instability of a shared sense of authority as we speed toward the horizon of the next cataclysmic post, news story, or presidential tweet.

I think that describing public discourse as exhibiting psychical structures homologous to those of individual subjects helps us to explain the increasing regularity of psychotic rhetoric as an emergent *style* and *genre* of discourse. I am suggesting that the constant and relentless parade of immediacy so characteristic of social networking seems to be producing the kind of discourse of someone who is constantly speaking certitudes, *in the moment*, like a switchboard for the communication pulsating in a charged and mediated sea of speakers and screens. I also think that cultural critics will continue having trouble contending with psychotic discourse because criticism is by default a neurotic disposition, especially in its more suspicious modes, even if we try to pervert its ways for insight. How we analyze and understand the popular, public discourse must shift toward thinking about the demise of the Third Thing or Other. If Žižek and Dean are right about the demise of symbolic efficiency, then Michael Calvin McGee's thesis about the fragmentation of "the text" in our time takes on a new character: the critic of contemporary, public discourse is now consigned to ceaselessly and unrelentingly constituting the context.[108] My doing so has been the point of this chapter, casing the contextual pulpit to better understand the rhetoric of the most perplexing and controversial public figure of our time.

CHAPTER 3

The Perverse Style, with Eventual Reference to Pee-wee Herman

Before moving on to the next episode of ohmygodness, it is worth considering the possibility that this constant, daily, often more than once-a-day, pileup of events—each one canceling out the one before—is the true aberration and novelty at the heart of the Trump presidency.

MICHAEL WOLFF[1]

Episodic "ohmygodness" is an offbeat but accurate caption for the high-speed whiplash journalists claim to experience when attempting to (re)cover the forty-fifth president of the United States.[2] Wolff's neologism captures a somewhat complacent violation of the third commandment of the Hebrew scripture—reflecting the presumed godlessness of mainstream media journalism by Trump's supporters[3]—but it also connotes the sort of breathless befuddlement we see or hear on the more conversational news and political programs, especially cable talk shows.[4] When I started writing *Political Perversion*, blurting deity's name in vain was often my own reaction to Trump's outlandish behavior. Just as I completed the first draft of this chapter, for example, Trump's campaign almost derailed after a series of sexual misconduct allegations, roused by his now infamous boast that his celebrity permitted him to "grab [women] by the pussy."[5] Given the daily flood tide of scandal that flows from Trump's tongue and thumbs, book scholars are perhaps wiser to leave the ceaseless chronicling of Trump's contempt to journalists and focus instead on the larger cultural forms and structures his rhetoric rehearses. (Thank deity!)

Of course, Trump's (alleged) assault on Lady Liberty began long before assuming the White Throne (it is no longer a "House").[6] On the stump Trump had been widely critiqued for asserting that he could "stand in the middle of Fifth Avenue and shoot somebody" without losing voters; for ventriloquizing a woman at a New Hampshire rally who declared rival candidate Ted Cruz a "pussy"; and for bragging about the size of his penis during a presidential candidate debate.[7] After appropriating the presidency, more recently Trump's administration has been dogged by a years-long investigation into "Russian meddling" and possible collusion by the Trump campaign in the 2016 presidential election.[8] The consensus of the intelligence community is that Russian leaders deliberately influenced the 2016 election, but undeterred by his own naysaying cabinet, Trump forced a "summit" with Russian president Vladimir Putin in summer of 2018:[9] "I have President Putin," Trump said at the meeting in Helsinki. "He just said it's not Russia [that meddled]. I will say this. I don't see any reason why it would be, but I really do want to see the [hacked Democratic Party] server."[10] Despite a publicly avowed and well-known distrust of intelligence advisors in his own administration,[11] in a scripted statement Trump later claimed he "misspoke" in the conference with Putin[12] but not before former CIA director John Brennan tweeted that Trump's performance was "nothing short of treasonous" and CNN reporter Anderson Cooper described it as "perhaps one of the most disgraceful . . . by an American president . . . truly that I've ever seen."[13]

Because of these and hundreds of similar petulant proclamations, some historians and critics have compared Trump's presidential rhetoric to the likes of Andrew Jackson and Barry Goldwater.[14] Presently, however, the dominant sentiment on screen and in print is simply that the republic has *never witnessed anything like it*.[15] " 'Unprecedented' has become one of the most popular terms to use when discussing President Trump," argues Julian E. Zelizer for the *Atlantic*. But Trump "is the symptom of our divided, polarized times, rather than the root cause."[16]

A case for Zelizer's diagnosis is easier to make with an attention to the *patterns* or formal regularities of Trump's speech, which advance a number of rhetorical conventions identified over two thousand years ago by Greek thinkers.[17] Indeed, rhetoricians have a bunch of very old labels for Trump's "tropes" or figures of speech: what is *not* unprecedented in Trump's rhetoric are the recurrent iterations of *occultatio* (that is, introducing a topic by disavowing it),[18] such as the *paralepsis* that Jennifer Mercieca has isolated as Trump's tropological calling tweet,[19] or the *preteritio* that Martin J. Medhurst finds coupled with a penchant for a simpering hyperbole.[20] Examples of Trump's "favorite rhetorical device" are not difficult to come by because they are apparently compulsively manufactured.[21] For example, after a debate in which a Fox News moderator questioned him about his misogynistic sensibilities, Trump tweeted, "I refuse to call Megyn Kelly a bimbo, because that would not be politically correct. Instead I will only call her a lightweight reporter!"[22] Because *occultatio* affirms a reality at the same moment of its disavowal, both Trump's allure and repulsion for many is that he seems incapable of hiding the pudding of his truth.

Having a handlist for identifying Trump's tropological tricks helps us to grapple with the specialty of his statements,[23] but we are still not quite sure how his ironic and often mean-spirited repertoire coheres into a patterned archive. Irony or *occultatio* notwithstanding, Trump's rhetoric remains elusively shrouded, as our social scientific friends might say, in an "$N = 1$."[24] "I've been studying presidential rhetoric for 40 plus years now," Medhurst concedes, "and I cannot recall an instance in any campaign or in any presidency where people have used language the way Donald Trump is using language."[25] So, how do we grapple with devices that we can name but that are advanced in seemingly unpredictable, novel performances?

The overdetermined recourse—of course!—is "to the man." That is, one is tempted to reckon with Trump's rhetoric with either defensive praise or character attacks instead of the words and arguments themselves, which is a ubiquitous and fractious form of reasoning termed the *ad hominem* fallacy.[26] As tempting as it might be to impugn Trump's character here, before we go there it is important to first situate the speaking subject—that is, most of us who attempt to communicate—as a kind of rhetorical switchboard for patterns and forms of thought that both comprise culture and *speak us*.[27] In what follows, then, I keep ethical judgment in abeyance in order to continue developing a rhetorical rendition of what Lacan dubbed "Freudian structures" or, more simply, psychical structures, which for Lacan reference three different, culturally specific strategies for relating to others that build the scaffolding for selfhood. Having detailed neurosis and psychosis in the last chapter, we can now take up the more complicated structure of perversion.

So far I have explained that the default relational strategy or disposition of Western culture is neurosis, which is expressed when an individual or community shares a common referential authority (the big Other) and has a more or less firm understanding of ignorance and limitation—including feelings of guilt and a willingness to "take 'no' for an answer." With a number of examples, I explained how the neurotic norm is short-circuited by the attentional habits cultivated by the *speed* of contemporary media technologies; a sense of immediacy and instantaneous communication disintegrates or obviates the time for reflection and recognition of commonly shared authorial points of reference, especially the one we term "the rule of law." With the eradication of the interval or episode central to a sense of continuous temporality, public space becomes an arena for addictions to the ecstasy of the ever-present interface.[28] A mundane example is that one may no longer be reluctant to say something offensive on Twitter because, in the scheme of things, such phatic rhetoric is fun, fleeting, and comes with limited fallout, replaced and forgotten in the next moment by something else.[29]

Although I am not certain, my sense is that a cultural trend toward psychosis is still largely behavioral and only momentarily structural at present, but this may be changing. It is, however, only within the *perception* of a characteristically psychotic *context* or environment that perversity can thrive for any sustained period of time (e.g., a presidential term). This is because in a psychotic environment only two dispositions toward others, neurosis and perversion, can continue without a crash. A culturally psychotic context could, of course, lead a public toward a more permanent psychotic disposition, but were this a widespread possibility, the social world would assuredly explode.

In this chapter, then, I move into a discussion of the psychical structure of *perversion*. Unlike psychosis, perversion bears the mark of *some* reflection or some sense of continuous temporality, which makes for a kind of predictable or cyclical volatility. Whereas neurosis is functionally self-reflective and psychosis is not, one might say that perversion as either a temporary or sustained structure is "quasi-reflexive." The quasi-reflexive character of perversion, I argue, is almost perfectly, rhetorically realized in the ironic trope of *occultatio* and its related formal patterns of disavowal: *I am not going to speak about the reality I affirm by denying it*, or *I know what I am doing is bad, but I am going to do it anyway*. Deploying the tropic form of *occultatio* (alternately *paralepsis* or *preteritio*) in political discourse is both a defensive disposition and demand factory: one denies a reality they affirm because they insist on something, at the very least the adoption of a particular point of view, but more grandiloquently for the restoration of a social order that never existed. Frustration is the marquee light and letter of the perverse, as disavowal and demand go hand in hand. Moreover, the logic of disavowal is not limited to simple statements of speech; as a strategy for relating to others, disavowal is composed of formal parallels among different aesthetic and rhetorical strata, or what I term *the perverse style*. Ultimately, I aim to show that Donald Trump's rhetoric is the most evident execution of the perverse style in our time.

PERVERSION TERMINABLE AND INTERMINABLE

It is not only that neurotics in themselves constitute a very numerous class, but it must also be considered that an unbroken chain bridges the gap between the neuroses in all the manifestations and normality. After all, Moebius could say with justice that we are all to some extent hysterics. Thus the extraordinarily wide dissemination of the perversions forces us to suppose that the disposition to perversions is itself no great rarity but must form a part of what passes as the normal constitution.

SIGMUND FREUD[30]

Perversion popularly denotes a swerving from cultural and purportedly biological norms in general, especially the widely assumed relation between sexuality and reproduction.[31] In addition to the (then) scandalous observation that infants and children are sexual beings, Freud famously argued that people are fundamentally "polymorphously perverse,"[32] meaning there is no "pregiven natural order" to the sexual drive and that its object of inspiration (either a person or a person's part) is ultimately interchangeable sans the constraints of cultural norms (homosexuality, for example, is no impediment to reproduction).[33] In short, to modify a lyric from Nirvana's Kurt Cobain, Freud knew what to cheer: everyone is queer.[34] A major reason for Freud's objection to popular theories of perversion in his time (such as Kraft-Ebbing's)[35] is that they wrongly import cultural and moral censure to bear upon a disposition "of no great rarity" and that actually forms "what passes as the normal constitution."[36] Judging or condemning another as "perverted" both overlooks a shared disposition and subjects them to what we know at some level betoken the sorts of cultural sensibility that lead to dehumanization and death. Properly perceived, perversity as such is a universally shared human trait that must be understood and accepted as universal before it is judged.

Despite the fact that "Freud effectively 'queers' all sexuality,"[37] the moralism attached to the term "perversion" and those who suffer the label has been hard to shake, both in popular culture and in legal and medical communities. Today many of the fetishes, behaviors, acts, *and thoughts* associated with perversion, from footwear worship to using a rather "innocuous plumed feather" in bed are still regarded and judged as "kinky," however commonplace.[38] To ward against pathological moralism and the conflation of clinical and juridical diagnoses, mental health professionals have moved to the term "paraphilia" to denote nonnormative, cultural compulsions and the pervasive prohibitions of "religious education."[39] Insofar as Western culture has come to accept classical perversions as more or less expected expressions of humanness—what else is the exchange of the fetishized commodity?—only "extreme" perversities with moral and legal implications (e.g., incest) remain as unacceptable aberrations inside and outside of cultural, legal, and medical contexts. The decision rule between a more common perversion and the kind of pathological perversion subject to punishment and hospitalization—the juridical domain—is *mutual informed consent.* "Nothing is true—everything is permitted,"[40] William S.

Burroughs once wrote, *but not without some self-aware agreement* among those who enjoy the "thing." Or as Andy Partridge explained to his newborn in the late 1980s, "Welcome to the garden of earthly delights / . . . This is your life and you do what you want to do / Just don't hurt nobody . . . 'less of course they ask you."[41] Nevertheless, to help us grapple with the limitations of the term "perversion" itself, I have advocated for a distinction among common, juridical, and ideological perversions. Common perversion is the universal queerness elaborated by Freud, juridical perversion primarily concerns perversions deemed morally or legally transgressive (e.g., rape), and ideological perversion references structural forms of oppression and violence that are misdirected or obscured in fantasies of the common good or public interest.

On the loop of perversion that spins from the common to the ideological, where do we conceptually locate the perverse structure? And what does it mean to say something or someone is *structurally* perverse? Unlike the more conspicuous expressions of neurotic and psychotic structures, perversity does not neatly lend itself to plotting: perverse behavior can range from the relatively common to the depraved, and one can sense how juridical and ideological expressions of perversity are much closer to an undergirding structure than fuzzy handcuffs. Even so, the difficulty in distinguishing between perverse acts or traits and structures has to do with a kind of mezzo castration between the neurotic and psychotic: the perverse subject knows at some level a second parent forbids an exclusive identification with the primary caregiver ("No!"), but s/he refuses to share and "disavows" knowledge of the prohibition. Put in Oedipal terms, the pervert hears the dad's negative demand for substitution, knows that there is supposed to be a break with Mom, but refuses to give her up. Returning to the diagram of the Oedipal triangle, then, the perverse structure could be envisioned as shown in figure 8.

For the pervert, there *is* an alienation from the primary parent because the "No!" is heard and registered, but he, she, or they *deny* having ever heard it and refuses a *separation* from an assumed "unity" with the maternal body. The pervert acknowledges and denies the social logic of substitution at the same time, even though they are capable of pretending compliance. Typically, the neurotic complies through the substitution of *repression*; the psychotic is oblivious and thus *forecloses* the process altogether; and the pervert knows what to do or say but *disavows* having such knowledge. The neurotic fumbles, though, with a more or less widely shared sense of what is right and wrong. Whatever the psychotic says, at base there is no understanding of what is or isn't culturally appropriate. And the pervert *knows what they do or say is wrong, but do or say it anyway*. It's this strange, unspoken acknowledgment of social order and the

PARENT II

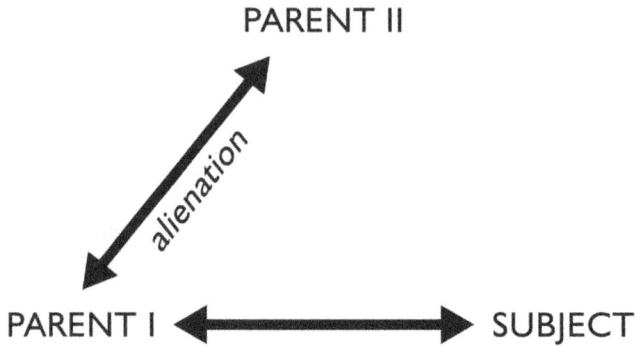

PARENT I ⟵⟶ SUBJECT

FIGURE 8. Perversion envisioned as a failure or absence of separation.

simultaneous denial of the same that makes the structurally perverse so per-plexing and (purportedly) unpredictable. Despite its obvious shortcomings, the asymmetrical and unstable confusion that results from alienation without separation and the consequent simultaneous affirmation and denial of consen-sus reality is why mutually informed consent has become the central arbiter of pathology and criminality: insofar as perversion is universal, it's just the best we got.

Still, as an *act* or *trait* perversion is pervasive—one could argue it is stan-dard in the "act" of abandon, for its perception is what we call "fun"—but as a structure perversion is very rare. The structurally perverse subject relates to others in alternately seductive and cruel ways—in ways that may seem to "con-nect" but in reality do not: the pervert refuses to accept the normative rules to which everyone else seems to submit like so many suckers, and the pervert observes them only insofar as they constitute a kind of game to get what they presumably want. The pervert may "play along" for a while but will eventually mete their own rules or sense of order onto others, even fashioning themselves as an instrument or tool of some grander, often cosmic purpose. The pervert issues different rules as a kind of defense or shield from accepting the norms everyone else seems to sheepishly follow. For example, in her careful study of clinical perversion from a Lacanian perspective, psychoanalyst Stephanie Swales points to the textbook exemplar of Anton Chigurh's coin-toss "game" in Cormack McCarthy's disturbing novel *No Country for Old Men*:

> When Chigurh encounters someone when he is not in need . . . he appeals to his law, which might be called the law of fate or chance. . . . Chigurh takes a coin from his pocket and instructs the other person to "call it." If the person

chooses correctly, then Chigurh lets him [or them] live. . . . On the other hand, Chigurh insists that the other person "call it" rather than he, which raises the meaning of the coin toss . . . to an event of fate in which the potential victim makes a choice. . . . Chigurh's role in the coin toss is that of the enactor of the Other's will (the god of fate).[42]

In a climactic scene from the novel, Chigurh's victim refuses to call a toss: "God would not want me to do that," Carla Jean protests. "Of course he would," replies Chigurh, "you should try to save yourself." She calls heads when tails would have spared her life. "You make it like it was the coin. But you're the one," she objects. "The coin didnt have no say. It was just you." He denies her pleas for life, explaining that her murder was fated and that "you're asking that I make myself vulnerable and that I can never do." He shoots her dead.[43] Called on to recognize his moral and legal responsibility, Chigurh disavows normalcy both in the simultaneous assertion of his superiority and in the sadistic banality of some presumably truer order of things, for which he is merely an instrument and thus is not responsible.[44]

From the outside and especially from the more or less the consensual default of neurosis, the pervert seems to enjoy their transgressions, or appears to take great pleasure in manipulating, exploiting, or punishing others (sadism); the more commonplace neurotic may even regard the pervert with jealousy or admiration ("Oh, I can't believe she just said that; I wish I could say things like that!"). The stereotypical pervert stands before us in a trench coat and— FLASH—we are made to witness their private truth as if it were universalized; from their smile or laughter we assume that the pervert is taking great pleasure in our collective shock and sometimes secret admiration. But, Lacan avers, this is not so.

Somewhat counterintuitively, the pervert's apparent transgressions are not that at all: these are actually *defenses*. These defenses *are perceived by others* as transgressions, and so we can speak of perverse behavior as culturally transgressive, but for the pervert the "violated" norms are not really violations. This is because such defenses are not in pursuit of enjoyment (*jouissance*) but rather constitutive of various disavowals issued to contain it.[45] The pervert is beholden, in a sense, to a ceaseless reliving of a primary bond with the first Other, and consequently, reckons with a position of unbearable passivity. The impositions of their own symbolic regime are attempts to (re)assert an active role, to achieve a sense of stability through *control* and *mastery*. Enjoyment is usually regarded as a loss of control, a form, however temporary, of "giving up," or a "little death," but this is neither what the pervert is after nor what they can achieve. Far from "the neurotic's wet dream" of the "liberated erotic connoisseur," the pervert is "fundamentally unfree, compulsively driven to repeat the same thing."[46] Inviting the gaze of others and controlling it, often with presumably unpredictable shifts in position or passion, is paramount.

The reason the distinction between perverse acts and the perverse structure is so perplexing is because the pervert is ultimately posed between two Others, so to speak: the bond with the inaugural Other of the primary parent, and the second Other of the paternal figure and the social rule of law it ultimately represents, the symbolic order of experience. The structural pervert behaves as if s/he can make the first Other whole or complete (Hooray!), but this is ultimately a passive position (Boo!).[47] The pervert thus attempts to achieve an active position, the metaphorical cake *and* its eating, through a perpetual parade of disavowals, both recognizing and denying social order simultaneously (precisely because, of course, the denial is ultimately a kind of recognition). The grown-up pervert is aware of social norms but denies them or only abides some norms insofar as compliance can be parlayed to an advantage, and often in the expressed service of some grander (second) Other that only they alone can perfect (God, the nation-state, "the people," and so on). This is why the pervert registers a kind of quasi reflexivity, because there is some time for reflection; there has to be for disavowal to occur. This cyclical in-betweenness is also why the pervert often seems to speak in the tones of prophecy, declaring a new path to law and order by punishing an exogenous threat, perhaps through exorcism or, as we have heard, by erecting a "big, fat, beautiful wall."[48]

TRUMPETEERING, OR, DISAVOWAL ON A ~~STICK~~ STUMP

> As I told everyone once before, [Anthony] Wiener is a sick puppy who will never change—100% of perverts go back to their ways. Sadly, there is no cure.
>
> DONALD J. TRUMP[49]

Of course, dear reader, you know where all of this is going.[50] The overwhelming temptation of the preceding explication is to rehash replays of "The Donald's" obscene oeuvre of *occultatio*, such as the voluminous orgy of perverse tweets that disavow backhanded affirmations:

> Sorry losers and haters, but my I.Q. is one of the highest—and you all know it! Please don't feel so stupid or insecure, it's not your fault.[51]

Happy New Year to all, including to my many enemies and those who have fought me and lost so badly they just don't know what to do. Love![52]

Why would Kim Jong-un insult me by calling me "old," when I would NEVER call him "short and fat?" Oh well, I try so hard to be his friend—and maybe someday that will happen![53]

We should locate Trump's perversity not so much in this or that single statement—which can be a violence in itself—but rather in the patterned disposition toward others implied by a collective corpus of acts in speech and deed: not one tweet but many. In its instance, an outrageous statement can be commonly perverse, but only those remarks that index an above-the-law sovereignty systematically or through an incessant denial of responsibility begin to outline the contours of a perverse style. A single tweet boasting of genius does not a style make. Three tweets do, however, demonstrate a pattern; a years-long chronicle of them reveals a particular public style of humor, irony, and meanness, almost in equal measure, which is arguably the trademark of disavowal and the tropic logic of *occultatio*.[54] Behavior and speech in a singular instance can point the way, but the signature of a perverse structure is often a *stylistic* disavowal—not once, not twice, but repeatedly and compulsively.

We have already noted that Trump's transcendental trope is *occultatio* (or variously *paralepsis* or *preteritio*), most recognizably in speech that references something by denying it: at a riotous rally in August 2016, after underscoring the Obama administration's failure to stabilize nation-states in the Middle East, Trump remarked that Obama is "the founder of ISIS [The Islamic State of Iraq and the Levant]. He's the founder of ISIS. He's the founder. He founded it. . . . And I would say the co-founder would be crooked Hillary Clinton."[55] The next day at a rally in Erie, Pennsylvania, Trump *appeared* to walk back his remarks—but then didn't: "So I said 'the founder of ISIS,' obviously I'm being sarcastic. But not that sarcastic, to be honest with you."[56] We do not need to cherry-pick for examples of *occultatio*, only to hold out our aprons to catch the strange, overripe fruits of the Trumpian disavowal.

In his monograph elaborating the artistry of "political conduct," Robert Hariman defines *political style* as a "coherent repertoire of rhetorical conventions depending on aesthetic reactions for political effect."[57] Hariman's approach suggests that political style is a shrewd or consciously chosen aesthetic that may or may not include speech or language but can include visual ornamentation, a gait or bearing, and so on.[58] From the psychoanalytic perspective, however, style can also be read symptomatically as the trace of a psychical structure, which implies that style is also a habitual repertoire of other relations. Consequently, any discernible aesthetic qualities will be infused with an affective juice.

Understood as disavowal, Trump's single-minded, splenetic salutations provide at least a partial explanation for why he is said to get away with the kind of hateful harangues and garrulous gaffes that would quickly disqualify others: as the currently visible trailblazer of the perverse political style, Trump's rhetoric registers the kind of reversals and semantic summersaults that signify *some* acknowledgment of the order of consensus and a denial of it at the same time. For disavowal, the indirect acknowledgment at some level is key—and it often inheres in parallel but distinct semiotic systems or communicative modes. For example, Trump's fevered rain of innuendo is symptomatic of a perverse manner of speaking that complements his deliberately cultivated comical appearance: he knows he *looks* silly to others, and yet . . .[59] Trump's self-styled, bleached-blonde comb-over and frequently disparaged orange facial tone have been ridiculed for over a decade.[60] Trump unquestionably knows others make fun of *how he looks*, but he refuses to directly acknowledge the critiques or adapt his appearance; the acknowledgment here is the act of refusal itself. In this respect, a tweet designed to insult North Korean president Kim Jong-un participates in the same rhetorical logic of Trump's trademark hair art. Although I had rather not dwell on Trump's appearance for good reasons,[61] the point here is that as a series of lateral disavowals in appearance, speech, and deed, we are not wont for examples of a perverse style, the hallmark of which is *occultatio* in speech, *but which should be traced in the disavowals of deed, look, gesture, tone, attitude, and ideology also.*

The key to the conceptual discernment of a given style in these parallel expressions is the homology. Originally inspired by the anthropological perspective of Claude Lévi-Strauss, the concept of homology references formal or patterned parallels among disparate representational resources, acts, and self-presentations (e.g., punk music and the chaotic coherence of punk dance, dress, and so on); style is thus wrapped up in a homologous "how," often aesthetic and affective in character but not necessarily so, that expresses a particular worldview.[62] By "style," then, I mean to reference conspicuous homologies netted into what Barry Brummett identifies as a "complex system of actions, objects, and behaviors" that is intended to mediate, distribute, and struggle over power.[63] (Insofar as it concerns power, style is always already "political.") Although it is a notoriously slippery concept, Brummett has insightfully demonstrated a way of grasping a given style by mapping it as a tangle of homologies.[64] From a psychoanalytic perspective, such cartography plots style beyond the statement to the serial enunciation of a tendency or bent; a style is a style only insofar as it registers as conspicuously compulsive.

Although we tend to associate style with the performative presentation of *particular* persons or groups, Brummett is careful to note that "style performs us as much as we perform a given style," which is suggestive of its ultimately mimetic and structural foundation.[65] Relatedly, we might qualify Robert Hariman's elaboration of political style as sometimes deliberately strategic but more often as *unconscious* displays of political power that recur in realist, courtly, republican, and bureaucratic flavors.[66] To this roster we can add the default political style of neurosis (supposedly rational or overtly deliberative rhetoric goes here, whether princely, managerial, or, in the end, Habermasian), the perceived anarchy of psychosis, and then the more befuddling stylistic villainy of perversion.[67] As a cache of recurrent, power-laden homologies, *the perverse style* is a mode of political presentation characterized by innuendo and irony, misdirection and contradiction, and deliberate instabilities in look, speech, and deed. The perverse style is often advanced in the service of humor but, in the final instance—and precisely because others are caused harm—a form of meanness if not irresponsibility.

Although I am arguing that Trump's discourse is most accurately typified by stylistic disavowals on multiple levels across many discernable contexts, I would be remiss not to include the "paranoid style" explicitly linked to Trump in the popular media. Trump's response to allegations of sexual misconduct or collusion with Russia are classically paranoid and parrot a pattern Richard Hofstadter described as reflective of a "feeling of persecution and of one's own greatness," which is "systematized in grandiose theories of conspiracy"—an alternative order if there ever was one.[68] "This [allegation of sexual misconduct] is a conspiracy against you, the American people," decried Trump at a rally in West Palm Beach in October 2015. "These people are horrible people, they're horrible, horrible liars and interestingly, it happens to appear 26 days before our very important election, isn't that amazing?"[69] The same evening on *PBS NewsHour*, presidential historian Jon Meacham remarked it was "as though Richard Hofstader wrote 'The Paranoid Style in American Politics'" for Trump instead of Goldwater "but in a Jerry Springer context."[70] Meacham's qualifier is important: Jerry Springer is a former mayor of Cincinnati but most known for his semiscripted, sleazy, eponymous talk show, typified by popularly perverse confessions and outrageous on-screen fights.[71] In this respect we should underscore that a given figure can simultaneously exhibit any number of styles, and Trump certainly exhibits *both* perversion and paranoia. I would argue, however, that paranoiac styling is usually and ultimately *in the service of the perverse*: A relentlessly consistent paranoid style would be more indicative of a psychotic structure that is, by definition, destructive and difficult to sustain without a so-called break.[72] It's this "Jerry Springer context," redolent of fakery and fighting and screamed demands, however, that suggests the perverse and paranoid styles are of a piece, the former a larger stylistic category, whereas paranoia is a free-floating one that can appear in neurotic, psychotic, and perverse contexts. Regardless, as a dispositive and stylistic strategy, perversion and paranoia are pointless without their principle purpose: the circus of demand.

HAND IN HAND, DISAVOWAL AND DEMAND

Mother should I build the wall? / Mother should I run for president?

PINK FLOYD, *The Wall*[73]

Flashback: June 15, 2015. In a tower that bears his name, just a worn coin's throw from the New York Stock Exchange, Donald Trump descended a gaudy, golden escalator with his spouse Melania to a flag-rimmed podium in a food court atrium.[74] Sensationally concluding that "the American Dream is dead," in a rambling, forty-five-minute address Trump announced his candidacy for the US presidency and introduced a platform more meticulously outlined on a 1979 Pink Floyd double album than any subsequent press release or policy paper to date.[75] "I would build a great wall, and nobody builds walls better than me, believe me," Trump barked, "and I will have Mexico pay for that wall."[76] Such an unlikely structure would have been dismissed out of hand were it not for the raison d'être of Trump's erectile injunction: Mexico's immigrants are "bringing drugs. They're bringing crime. They're rapists," and while he assumes "some . . . are good people," Trump averred, "border guards" say that Mexico is "sending us not the right people."[77] "Build the wall!" has subsequently become a taunting demand for Trump's supporters, not simply at the political rallies Trump routinely conducts but at sporting events, vacation resorts, and other crowding contexts racists deem ripe for segregation.[78]

Flashforward: Friday, July 13, 2018. In a manner recalling Pink Floyd's live show staple of a giant flying pig, a bright orange, twenty-foot blimp depicting the president as an enraged infant clutching a cell phone floats above Parliament Square at a "Carnival of Resistance."[79] Although the US president mostly avoided London in the summer of 2018, tens of thousands of British Islanders, many shouting "No Trump, no KKK, no fascist USA!" assembled to protest his meeting with Prime Minister Theresa May during a visit that proved to be a diplomatic disaster.[80] Environmental activist Leo Murray crowdfunded the creation of "Baby Trump," which he argued "captured something of the essence of the president's character"—so much so that the blimp is in demand for protests around the world, making appearances in Argentina, France, Ireland, and the United States so far.[81] Noting the unanticipated amount of money the blimp campaign raised, Murray said, "We are going to send Trump Baby on a world tour . . . to just make sure he carries on trolling Trump throughout this awful, grotesque presidency."[82]

Insofar as the delivery of reality in (post)modernity is mostly conducted with and through screens, it makes rhetorical sense to deploy a term typically reserved for the virtual: "trolling" typically refers to a deliberately provocative statement designed to offend or upset others online. Using an inflatable infant to make Trump feel unwelcome in the places he visits is a material counterpoint to Trump's own trolling via Twitter tirades, as if trolling in the nonvirtual trumps the presumably inconsequential effects of online obstinacy. Nevertheless, the blimp-flying culture jam bespeaks the same infantile logic it critiques, however perfect the "Trump Baby" captures the commander in chief's "character": both are forms of crying.

Much better than the "Trump Chicken" blimp that probably inspired it,[83] the "Trump Baby" balloon indexes a public awareness of the regressive logic that Trump's political rhetoric represents: infantile omnipotence, a mistaken narcissism ubiquitous in early life, that one can control the universe or bend reality toward one's will through urination, defecation, and finally, crying—in multiple senses (it must be underscored that the eyes, ears, and mouth are leaky orifices). In adult life the persistence of this feeling often goes by the term "magic," its rhetorical key terms consisting of "spells" and "rituals," but in politics it is almost always in terms of *the demand*. From a Lacanian vantage, the demand is an expression of speech (say, for refusing to bake a cake for a gay wedding) that is situated between "need" and "desire," but it is ultimately founded in Freud's conception of crying. Rehearsing how the demand operates as a permitted form of crying in politics (or "demand politics," as it is sometimes called) helps us to better grapple with the perverse style as one that presses disavowal into the service of the demand. Strangely to some, Trump's rather snug relationship with the National Rifle Association will help us toward this end.

On Crying

As Sigmund Freud said of religion, the condition of speech is an original helplessness.[84] Incapable of meeting its needs alone, the infant's yelps pierce "a synchronic world of cries" already arranged in a symbolic order, enabling a caregiver to assign meaning and, in effect, to speak for the babe ("Herman is hungry!").[85] This is to say that infants are caught up in the symbolic world before they can understand it—indeed, many people are given names before they exit the womb. The cry, then, has a double character that is always already instinctual *and* symbolic, hence "the drives." Initially, the cry is made to have a *need* addressed. Lacan argued, however, that the cries of helplessness already signal the emergence of the demand, a plea for recognition. Need typically yields to the dominance of the demand in toddler (thug) life. At a later stage, cries are demands because the toddler *actually* wants the attention or love of the parent; the object of the demand is a proxy.

Once one is a subject of language, then, within every *manifest* demand—however reasonable ("Can I have some water, please?"), unreasonable ("Make it stop raining!"), or silly ("I can haz cheezburger?")—is a *latent* demand for recognition ("Love me!").[86] In this way, a maturing person may begin to realize that her demands for various things may not or cannot be satisfied by getting those things, that there is something extra or impossible *about* the things that has more to do with the Other they re-present than the things themselves. This excessive dimension beyond the object of the demand is the domain of "desire," and a lot of us have trouble speaking about it because doing so means we have to give up on the fantasy of a love that would make us whole. Realizing the truth of one's desire beyond demands, that no object or Other can "fix" you or me, is a difficult reckoning and is the hardest part of being a "grown-up." Learning to *desire*, to spend one's life as a series of substitutions and compromises that never lead to total satisfaction, means that one has to reckon with the fact that the Stones were right, you never really get what you want; one is lucky to get what one needs. Such is the ideology of neurosis and, as I elaborate below, why the pervert doesn't desire.

The demand and its various genres (the cry, the call, the request, the petition, the love letter, the ultimatum, and so on) are indispensable for politics, which is to say indispensable for living at all. One must make demands from time to time to satisfy a need or to get what one wants. This is particularly true of politics as such, which is why the philosopher of social movements Ernesto Laclau argues that the "social demand" is the "smallest unit" for any analysis of politics.[87] An exclusive focus on the politics of demand is usually posed against a more reflective "politics of desire," which tempers the stridency of any sociopolitical demand. Ideally, the political would progress as a dialectic between demands and desire—the neurotic disposition requiring some time for reflection. Christian Lundberg warns that a pure politics of demand, however, is functionally perverse because "demands also entail a perverse dialectic of political agency as resistance and simultaneous interpassive political constraint. Demands empower forms of political agency by generating an oppositional relationship to hegemonic structures, and by providing the equivalential preconditions for identity."[88] One should not be surprised that the interplay of resistance and "interpassivity," a term that denotes a kind of vicarious feeling of activity done by someone else (e.g., canned laughter in sitcoms),[89] is locked into any one demand. Participating in a politics of resistance while doing nothing is perversely homologous to the strategy of disavowal—and in a certain sense a demand *is* disavowal: to make demands is to disavow that the object of the demand *cannot* satisfy because it is not really what one wants. Such a political disposition is classically perverse, as Astrid Gessert explains: "Neurotics will always struggle with their desire. . . . The problem for the perverse subject, on the other hand, is that they think there is an object that can satisfy. There is, as Freud said, fixation instead of desire. . . . The perverse subject does not desire but demands, and demand is directed at an object."[90] That a perverse person or group believes that an object *can* satisfy—locking her up, building that wall—reflects the quasi-reflexive temporality of perversion: each time the object is achieved, it is not the right one, so the fixation on another object begins anew in a ceaseless cycle of demands. Moreover, this push for a purer politics of demand, which is precisely the story of the radical right crafted by Newt Gingrich,[91] is perversely addictive; a pervert's repetitive violations and disavowals register the repetition compulsion so characteristic of addiction. Resistance to the art of substitution, which is the way of desire, can throw a person or group into an endless, addictive loop of demands, or as Robert Smith sings, "Whatever I do to make it real / it's never enough."[92]

The overwhelmingly addictive and perverse politics of demand is insightfully illustrated by Laura J. Collins in an essay on Second Amendment fanaticism.[93] Gun rights discourse, she argues, has been almost completely taken over by a politics of demand, seemingly independent of satisfaction, leading to a larger impasse or deadlock over regulation in the United States.[94] This deadlock is easily gleaned by contrasting the rhetoric of a National Rifle Association convention and the speeches of the youth-led "March for Our Lives" protest in the wake of a high school shooting in Florida.[95] Collins analyzes an interesting and related case, showing how a politics of demand is articulated around an identity of traumatic victimhood.

Collins tells the story of gun journalist Dick Metcalf, whose career was ended after he published a column in *Guns & Ammo* magazine in 2013. He wrote that "way too many gun owners seem to believe *any* regulation of the right to keep and bear arms is an infringement. . . . The fact is, all constitutional rights are regulated, always have been, and need to be."[96] Metcalf's remarks were received by the gun rights community as a wounding betrayal, leading to his firing from the magazine. Despite what would appear to be a satisfying "win" for those deeply offended by Metcalf's defense of regulation, it was not enough and outraged demands continued long after his firing. Collins details a strange, cultivated dependency on experiences of offense that accrue gun lovers an outsider or minority identity, weirdly reinforcing a sense of self-sufficiency in victimhood and betrayal—the preconditions of an identity Lundberg warns us about, the demanding subject.

What accounts for an addiction to the demand is the motor of *jouissance*,[97] usually translated as "enjoyment," a term that indexes a drive to escape the limits of language, beyond any moderation of pleasure or satisfaction or labeling, into a kind of painful perseveration or "suffering."[98] Consequently, the manifest content of gun rights discourse is secondary to the formal patterns of the demand and the affects they organize. Describing *jouissance* in the abstract—well, in any language at all—is difficult and so another example is helpful (and not quite so dark). Insofar as the politics of demand is figured in form, we should be able to switch out the high court, gun rights tragedies with a bit of low-brow vulgarity and still find a similar kind of dependency. We do (of course!) in the first act of Tim Burton's 1985 directorial debut, *Pee-wee's Big Adventure*. After a complex morning ritual in his toy-strewn bungalow (so many objects to love!), a precious Pee-wee Herman goes outside and excitedly removes his cherished red beach-cruiser bicycle from its secret hiding place. As he is preparing to go for a ride, Pee-wee is approached by his neighbor Francis Buxton, a rotund figure wearing blue coveralls:

FRANCIS: *[snide tone]* Morning, Pee-wee.
PEE-WEE: *[resigned tone]* Hello, Francis.
FRANCIS: Today's my birthday, and my father said I can have anything I want.
PEE-WEE: Good for you and your *father*.
FRANCIS: So guess what I want?
PEE-WEE: A new brain!
FRANCIS: No! Your bike.
PEE-WEE: *[falls on the ground, exaggerating laughter]*
FRANCIS: What's so funny, Pee-wee?
PEE-WEE: *[gets up]* It's not for sale, Fran-*cis*!
FRANCIS: *[pulls out a wad of cash]* My father says everything's negotiable, pee-wee *[flips through bills]*

PEE-WEE: I wouldn't sell my bike for all the money in the world. Not for a hundred million, trillion, billion dollars!

FRANCIS: Then you're crazy!

PEE-WEE: I know you are but what am I?

FRANCIS: You're a nerd!

PEE-WEE: I know you are but what am I?

FRANCIS: You're an idiot!

PEE-WEE: I know you are but what am I?

FRANCIS AND PEE-WEE: *[in unison]* I know you are but what am I? I know you are but what am I? I know you are but what am I?

PEE-WEE: Infinity!

FRANCIS: No, I'm not. *[In unison with Pee-wee]* You are!

FRANCIS AND PEE-WEE: *[Pee-wee mocks Francis by mimicking his comments; in unison]* No way! Knock it off! Cut it out!

FRANCIS: Shut up, Pee-wee!

PEE-WEE: Why don't you make me?

FRANCIS: You make me!

PEE-WEE: Because. I don't make monkeys, I just train 'em.

FRANCIS: *[plaintively]* Pee-wee, listen to reason.

PEE-WEE: *[uses hand as a cone over his ear, feigns listening]*

FRANCIS: Pee-wee!

PEE-WEE: Shhhhhh! I'm listening to reason.

FRANCIS: Pee-wee!

PEE-WEE: That's my name, don't wear it out.

Queering the gun lover's script,[99] Pee-wee cherishes his bike more than anything in the world, but Francis asserts the eminent domain of paternal authority and wealth. When the Oedipal appeal doesn't work, Francis retorts that Pee-wee is "crazy," a "nerd," and an "idiot," echoing the types of people typically excluded from public deliberation (the unmanly, the childish, and the mentally unstable).[100] The resulting bandy of juvenile objections leads Francis, finally, to an appeal to the logos—which also fails. The failure of the appeal to "the economy" or its surrogate "reason" is telling: both boys (well, grown actors pretending to be boys) *enjoy* the demand and its refusal, and aside for the spectator's mirth, in the diegesis or film story world neither character experiences the encounter as pleasurable.

My focus on the demand here is formally rhetorical: it is a gesture that is, in the end, a cry for recognition; as such, the demand is not fixed to any psychical disposition (which is to say, we all make demands). Moreover, in respect to Second Amendment fanaticism, there are myriad intersecting discourses that complicate the character of the demand, including class anxiety, whiteness and racism, perceptions of a besieged masculinity, and so on. The same can be said about rhetorically similar conflicts where demands are clearly present despite different material and historical contexts: demands about the English language, capital punishment, abortion, the minimum wage, the US border, or same-sex marriage in our political discourse intersect with a host of difficult tensions and issues (class, race, misogyny, sexuality) yet nevertheless evince similar insistent cries for recognition that indicate that identities are as much a part of the conflicts as the objects of demand themselves. This is *not to say the objects are unimportant*, only that something in addition to "the bike" is at stake. An affective dimension of rhetoric is tied to phatic utterance and identity as much as it is to the content of claims.

Precisely because it is absurd, it is difficult to avoid comparing Francis and Pee-wee's infantile exchange to the stale story of civil decline that has become so familiar to us in the last decade. Both Francis's and Pee-wee's feigned fealty to reason also reflects, in many ways, the cynicism that is supposed to follow the critiques of civility and public reason gleaned from the work of Nancy Fraser and Michael Warner,[101] and closer to my home field, from the work of Nina Lozano-Reich, Dana L. Cloud, and others on incivility, as well as from the cautionary tales advanced about the civic mission of speech education by Pat Gehrke, Ronald Walter Green, and Darrin Hicks.[102] As is the case with these critiques, however, the criticism of demand politics does not present us with a cynical prognosis but rather *a diagnostic* to better enable us to get over our contemporary addiction to the demand. To this end, we should attend to the *enjoyment* Francis and Pee-wee are getting from their banter, related to but distinct from what they say. We can "read" the cinematic exchange on the two levels of the demand, the manifest and the latent:

- On the first level, the manifest level of meaning, image, and (feigned) rational exchange, Pee-wee and Francis argue over a bicycle. This is the level of the disavowal, as this is really not the reality in play.
- On the second level, however, is a deeper deadlock that indicates a repartee over seemingly substitutable objects: Francis offers paternal authority, money, and reason as *substitute* objects for the bike, which reveals that what's really negotiated here is a classed relationship between two people vying for recognition. Who is Francis to Pee-wee, and who is Pee-wee to Francis?[103]

It is this second level, where *love* is lodging in demands and refusals: insofar as the plot of *Pee-wee's Big Adventure* concerns the theft of Pee-wee's bike and his attempts to find it (at one point he is misled to find it in the "basement" of the Alamo), focusing exclusively on the content of the argument we would be led to believe the conflict and quest *is about the bike*. But the bike doesn't really satisfy a need for either Francis or Pee-wee, so we know to look for the latent demand for recognition: Francis wants to purchase his love and has his selfhood reaffirmed when his demand denied; Pee-wee's sense of self-worth is reaffirmed knowing that someone wants what he has, most especially when it is taken away. In this way, Francis and Pee-wee are not taking *pleasure* in their banter as much as they are confirming their own identities in pain, a paradox of enjoyment. Consequently, there can be only stalemate or an escalation of aggressivity.

All You Need is Love? No Thanks!

I'm just trying to find out what you're hiding
What is the mystery?
What you get is what you seek (sugar)
Desire

GENE LOVES JEZEBEL[104]

So the pseudointerrogative "I know you are but what am I?" is a kind of demand for love that obscures a deeper question harbored by all subjects, "What do you want?" "I know you are but what am I?" is, in fact, disavowal on a stick, implicating a close relation between demands and disavowals as relational strategies. The deeper question, "What do you want?" or "*Che vuoi?*," is the question of desire, which Lacan deploys in both directions: from the place of the subject, "What do you want from me?" and from the place of the Other, "What do you *really* want for yourself?" From either vantage, the question "What do you want?" implicates an uncertainty about what the Other wants from me and what I actually want myself, a disposition of uncertainty. Although such a disposition is difficult to sustain all the time, it is one that keeps us receptive to contingency, reflection, and possibility, which denotes the psychical structure of neurosis. In this respect, if we can make a scholarly project of the structural relation between subjects, demand politics poses us with a question: How can we refigure "I know you are but what am I?" in such a way that a more fundamental and common question at the core of selfhood can be continuously intoned instead: *What do you want?* The condition of the possibility of a democracy (yet to come) rests on the question of desire and a striving to keep this question an open one; the condition requires a disposition of listening.

At this juncture I've wandered pretty far into the pastures of psychoanalysis, and I do not need to drag folks out there all the way—it's much too easy to get mired in Lacanian patties and Kleinian placentas. We do, however, need to graze around another psychoanalytic question intoned more famously by Tina Turner than Sigmund Freud: What's love got to do with it? The answer is, predictably, everything. We know, for example, that the latent dimension of the demand is for recognition or love. But there is another kind of love, a bigger fantasy of courtship that underwrites public deliberation and that Trump has worked hard to undo. In this respect we might identify two levels of love, the love of the demand or lowercase "love" ("Recognize me!") and the uppercase "Love" of desire ("What do you want?"). Whereas the former is thoroughly narcissistic and driven by *jouissance*, the latter denotes the disposition of desire as a question mark, open to the Other.[105]

If it's not already clear, I've been arguing that the perverse style references a politics of demand, while a more democratic or deliberative style points to a neurotic politics of desire. Neither of these are ever truly "pure" and, in general, persist in contemporary politics as an admixture. The dominance of Trump's perverse style in (post)modern politics suggests, however, a swerve toward increasing, generalized perversion if only because demands seem to be outpacing calls for moderation and deliberation. Every wish is cast as an uncompromising and absolute demand. So why are we getting stuck today in political demands? Why the little love of enclaves instead of the big love of the demos? Why aggression instead of compromise? The answer has something to do with Francis's father, or rather, with the erosion of the kind of Oedipal authority the rich daddy represents.

In a paper elaborating the theory of the political demand,[106] Lundberg argues that our assumed model political deliberation is analogous to courtly love: for Lacan, the fantasy of romantic love as an illusory union of different subjects is a *necessary* and rather elegant solution to our common, existential alienation: we are not, nor shall we ever be, "one." This brute fact drives all sorts of affects that get rendered as aggression or passion—at base these are two sides of the same coin—alternating between a drive toward independence (liberty!) and a desire for unity (consume!). Because an *unbridled enjoyment* of these intensities can lead to violence and destruction, we use speech to modify and rechannel them into socially valued expressions. This rechanneling is termed "sublimation," and for Lacan the paradigm example of sublimation is courtly love, an asexual, imaginary scheme or fantasy that checks aggressivity—that puts breaks on enjoyment and the drives run amok—in favor of social belonging. As the figure of the fool teaches us, the fantasy of love is not without its unforeseen pitfalls, but even so, within its coordinates the question "What do you want?" remains an open one, even in the parade of temporary bridges (especially the bonds of deceit).

Drawing on Herbert Marcuse and John Dewey, Lundberg suggests that political sublimation is a principled and "healthy" approach to democratic antagonism that resembles the structure of courtly love: while the demos is far from stable, the story goes, there used to be *faith* in a kind of public deliberation or reason in which compromise or bipartisanship puts checks on getting what one wants, tempering the demand. Faith here is better placed in the Stones than the Beatles: love is not *all* you need, because you can't always get what you want. The authority of the demos was *never* based on the promise of a perfect union, as if there were some total satisfaction to sublimation,[107] but rather on the *more* perfect union—a dream functionally and deliberately deferred, a love that was recognized as impossible yet necessary. If we agree with Lundberg that there has been a shift in our "affective ecology,"[108] indexed in the superstructure of public arguments (e.g., about the Second Amendment), then what has changed in our time is the *perception of* the character of democratic courtship. Love is a variant of aggressivity, as even political anger is founded on the conditions of conciliation; it is a *mean* love or hate, but a love nonetheless, still a courtship in a mirrored hallway.

CONCLUSION: ELEMENTS OF (PERVERSE) STYLE

> You do not know what wars are going on
> Down where the spirit meets the bone.
> MILLER AND LUCINDA WILLIAMS[109]

So what accounts for the *mean* love of our time so well represented by the perverse style? How do we account for the sadism of our present political climate and the seeming masochism of the electorate? Although the language of symbolic efficiency and its decline outlined in the previous chapter was not yet available to him, it is not surprising that the most psychoanalytic of the Frankfurters, Herbert Marcuse, argued it was the decline of authority as represented by a parental figure, or to reference Pee-wee and Francis's melee, the ultimate irrelevance of Francis's rich papa. As the big Other erodes, demand politics is all that you're left with. For Marcuse, the obsolescence of Freud's conception of subjectivity in modernity had to do with the fact that the family "is no longer the primary agent of socialization," which depended on an authority of parenting. Rather, in our time "the child learns that . . . the playmates, the neighbors, the leader of the gang, the sport, the screen are the authorities on appropriate mental and physical behavior."[110] A strictly Freudian characterization of political sublimation required a *leader*, although Freud made room for the possibility that an "abstraction may . . . be substituted for the leader," which is in some sense the function of Lacan's big Other. Nevertheless, Marcuse argued that our current surrogates, "the United States" or "the Economy," are no more "unifying" than Francis's "money" or "reason."[111] Marcuse argued that the entire apparatus of mass culture offers up a series of fungible proxies: "the stars and starlets of politics, television, and sports" are merely the "functionaries of a higher authority which is no longer embodied in a person" but a "productive apparatus" that strongly resembles Foucault's characterization of governmentality.[112] In many ways, then, the deadlock of demand politics cannot be undone because we are increasingly leaderless (the "big Other," as 'dem Lacanians say, is becoming dead to us). The ascent of the politics of demand registers the erosion of authority as embodied in political leaders and conceptual abstractions.

In a "society without leaders,"[113] we are left with the fragility of the authority of the demos and a never-ending parade of popular inducements toward what we might term "microsublimations" for individual transiency, from our walking about campus compulsively looking at our phones, to a turning toward peer groups and screens, to most alarmingly, the celebration of tragedies—of school shootings and train wrecks, of forty-eight-hour murder mysteries and the elevated beating of Jay-Z by Beyoncé's sister. In the looping of antagonistic enjoyment that is the key tonal quality of the perverse style, argument forms are only *one* way in which the motors of enjoyment continue to combust: since 9/11, the trauma industries that arose in the ashes of the World Trade Center relentlessly feature the failures of sublimation as entertainment, which Freud somewhat infamously footnoted as an inability to "renounce" the desire to piss on the fire.[114] A horrific scandal created by the hipster clothing retailer Urban Outfitters is another example of what we get with the perverse style: a bloodstained Kent State sweatshirt. They just had to sell it.[115] Smoke ensued.[116] We enjoyed our mutual but temporary outfitting in moral outrage, but then we went back to work, just as we have resorted to doing with the daily news of adventures in Trumpeteering. In the place of shared principles and the collapse of authority, slack-jawed shock and awe fills in the gaps.[117]

The perverse style names an affective and aesthetic repertoire of disavowal and demand. Its master trope is *occultatio*, and its logic reflects a quasireflective temporality of indirect acknowledgment through denial. When the style reflects a common perversion, it is mostly harmless, often humorous, and fun: most jokes, for example, are a "lite" form of disavowal. Yet at the deeper juridical and ideological levels reflected in demand politics, the perverse style is functionally destructive and a danger to the fantasy of democracy. The arrival of Trump to politics, with props to George Orwell and Kenneth Burke, is turning the comedy of the barnyard into the tragedy of war. The ruptures of enjoyment that public humor used to inspire have become so much schadenfreude. Instead of seeing Pee-wee and Francis's verbal melee as two actors trying not to crack up when delivering their infantile lines, we attend too closely to the letter of refusal: *I know you are but what am I?* Maybe, then, this perceived shift in our affective ecology questions the effectiveness of the form of public argument itself? Maybe it heralds the final arrival of the hegemony of perverse politics?

To make good on the hope of a politics of desire and the more stable scene of a neurotic republic, perhaps one of the tasks of scholars in the humanities is to transmute the closed claims of demands into the open questions they harbor, tickling the underbelly of the political at the ribs of social values? To this end we would need to get closer to the *structure* of perversion and take up the question of responsibility and judgment. Style tells us where to look, but it is effectively a repertoire and not yet the archive a structure connotes: when style becomes immutable as an ideology it becomes a kind of genre of subjectivity. Having an account of the ideological moorings of perversion will help us to see better and make the call.

CHAPTER 4

Showmancing the Presidency: Perverse Genres and the Problem of Judgment

One certainly does best to separate an artist from his work to the extent of not taking him as seriously as his work. He is in the end only the precondition of his work, the womb, the ground, in some cases the fertilizer and manure on which it grows—and thus in most cases something one must forget if one wishes to enjoy the work itself.

FRIEDRICH NIETZSCHE[1]

To seriously discuss this presidency, you have to open your mind to the obscene.

MICHELLE GOLDBERG[2]

For the last seven months of 2016, a former MI6 secret intelligence head for Russian affairs dashed off seventeen memos to his employers at the DC-based Fusion GPS, an investigative firm that produces "oppositional research" for political actors. British bloodhound Christopher Steele did not know for whom he investigated, only that he needed to provide leads for further research to verify his answer to the following question: "Why did Mr. [Donald] Trump repeatedly seek to do deals in a notoriously corrupt police state that most serious investors shun?"[3] It turns out the private intelligence dossier that Steele helped to produce was paid for by Hillary Clinton's presidential campaign and the Democratic National Committee—routine "oppo" politics, of course.[4] The report gradually landed in the hands of US intelligence officials and in front of the alarmed gazes of President Barack Obama and Vice President Joe Biden.[5] The distressing dossier alleged that the Trump campaign colluded with Russian operatives to interfere in the 2016 election, in part by publicizing damning, private information illegally hacked from the DNC. The report also included nocent notice about candidate Trump's susceptibility to blackmail.[6]

Although news of the existence and details of the dossier had been circulating "among journalists and politicians in Washington" months before it was reportedly revealed, much of the information was unsubstantiated, and intelligence officials worried it would leak before Trump could be briefed on its existence.[7] After the election Trump was informed, but CNN reported on the existence of "classified documents" ten days before the inauguration, deciding to omit the unproven details.[8] The online, tabloid news(ish) and media website BuzzFeed shared no such caution, however, and later on the evening of January 10, 2017, published the entire leaked dossier "so that Americans can make up their own minds about allegations about the president-elect that have circulated at the highest levels of government."[9] BuzzFeed was instantly pilloried by the press and government officials for violating journalistic ethics and compromising national security.[10]

The possibility of a conspiracy with Russian officials is bad enough, but Trump's station was worsened by his repeated attempts to inhibit further investigation, which compounded the allegations of collusion with charges of obstructing justice: when the former Trump surrogate and attorney general recused himself from a special counsel investigation, Trump bullied and publicly humiliated the (formerly) fiercely "loyal" Jeff Sessions,[11] and soon thereafter fired the director of the Federal Bureau of Investigation, James Comey.[12] Yet despite the high drama of political intrigue, and regardless of an almost two-year-long investigation of high crimes by former FBI director Robert Mueller, at present the dominant catalysts for popular fascination are projections about Trump's aberrant proclivities in the bedroom: while attending the Miss Universe pageant in 2013, Trump allegedly watched two prostitutes urinate on a bed that the Obamas previously slept in at the Moscow Ritz-Carlton Hotel.[13]

If only because the rumors about the Trump "pee tape" continue to circulate—which Comey's tell-all memoir rallied again in 2018[14]—the argument that his political figure is perverse is hardly new: until the tape publicly appears or Trump leaves office (or both), late night talk-show hosts will never let the rumors rest.[15] Among a number of related salacious stories, the pee tape fantasy has become the centerpiece of *kompromat* conspiracy theories elaborated to explain Trump's public flirtations with Vladimir Putin.[16] Speculation about Trump's erotic escapades has almost become, at least on living- and bedroom screens, a national pastime. In the fall of 2018, for example, actor and comedian Tom Arnold hosted a Viceland "documentary" series, *The Hunt for the Trump Tapes*, in search of *any* incriminating recordings he could find; the Holy Grail would be filled to the brim with whizz and piddle. Arnold found nothing.[17]

Of course, given the fodder for entertainment that the maybe-existing tape has provided, the golden shower fantasy doesn't depend on whether it actually exists. As columnist Maureen O'Conner insightfully argues, the rumor or myth is *wabi-sabi*, "a Japanese term for that which is perfect . . . because of its imperfections." She elaborates: "Wabi-sabi rumors are stories that are so unbelievable, they become perversely believable again. They feel right, even when you know they aren't, so they take on the force of legend. Examples include Richard Gere's gerbil [that the famous actor enjoys putting rodents in his behind]. . . . They're rumors so compelling that even when you realize they're false, you stay up all night reading about parallel universes."[18] What would the discovery of a pee tape prove? That "Trump is sexually debauched and longs to desecrate everything Obama touched[?]," quips Michelle Goldberg of the *New York Times.* "We already know that."[19] Yet despite the "sheer perfection" of the near mythic status of the pee tape, many commentators have marveled at how Trump's "truly outrageous actions never seem to stick to him."[20] Goldberg opines one reason is that "Trump benefits from the fact that looking too closely at his behavior, sexual and otherwise, feels soiling."[21]

Perhaps.

Insofar as Trump's cyclical style of disavowal and demand screens perversion in plain sight—in appearance, word, gesture, and deed—and insofar as revelations of his porn star philandering keep coming,[22] perhaps the reason why the "perverse" label fails to (sus)tain him has more to do with a widespread quasi-conscious recognition of our common perversity? Any sense of soiling elicited by studying Trump's salacious scandals also secretly saps our own nonnormative fantasies, most of which only get traversed by proxy anyway. "Every neurotic subject dreams of being a pervert," observes Paul Verhaeghe. "He or she dreams of the unlimited gratification the pervert is imagined to enjoy."[23] Becoming too (publicly) engaged with our perverse imagination—at least outside of a darkened cinema or domestic screening room—risks outing, which is perhaps why labels like "crazy" or "genius" are more readily deployed: they either distance or disregard.

To reckon with Trump as a pervert risks confronting our own aberrant teacups, making it much more difficult to dismiss or claim his figure as "one of us." When accepting the common perversion that we all share, our enjoyment of Trump's spectacles and his compulsive need for witnesses makes the moorings of ethical judgment much harder to discern.

Trump certainly seems to enjoy a need to *at least appear* as an agent of "unlimited gratification" by staging an array of transgressions, even though a structurally perverse person's perceived transgressions are in reality a loop of defensive demands.[24] That he is a textbook exemplar of a perverse style of political rhetoric is palpable. But can we claim that Trump's perverse style is solidly structural and not, simply, a put-on? In this chapter I take up the question of what happens when a style also expresses a more or less *unmanageable* series of rhetorical disavowals and demands or, simply, the idea of an entrenched cultural genre as a psychical structure.[25] I argue against the common suggestion, coming from sources from journalists to scholars like Princeton University historian Julian Zelizer, that "Trump sounds normal in private" or that "the norm-breaking, in-your-face conservative populist" is a role played for microphones and cameras.[26] Whereas a style might be adopted, I suggest that genres preexist us—and that *roles play us too*. For example, one common trait of the perverse subject is the cavalcade of endlessly deployed prefab defenses, enactments of ready-made cultural fantasies for what an impossible, unlimited satisfaction is *supposed* to look like (perversion, for example, is always supposed to look sadistic when, I would argue, ubiquitous examples are readily available for fieldwork in chow-mart chains like Golden Corral, Luby's, and Western Sizzlin). This is all the more reason why Trump's confirmed lewdness and lawlessness is so cartoonishly grandiloquent: mob boss fantasies of wealth involving Russian oligarchs; gilded furniture; self-serving economic conflicts of interest (such as having state events in Trump-owned properties); gilded picture frames; an above-the-ground courtship of white supremacists which was, hitherto, a sub-rosa "Southern Strategy";[27] and the peeing prostitutes of a gilded rage.[28] Trump's extramarital affairs were no variety of the everyday adultery garden, either, but rather trysts with famous adult entertainment industry stars.[29] It is as if Mr. Trump bought the US (graphic) manual *How to Be a Bad Boy*, and started following its vapid lessons a bit *too* perfectly, a bit *too* mindlessly.

The actual archive of Trump's bad-boy playbook is, of course, television, and, more specifically, the genre known as reality TV. Many cultural critics and journalists have referenced both Trump's campaign and his presidency as extensions of the televisual script of the show that brought Trump to popular prominence, NBC's *The Apprentice*.[30] In this chapter a primary claim is that the logics of reality television and Trump's brand of governance are both *perverse* at the level of structure. These logics go beyond style, which still has an elective quality, getting closer to a more or less stable cultural structure coherently understood as a *genre*. A perverse style of disavowal and demand can show us where to look for a psychical structure; however, it is a perverse genre—dynamic, formal repetitions of plots, schemes, or strategies that are felt as rhythms—that secures a psychical structure in the popular imaginary. Yet the ultimate reason for figuring perversion as a popular or public genre is that it helps us to get our bearings for making judgments about political figures as expressions of culture. Outside of the deliberate staging of outrage for ratings, in both public culture and scholarship critics have been reluctant to criticize televisual *persons*, turning to behavior, performances, or personae instead. Is it appropriate to critique *a person* as such in scholarship? Is it ethical to say Donald Trump is a pervert in public at all? I think so, but this depends on what one thinks constitutes a person; such claims should not be made without ample qualification to avoid the disavowal such a claim would critique.

HOMINA, HOMINA, HOMINA:
GOLDWATER AND THE GREAT AND POWERFUL OZ

If . . . we inquire among . . . neurotics to discover what were the deeds which provoked [guilt], we shall be disappointed. We find no deeds, but only impulses and emotions, set upon evil ends but held back from their achievement. What lie behind the sense of guilt of neurotics are always *psychical* realities and never *factual* ones.

SIGMUND FREUD[31]

From the wildly successful BDSM fantasy of the novel and film *Fifty Shades of Grey*[32] to the complaint that the critique of Trump's priapic weaknesses is "kink-shaming,"[33] permissible perversion among consenting grown-ups is more popular now than it has been in recent history.[34] Even so, the moral opprobrium attached to juridical forms of perversion still shades the *term* with a sense individual imperfection or illness that makes us reluctant to use it outside a jocular or flirtatious context. Despite the pee tape rumors that won't go away or Trump's repeated statements that tempt the most widespread cultural taboo there is ("If Ivanka weren't my daughter, perhaps I'd be dating her"), very few critics, commentators, or scholars reference the president as a "pervert."[35] Even so, in the years since Trump's announcement of his presidential ambitions, his perverse style and the interminable dissemination and global circulation of his branded "truthful hyperboles" has given his rhetoric a stylistic consistency that simply begs for a character assessment![36] The call of the ad hominem is all but deafening, but still, almost no one describes the current sitting president a *pervert*.[37]

Writing for *New York* magazine, Annie Lowrey suggests Trump's rhetoric is emblematic of both his "magnetism and psychosis."[38] Along similar lines, Trump's xenophobic statements have led many to suggest he is a fascist or "borrows from the fascist playbook"[39]—or at least Leni Riefenstahl's.[40] Trump has also been widely dismissed—and then taken very seriously—as a demagogue too,[41] and largely because the success of his populist appeals appears to transcend reason, if not dumbfound political scientists overly wed to a "rational choice" model that cannot account for affect and feelings.[42] In an early attempt to apprehend the role of political feelings, a number of mental-health experts even violated professional propriety to diagnose Trump as a textbook example of "narcissistic personality disorder," characterized by grandiosity, an exaggerated sense of self-importance, and a lack of empathy.[43] "Narcissist" seems to be the most popular epithet for Trump.

I have suggested that a confrontation with a commonly shared perversity is at least one reason why we avoid discussing another's perversions ("To each their own," one might say, but the unspoken warrant here is "unless it makes me reckon with my own," the motto of liberal homophobia). There is, however, another reason that concerns professional *ethics*: although the narcissism of Trump's speech is difficult to deny, the printed and screen-based diagnoses of his character and psyche were so frequent in 2016 that the president of the American Psychiatric Association issued a press release, presumably admonishing psychiatrists—but really, all political commentators—to refrain from publicly "psychoanalyzing" Trump.[44] "The unique atmosphere of this year's election cycle may lead some to want to psychoanalyze the candidates," wrote Maria A. Oquendo, "but to do so would not only be unethical, it would be irresponsible."[45] To proffer pronouncements about Trump's mental health violates the so-called Goldwater Rule adopted by the APA in 1973, an ethical guideline developed to protect public figures from the stigma of mental illness and to insulate the professional reputation of psychiatry itself.[46] The rule, which holds that psychiatrists cannot offer psychological opinions about someone whom they have not personally analyzed, was developed after a short-lived magazine published a survey of 2,417 psychiatrists in 1964, over half of whom declared Barry Goldwater psychologically unfit to assume the presidency.[47] Ultimately, of course, the problem the rule is designed to manage is the suggestion of subjective political or moral humiliation in the guise of objective, "scientific" truth.

Rhetorical critics have wrestled with similar issues of professional propriety regarding the character assessments of speakers, initially in regard to the role of the speech or composition teacher in the classroom[48] and later "speech criticism" in the postwar period.[49] In the handbook that guided the emergent field of rhetorical studies in the mid-twentieth century, Lester Thonssen and A. Craig Baird afford the critic license to assess the "probity" of a speaker's character if they advance an "ethical proof" (ethos) dependent upon credibility, moral esteem, and goodwill.[50] Although Edwin Black's *Rhetorical Criticism: A Study in Method* helped to unmoor a long-standing focus on authors in favor of audience psychology, emotion or "exhortative" rhetoric, and larger social and ideological contexts in the late 1960s,[51] since World War II the dis-ease about the discussion of the character of a speaker or writer was and remains registered in the repeated displacement of specific speaking bodies with an ethical proof (demonstration or argument), traditionally the notion of character as constituted in writing or the delivery of a speech, echoing in some sense an avoidance of the "intentional fallacy" inherited from literary criticism and the formalist turn in cultural criticism.[52] In recent memory, tensions over the critical distance effected by a focus on proofs instead of persons came to a head over the rhetoric of a particularly "tricky" rhetor who, not coincidentally, is frequently compared to Trump:[53] Richard Nixon.

In an influential academic exchange between Forbes Hill and Karlyn Kohrs Campbell in 1972, Nixon was praised as a shrewd technician and denounced as a liar, respectively, but both scholars were careful to underscore their assessment of the speaker's "perspective" instead of Nixon's person.[54] From a presumed scene of Aristotelian objectivity, Hill praised Nixon's 1969 "Vietnamization" address as a calculated masterpiece and criticized Campbell's explicitly moral critique of the same. In her rejoinder Campbell argued that Hill's praise of Nixon's instrumentality was "covert advocacy" and that the critical act is unavoidably a political one demanding some degree of reflexivity. In so doing, Campbell tacitly underscored the ancient, moral dimension of ethos and asserted the role of the critic to make "ethical assessments" of a speaker's integrity based on standards *internal to a discourse* as well as established facts of record.[55] The exchange between Hill and Campbell can be said to inaugurate the so-called ideological turn in rhetorical studies;[56] however, in so turning the dispute also helped to authorize, recommend, and reinforce a critical summersault first executed by Edwin Black two years prior: rhetorical personae.

In the tumultuous, televised context of the first Nixon term, the end of free love innocence in California, civil rights struggles, and the unprecedented "embedded" coverage of the carnage in Vietnam, Black argued that "our politics seems at times a public nightmare privately dreamed," necessitating "some adjustments" to "the ancient doctrine of ethical proof."[57] Black underscored a commonly accepted critical distinction "between the man and his image" or "reality and illusion" and the consequent evasion of moral judgments by critics. "The whole subject has the forbiddingly suspicious quality of a half-hidden scandal," he opined.[58] Black found footing for ethical appraisal in terms of the figural agents implied by a discourse, which kept "before us the possibility, and in some cases the probability, that the author implied by the discourse is an artificial creation" and not "necessarily a person."[59] Although

Black would later find a more robust role for an analysis of the first persona—and not surprisingly, with Nixon[60]—he advocated for the critical discernment of the "second persona," or the implied audience of a speech or text as an index of ideology.[61]

The analysis of other kinds of personae in cultural and rhetorical criticism would follow in succeeding decades (the third persona, the fourth persona, the null persona, and so on), producing a number of insightful landmark studies that illustrate, as Kenneth Burke once put it, how words use us and how ideology "makes a body hop around in certain ways."[62] In this respect persona criticism and its critical cousins in style, genre, and ideology criticism implicitly rest on a version of the Goldwater Rule that is still observed in criticism today: a showperson's show does not necessarily align with "that man [or woman or person] behind the curtain." Let us dub this familiar habit of analytical restraint in criticism, rhetorical and otherwise, the Wizard of Oz Rule.

The Wizard of Oz Rule is not particular to criticism, of course, and is a cognate to something like the Goffman Rule of Self-Presentation shared by scholars in performance studies and in the social sciences (e.g., the concept of "face").[63] While less restrained, the widely circulated notion that there are "two Trumps" in the news media,[64] or that Trump is pretending, or that he *is akin* to the Wizard of Oz lurking behind a fog machine as Hillary Clinton observed,[65] implies that the rule is also a popular one beyond the domain of scholarly critique, albeit toward much different ends: whereas the critical distance afforded by the analyses of personae, genres, and styles enables a critic to make depersonalized, ethical observations about figures and phantasmagorias, pundits and politicians exploit the presumed divide to diagnose hypocrisy and impugn the sincerity and conviction of "real" persons. Regardless, whatever the iteration and wherever we find it, the Wizard of Oz Rule seems to rest on at least two central assumptions: (1) there is an authentic or "true" self or group orchestrating, conscious or unconsciously, the persona(e) in performance; and (2) the assessment of personae entails some kind of implicit or explicit moral judgment, usually in the register of responsibility or accountability.

However unavoidable in day-to-day interaction—it is, in fact, inevitable—the first assumption has been rigorously critiqued as a humanist conceit that has lost some explanatory power: the linguistic turn, the ideological turn, and the introduction of poststructural perspectives (especially deconstruction, performativity, and rhetoricity) have collectively undermined the idea that there is something essentially substantive *behind* the curtain of speech.[66] While there are certainly discrete histories and experiences, and particular historical exigencies, while there *are* discrete "bodies that matter" and feel and think, we are not so sure there is more to our drapes in any *meaningful way* other than how they hang.[67] Nevertheless, however we regard the status of agency,[68] understanding, naming, and explaining how discourse hangs together remains the guiding protocol of the enterprise of criticism.

The moral connotations of the Wizard of Oz Rule are much harder to negotiate, especially after critical scholars began to acknowledge the critic's emotional and political investments in the critical act, and this even *despite* a tacit agreement to keep the closure of moral judgment in abeyance.[69] Approaches to personae and formal patterns like style or genre have been developed to manage this impasse, but still, the problem with these middle-range metamoves is that they *feel* dissatisfying, pushing the persons attached to and produced by the rhetoric we critique to some peripheral place (e.g., "What I am saying about Nixon is limited to his language and actions, and yet . . ."). The discernment of implied personae in a given discourse, for example, imparts a kind of disembodied disposition,[70] while related approaches to style, genre, and ideology seem even more abstracted from the mouths, ears, and brains they activate and animate. The case of Donald Trump is particularly apropos because so many commentators and critics are passionately drawn to dismissive ad hominem: the frequently bandied assertion that he is "unfit" for the presidency—an assertion that I share, if this is not already obvious—intones a judgment of responsibility that rests, however naively, on an assumed divide between an erratic persona and some immor(t)al essence.

What if, however, scholars more deeply commit to our posthuman convictions and begin our critical analyses of public figures and their rhetoric with the assumption that the divide between persons and personae is merely an inevitable but illusory contrivance? What does it mean for critics to say that rhetoric is an index of roles and "complex linguistic formulations" constitutive of speaking subjects, including the one writing this question?[71] Admittedly, such a collapse is hardly homey.[72] Conflating personae and persons displaces the moral judgment of criticism from essentialist-tinged "stands" against the monstrous Other of demagogues and fascists to dynamic and contingent contexts and consequences, thereby subjecting ethical observations to ceaseless revision and reevaluation. And yet I think that this place of dead roads,[73] this intersection of the unsatisfactory and unresolved contingency, is where critics have arrived, *at least in theory*: the subject as such is and remains dead, or at least is on display as an open question or casket.[74] Although the admission is frustrating, this means that scholars and cultural critics have already resigned the Wizard of Oz Rule toward this or that limited strategic purpose (such as the work of the public intellectual or social activism) in favor of more complicated and tentative reckonings with subjectivity, which is precisely all the more reason why someone like Donald Trump both amuses some and infuriates others. While it is also unsatisfying, and deliberately so, I think a psychoanalytic perspective provides at least a modicum of relief in a space of pause or at least gets us a little closer to handling the *homo* that stalls a familiar, habituated rush of righteous praise or outraged condemnation.

PRESS CONFERENCING PERVERSION, OR, WHERE THE JURIDICAL AND STRUCTURAL CONVERGE

The predetermined character of ethical judgment in criticism is forestalled by the abandonment of subjective essentialism on one foot and a generally assumed commitment to acknowledging complex personhood on the other.[75] To this end I'm suggesting that a focus on discursive structures or articulations such as genre, ideology, and persona have provided a useful response for the critic, but that these leave us somewhat dissatisfied when confronting controversial figures and their rhetoric.[76] Part of that dissatisfaction concerns the often forced critical distance that disarticulates a persona from a person, and the strong feelings that we sense are really provoked by *both*. Insofar as there is an uneasy consensus that the subject is discursively produced, Lacan's conception of psychical structures provides an alternative but complimentary perspective. Notably, however, thus far I have stopped short of endorsing psychical structures as a basis for moral judgment. The perplexing psychical structure of perversion helps to explain why.

One of the primary reasons Freud and his followers went to great lengths to elaborate fantasy and psychical structures is in order to heed the good warning that both the Goldwater and Wizard of Oz Rules underscore: As Black put it, moral judgments are "terminal" in character and work to "close critical discussion rather than open or encourage it";[77] the labor of psycho-, critical, or any kind of analysis would be finished before it began. Whether we call it hope, the noumenal, chance, or the persistent, complaining mote of an odious determinism, we take it as axiomatic that things could be otherwise, the promise of "futurity"; as thinking things, how can we not? Moreover, and precisely because any given subject is a performative repertoire of various cultural codes and scripts, absent sustained engagement it is difficult to determine the difference between a psychical structure (a settled archive, broadly conceived) and various traits or behaviors of which anyone is capable.

Perversion denotes an especially queer exemplar because of what I have called a common perversion—we all share it.[78] For example, one significant and widespread experience of a common perversion is spectatorship as such, the voyeuristic enjoyment of suspending one's life for a moment in time in front of a screen of one sort or another. Since the 1970s, the British film journal *Screen* has been dedicated to explicating our common perversion in cinematic enjoyment, especially in regard to "investigating the terms in which cinema constructs and deconstructs" gender, race, and class in structural, semiotic, and psychoanalytic perspectives.[79] In film studies today, the "perverse spectator" is simply a redundant term. Film scholars have elucidated, for example, how the identificatory pleasure of staring at screens is classically perverse because it ignores "dominant notions of 'right' and 'good.'"[80] With a particularly (and politically deliberate) productive misreading of Lacan,[81] Laura Mulvey introduced the notion of the "male gaze" as an ideologically perverse default in Western cinema: all spectators identify primarily with the camera as a straight male and secondarily with masculinized protagonists on the screen. One of the pleasures of cinema, she argues, is that we can vicariously restage and work through the Oedipal triangle in cinema, and this has, historically, been at the expense of women as objects of unification and destruction.[82] Insofar as the assumed baseline of human interaction is the interpersonal encounter, absconding into the world of the woofer and screen is a perverse substitution for bodies in the flesh. Again, in general, perversion popularly denotes a swerving from cultural and purportedly biological norms in general—eating junk, watching television, *and* fuzzy handcuffs—especially the widely assumed relation between sexuality and reproduction.[83] Watching film or television has become a ubiquitously permissible perversion.

Because a common perversion is now the norm, "the norm is no longer a set of behaviors," observes Astrid Gessert. "Rather it has become a question of 'informed consent between adults.'" Such consent is not pregiven but negotiated between those involved in the "perverse" activity.[84] The acknowledgment of informed consent as the rule for deciding whether a perversity invites moral or legal judgment is the pickle of juridical perversion: What constitutes informed consent, exactly? Can consent be coerced, and if so, is it then mutual?[85] Can't contracts be rigged, and isn't this the lesson of human history?[86] Regardless, the point here is that if we limit our understanding of perversion to symptomology, style, or speech (p)acts we are confronted with a series of slippery traits that anyone can express and that are, in many contexts, often culturally encouraged. For this reason, Lacan parted ways with Freud by insisting on an important distinction between perverse acts, behaviors, and traits and a more stubborn perverse structure. Insofar as human sexuality itself is foundationally perverse and subject to constant cultural revision vis-à-vis the (social) contract, Lacan argued that a perverse *structure* must be located in a repeated disposition toward the Other that is relatively independent of the hegemony of compulsory heterosexuality (Freud is critiqued here "for forgetting at times that the importance of heterosexuality in the Oedipal myth is a question of norms and not nature").[87] While inextricably related, behaviors deemed "perverse" have changed dramatically over time at the level of the cultural norm, which includes, of course, the biological too; Lacan argues that the perverse structure has not.

While many would consider it inappropriate to diagnose Trump as a *clinical* pervert, it seems to me there is no question that his rhetoric evinces a perverse structure. As I noted in the previous chapter, that Trump's rhetoric is stylistically perverse is, at least, an explanation for why he is said to get away with statements and gaffes that would disqualify most public figures: he simultaneously denies the reality he asserts, which is both fun and infuriating to hear or watch. As the hallmark of perverse rhetoric, disavowal registers at almost every level of Trump's discourse. At the level of the statement, Trump decries journalist Megyn Kelly as a "bimbo" but later "pleads ignorance."[88] At the level of style, Trump's comb-over and ill-fitting suits are much derided, but he persists on sticking with the look. It is at the level of genre, a patterned discourse that cues audiences to *anticipate* the outcome, however, that we can assert with some assurance that the perverse structure is at play.

It is in the sustained episode of a press conference or a news program interview that Trump repeatedly upsets expectations but proclaims victory at following the form "beautifully." When orchestrated by his team, Trump's press conferences almost always begin with the restatement of some demand, the disavowal of some widely shared reality, and then praise *for his person*. One particularly operatic and conspicuous example is Trump's press conference with the alleged victims of Bill and Hillary Clinton's sexual improprieties.

Immediately prior to the second presidential debate with Hillary Clinton in early October 2016, Trump conducted a surprise press opportunity at the St. Louis Four Seasons Hotel with three women who claimed to have been sexually assaulted by president Bill Clinton and a fourth woman whose rapist was defended by Hillary Clinton. The conference was offered in the wake of the controversy ignited by the leak of a tape in which Trump bragged to an *Access Hollywood* reporter that he was able to sexually assault women because of his celebrity. "So, uh, thank you very much for coming," opened Trump, seated in the middle of a long table draped in black cloth with two women on either side. In the unsteady phone video taken for the event, top aid Steve Bannon can be seen moving to the back of the room with an ear-to-ear grin across

FIGURE 9. Trump holds a press conference with women who accused Bill Clinton of sexual assault and one who claimed inappropriate legal tactics by Hillary Clinton. From left to right: Kathleen Wiley, Juanita Broaddrick, Donald J. Trump, Kathy Shelton, and Paula Jones. Photo by Evan Vucci, courtesy of the Associated Press.

his face. "The four very courageous women have asked to be here and it was our honor to help them. And I think they're each going to make just an individual short statement. And then will do [*sic*] a little meeting, and we will see you at the debate." Paula Jones, who sued president Clinton in 1994 for sexual harassment, was nominated by Trump to speak first:

JONES: Well, I'm here to support, uh, Mr. Trump because he's gonna make America great again, and I think everybody else should vote for him, and I think they should all look at the fact, that, that, um, he's a good person, he's not, um, what other people have been saying he's been, like Hillary. So, think about that.

TRUMP: Kathy Shelton?

SHELTON: So I'm also here to support Trump, um. I, uh, at twelve years old, Hillary put me through, uh, something you would never put a twelve-year-old through. Um, and she says she's for women and children, and she was asked last year what happened, and she said she's supposed to defend, whether they did it or not. Now she's laughing on tape saying she know they did it.

TRUMP: You went through a lot.

SHELTON: Yes, yes sir I did.

TRUMP: OK. *[looks to his right]*

BROADDRICK: Hi, I'm Junita Broaddrick, and I'm here to support Donald Trump. I tweeted recently, and Mr. Trump retweeted it, that actions speak louder than words. Mr. Trump may have said some bad words, but Bill Clinton raped me, and Hillary Clinton threatened me. I don't think there's any comparison.

TRUMP: *[nods to Wiley]*

WILEY: I'm Kathleen Wiley, and, um, I'm here to support Donald Trump. The reason, the reason for that is, the first day that he announced the president [*sic*], he said, "I love this country, and I want America to be great again." And I cried when he said that. 'Cause I think that this is the greatest country in the world. I think he can do anything. I think he can accomplish anything. I think that he can bring peace to this world, and I think Donald Trump can lead up to that. Thank you.

TRUMP: Thank you. OK, thank you all very much. We're gonna have *[points thumbs to women on each side]*, we're gonna have a little talk.[89]

Immediately reporters began shouting questions like "Why do you say you touch women without consent, Mr. Trump?" The candidate does his best to appear stone faced. Jones shouts back, "Why don't y'all ask Bill Clinton that? . . . Go ahead and ask Hillary as well!" Laughter ensues, then applause. The conference lasted approximately three minutes.

A similar patterned spectacle would be staged eight months later, when the president invited news media to a cabinet meeting at the end of which, for ten excruciating minutes, Trump's appointees showered him with praise (e.g., former staff chief Reince Priebus said, "On behalf of the entire senior staff . . . we thank you for the opportunity and blessing to serve your agenda").[90] Both press conferences bespeak the common disavowal of denying a consensus reality but with a structured perversion that bleeds far beyond style. With the alleged Clinton victims, for example, the superficial claim was that the Clintons are guilty of legal and moral crimes, while Trump's "locker room talk" was merely talk: Trump's speech was commonly perverse; the Clintons' perversity was presumably juridical, a *truer* violation of mutually informed consent.

The affective or feeling-based "press conference" of victims of sexual assault was inspired by political consultant Roger Stone but was orchestrated by Charles Johnson, Steve Bannon, and Jared Kushner.[91] What is particularly perverse about the strategy is the way in which the conference rehearses an ideological perversion that asserts the use of women as objects of communication at the same moment that it presumably critiques it—disavowal on a stick. Notably, with this media spectacle sexual assault is *not* critiqued as much as it is underscored as a *norm*. This is to say, Trump's braggadocio with Clinton "victims" is in keeping with the actual order of things, where women are trafficked as objects to assert patriarchal power (recall that the primal father, in Freud's second Oedipal myth, controls all the women).[92] Trump is simply making explicit a political norm, the obverse of presumed propriety, disavowing that he has done anything wrong, unwittingly exposing the obscenity that underwrites political power in the United States. Here, too, is the "both-sides" logic of moral equivalency we will hear a year later in Trump's abhorrent press conference on Charlottesville violence, that antifascist protesters are just as responsible for racist violence as the white supremacists,[93] as if to say, "I'm not responsible because they did it too." The power of prophecy—of political perversion—is precisely its rootedness in feelings of infantile omnipotence and the demand that others watch.

THE REALITY TELEVISION PRESIDENT AND FUCK IT ELECTORATE

Rather than repulse potential voters, Trump's political perversion has obviously proved seductive to many, securing the presidency. So how do we account for the appeal and persistence of Trump's perverse style and performances over time? Who is Trump's public? I think a useful answer to such questions situates perversity as a *genre* that invites affective or emotional investment, which suggests at some level an expectation or priming: it's not only that Trump makes perverse statements or evinces a perverse style but that this seemingly novel or unpredictable style cues or *repeats* a more familiar, relational and thus anticipatory structure between self and other, a kind of mass or collective psychical structure (which is, well, what psychical structures *are* in the last instance). However novel we presume Trump's style to be, that we recognize it at all suggests the repetition of something we anticipate, something we have felt before, a kind of rhythm familiar to us in spectatorship as such.

Because representation implicates a subject position or disposition, a sustained and patterned rhetoric must ultimately index a more basic structural orientation ("because power," as the preposition-free kids of today might say). This is to say that the figure of Trump is as much a reflection of the attachment and disgust of followers and detractors as it is stylistic consistency: in our approving or condemning regard for his rhetoric—if you are reading this, dear reader, then you too are implicated by dint of your attention—we are cocreators of a perverse possibility, *especially* in the after-inhalation of objection and rejection. I suggest that this cocreative dimension of perversion is better discerned structurally as a series of relations that more closely cleave to *genre*, understood not simply as a stylistic mode or textured pattern but as the "signature of an affective apparatus that both presumes and produces bodies-in-feeling."[94] For our purposes here, genres are names of forms that are repeatedly felt, or instances of the linguistic sedimentation (in name and adjective) of affective recurrence into code and meaning. Although technically a genre helps us to reckon with affective repetitions in a meaningful manner, their relative stability is often in tension with the dynamism of the forms they designate, frequently registered in the objections of those who bridle at generic comparisons or labels because they necessarily and inevitably misname and constrain. Regardless, if a psychical structure is the term for a habituated disposition of relating to others—and ultimately the Other or symbolic order as such—we should expect something analogous for patterned discourses that specify or overdetermine a structural disposition in genres, either through a "text," a style, or any series of objects in manner, word, or deed.[95]

Genres have been productively theorized and elaborated in rhetorical studies but perhaps no more gainfully than by Karlyn Kohrs Campbell and Kathleen Hall Jamieson, who have critiqued the assumption that genres obtain in "texts" or objects and, instead, argue that genres persist as terms for relational patterns in the collective imagination, repetitions that can eventually become inscribed in social institutions (e.g., the inaugural address for the US presidency).[96] The social character of genre has also been extensively examined by many film and television scholars who have persuasively demonstrated how spectators are disposed toward the camera, screen, and narrative in ways that invite enjoyment in recognizably perverse ways, substituting interpersonal encounter with an identificatory fantasy. To say that film, television, or news media advance and reinforce an addiction to perversity *explicitly* in our time actually goes without saying, both because it is now obvious and because many have already said it.[97] Perversity is the screened logic and not-so-weird-anymore model of entertainment today; however, such an observation rests on the more or less accepted Freudianism that cinematic or televisual voyeurism is now widely practiced and simply regarded as sexuality by other means.

Considered as a perverse *structure*, however, genres require the specification of a subjective disposition that transcends the pleasure and pain of recognition or consumerism in order to limn the contours of *kind of orientation*. As a style, perversion lodges at the level of experience or trait; as a genre, perversion ceaselessly forges and reinscribes an identification that disavows established order and, morally and legally, regards others as real or imagined witnesses. To make the case quickly I resort to a personal anecdote about my own perverse enjoyments (but, trust me, don't hold your breath).

I confess that I originally became interested in understanding perversity as a persistent and now accepted cultural structure after watching and enjoying the recent prime-time "fictional" television programs *Dexter* (2006–2013), *Hannibal* (2013–2015), and *American Horror Story* (2011–present). These shows felt unusual because of their encouraged identification with violent antiheroes, which seemed to me more characteristic of cinema. Watching these shows, I found myself gasping at the absurd violations of social norms and puzzled by my enjoyment of them weekly or in days-long "binge watching" marathons: "Am I actually rooting for Hannibal!?!?" I worried in delight. "He eats folks' faces!" I started writing about what seemed to me a recent turn in popular televisual entertainment that I was calling "prime-time perversion,"[98] which I was arguing is a deviation from cinematic perversions because of its seriality and intimacy. But then, just as I had sketched an argument and started to write it up, Trump bombastically interrupted my thinking through the speakers and screens of my home. It then seemed to me that the success of these over-the-top televisual thrillers shared something in common with Trump's widely publicized stumping, that my gasping at the horrific violence of self-conscious fantasy worlds were of a piece with my gasping at the "real" exchanges of the Republican presidential candidate debates. Of course, we can argue that reality is composed of fantasies and the critical distance they afford is the work of ideology as such.[99] Even so, what does my fascination with *American Horror Story* have in common with a widely perceived presidential horror show?[100] And what do my televisual investments have to do with Trump's political investment scheme?

The answer to these and similar questions came quickly from journalists in the form of proclamations that the emperor of our time is naked in many senses.[101] No sooner did Trump announce his bid for the presidency than pundits characterized the campaign as a form of "reality TV," now an ubiquitous genre, and that this would-be president was advancing a campaign in the televisual format of *The Apprentice*.[102] Trump's penchant for press conferences that seat him at the center of a table while he is praised is very similar to "board room" scenes from the NBC reality show.

While its history and definition are still debated, reality television is now widely regarded as a dominant television genre, presumably unscripted and featuring personalities whose daily lives are documented or who are thrown into a conflict or competition (e.g., *The Bachelor*, *Keeping Up with the*

Kardashians, Survivor, Chopped, Project Runway, and so on). The more mundane perversity of spectatorship is achieved through a well-known duplicity: what viewers experience through the genre is the knowledge that "reality TV" is scripted and performed, or at the very least, manipulatively edited.[103]

Reality TV begins to mark a departure from the consensual voyeurism of cinematic and televisual fictions by warping its "informed consent" character, a tacit contract of viewership that has been debated most conspicuously in terms of representations of sex and violence (e.g., in the United States, the "TV Parental Guidelines" developed by the FCC and others in 1997). "Reality TV" is unique because of its invitation to a contradictory investment from viewers that Dana Cloud has insightfully dubbed "the irony bribe." Offered as a counterpoint to Fredric Jameson's conception of the "fantasy bribe,"[104] Cloud argues that reality television weirdly offers the rejection of the screened world at the moment of its revelation: "The *irony bribe* is a strategic mechanism of a cultural text that invites audiences to identify with the pleasures of the reaction against taking seriously the patently ideological fantasy. . . . Ironically, the irony bribe naturalizes the worldview of a hegemonic text in the process of denaturalizing it. Irony is the fantasy bribe's Other in its production of investment through disinvestment."[105] While such a conflicted identification *is* the labor of ideology as such for Slavoj Žižek,[106] for Cloud the reality TV genre is especially visible and invites an "ironic oscillation of investment and irony among viewers" that absolves viewers of responsibility in all but explicit terms.[107] All screened narratives disavow through fantasy; for Cloud the "irony bribe" elevates this function to an almost unequivocal abjection: "Can you believe she said that?" gasps the spectator. "That is too horrible, let us replay you the clip!" responds the producer. Without such a bribe, how else do we contend with the ways CNN framed all of its televised debates among candidates as "smackdowns" or boxing matches,[108] replete with rousing music, chiaroscuro facial profiles and odd introductory biographies? And aren't such spectacular contests often "rigged," as Trump continues to declaim?[109] Political contests presumably concern long-term decisions about policies that will affect the lives of millions of people, and yet by suggesting presidential debates are akin to reality TV or sports programs, cable news networks help to cultivate a kind of investment in ironic oscillation that would render voting either as an inconsequential game or only an optional responsibility.[110]

Of course, genres entail expectations, and thus the political disposition of the Trump supporter, perhaps better cast as the "Trump viewer," needs some explanation. A neurotic electorate votes for a more traditional candidate, any of whom represent a presumed consensus of established order. But who would vote—or claim to vote—for a perversion of the established order that Trump has come to represent? At first blush we might be tempted to say a public that supports a Trump candidacy is structurally psychotic; if the discourse of social networking is any measure, those of us in the developed West are increasingly part of a psychotic environment (a topic explored in chapter 2). Sustaining such a structure is implausible, however, if only because it is hard to imagine how a community of private Idahoes—or even Kansases, whatever is the matter with them—could agree about anything.[111] If Trump support is reflective of neither a psychotic nor a classically neurotic disposition (e.g., supporting a "traditional" candidate), then we might conclude that only a perverse electorate elects a Trump, an electorate that regards politics as reality television show, a playful contest from which they are distanced and even immune, much like a video game in which three lives are promised in the event of failure.[112] The upshot here is that when we consider genres as psychical structures, which is easier to do when we take them up as dispositions of spectatorship instead of discretely mediated conditions (e.g., cinema, television, social media), then genres are promiscuous. The imperative of media convergence and the "reality" of our present political circumstances suggest that perverse articulations transcend the scene or screen you're in.

Political perversion is a style and genre that evinces a patterned disavowal that is directly discerned in the ironic spectatorship of reality TV–cum–presidency. In this particular regard, Trump is a cultural production that is far from the aberration his figure is frequently said to be; if not fully fledged in traditional electoral politics, we have certainly experienced such perversion in "entertainment" (before the contemporary screamo talk show there was, of course, the artful deceptions of P. T. Barnum, who also ran for office).[113] Understanding genres as relational structures also suggests that Trump supporters are as much an invention of their discussion as they are any actually existing persons; the voter for Trump is brought into being by the same generic structure that makes notice of his aberration possible at all.

Cloud's isolation of the "irony bribe" as endemic to the reality TV genre helps us to see how the "voter" and "spectator" of our screened lives today are united in the structured project of *disavowal*: default or consensus order is affirmed in the same gesture of its veto, which is ultimately an enjoyment of renounced responsibility. Such an understanding of free-range generic structures, usually discernable retrospectively, makes a figure like Trump paradoxically an inevitable consequence of demanding publics that have been cultivated for generations. As one cultural critic puts it,

Look, Donald Trump was inevitable. . . . We have raised two generations of Americans who believe that anything the government does is horrible, all politicians are corrupt, ah . . . Washington is evil. And then every commercial we ever see, politically, on frankly on both sides of the aisle . . . is how the other guy is a bum, the other guy should be in jail, the other guy is a pervert, whatever. Well, if you raise two generations of kids to believe that about our own government . . . you can't then be surprised that eventually someone would run for president who is absolutely anti-government. . . . So, we should have seen it coming that eventually someone would run for president who was an entertainer and totally against government. . . . Did we know it would be Trump? No, but it would be someone like him. And that's what we are living with today.[114]

Such astute observations are from a cultivator of this kind of political disposition: Jerry Springer. We should also expect the political philosophy of a Trump supporter to be homologous to the Trump figure: spectacular, grandiloquent forms of protest akin to throwing chairs at a wrestling match,[115] "MAGA!" ("Make America Great Again!"), or "Fuck it, I'm voting for Trump!"[116] At this juncture it should no longer shock us that "Fuck it!" is an apt term for the disposition of the Trump supporter.[117]

"Fuck it!" is not, however, a revolution—quite the opposite, for such an orientation disavows both the presumed, dominant social order as well as any need to fundamentally and systematically change it: declaring "Fuck it!" and "Make America Great Again!" in the same breath is an almost perfect condensation of a disavowal and demand, the rejection of an order that one insists should be restored. That a number of Bernie Sanders supporters—a candidate who proposed a "revolution" of *reform*—would sooner vote for Trump than Clinton provides added evidence that the presidential election for the Trump supporter was less about policy than it was a sense of wounded identity.[118] Second Amendment gun fanatics opposed to "common sense" regulation policy are not really concerned about policy; they're concerned about an outsider or victim identity ("I know you are, but what am I?").[119] So, too, are Trump supporters: the social order as usual is a game they do not have to play, or if they play, only at a distance and without a sense of consequence or responsibility. For this reason, we can expect support for Trump to continue; when coupled with disavowal, demands are especially addictive.

At this juncture Žižek's thinking and the insightful elaborations of Matthew Sharpe and Geoff Boucher are useful for describing a public that would support a perverse presidency: Žižek argues that in the West, democratic cultures seem to be moving toward a kind of generalized perversion, a collective identity in which a people are losing faith in a shared authority or law (the decline of symbolic efficiency discussed in chapter 2). This is not to say that individuals are becoming clinical perverts but, rather, that collectively our speech and behavior evinces a perverse structure through a series of disavowals: the government is broken; Congress is dysfunctional; exogenous others are taking our jobs; or, of course, "Fuck it!" Such convictions both recognize the existence of the social order and deny it at the same time, having now dispensed with the kind of authority that used to be a stabilizer by proxy (originally a monarch, then a paternal figure or expert, and now what?). There is, in other words, a structural parallel between the perverted figure who hears the second parent but disavows the demand to separate, leaving the external authority in a position of powerlessness and a collective cultural denial of symbolic authority (e.g., the POTUS, climate scientists, and so on). In his earlier work Žižek described the average cultural subject of our time as a "pathological narcissist": "The narcissistic subject only knows the 'rules of the (social) game,' enabling him to manipulate others; social relations constitute for him a playing field in which he assumes 'roles,' not proper symbolic mandates; he stays clear of any binding commitment that would imply a proper symbolic identification. He is a radical conformist who paradoxically experiences himself as an outlaw."[120] A later name Žižek deploys for this narcissist is the "pervert," the person who no longer yields authority to social norms but rather regards them as rules that only those other idiots truly believe in. The erosion of the symbolic authority of the presidency, signified so starkly by South Carolina representative Joe Wilson calling president Obama a liar in the middle of a live, nationally televised address,[121] heralded the arrival of an explicit political perversion: a ceaselessly unstable series of challenges to order and the abject failure of anything resembling agreement, compromise, or consensus. Disavowal and demand.

One might suppose that the thrill of this brave new world of perversion is the possibility of radical self-fashioning: in the absence of anchoring authority, I can be who I want, I consume what I want, and so forth; there is no "No!" and so, well, I get to enjoy anything![122] Yet Žižek warns this is actually a scary situation, for "when the 'pacifying' symbolic authority is suspended, the only way to avoid the debilitating deadlock of desire . . . [is] a despotic figure which stands for the primordial *jouisseur* [master who enjoys]: we cannot enjoy because *he* appropriates all the enjoyment."[123] In other words, when the social order is presumed to have eroded, when there is no authority figure, the door for a master punisher, or what Freud described as the "primal father," is reopened.[124]

CONCLUSION? DONALD TRUMP IS A PERVERT

DOROTHY: Oh, you're a very bad man.
WIZARD: Oh, no my dear. I'm a very good man. I'm just a very bad wizard.

FILM VERSION OF *The Wizard of Oz*

What began initially as a pee tape parable for moral judgment has ballooned into an admittedly ambitious excursus on the genre of political perversion: Trump's discourse, from the level of the statement to the level of style and genre, features the gesture of disavowal and demand. Translated into our current political predicament, political perversion is the name for public demands that simultaneously disavow—fights over gun rights, same-sex marriage, abortion, immigration, and on and on and on—and thus are representative of a collective longing for a newer order, newer fundamentalisms, newer belief systems, renewed racisms, outbursts of violent individuals or groups laying down their own rules (e.g., mass shootings), forms of radical conformity, and, in the end, the demand for a powerful master who will *cut through all the crap*.[125] Trump says what he means, except that he doesn't. Trump's the real deal, except that he isn't. He will build a wall and keep them out, although we really don't believe such a wall is feasible. He will return an older sense of order, or rather, he will reinscribe an existing order without difference. One is tempted to characterize our political predicament as some psychotic, Hobbesian state of nature, because so many of our screens now regularly feature the "unspeakable" and "senseless" norms of violence—except that such violence has a certain sense and is spoken about all the time.[126] What makes our political moment perverse is that, to put it colloquially, we *know* that the ends do not justify the means, but we do it anyway.

With a widened sense of the generalized perversion endemic to postmodern culture, we are better able to take up again the perplexing problem of moral judgment—which, of course, I have deliberately withheld and commuted all the same in the familiar but serious gesture of the tease. From antiquity, the rhetorical critique of ethical proofs has been justified with reference to the conditions advanced and internal to a given speech or discourse, as Campbell has demonstrated so well with Richard Nixon's 1969 speech on Vietnamization.[127] Less constrained, Edwin Black's "long-standing antipathy" to Nixon finally went there,[128] to the first persona, "to the man," but only the *homo* as a vehicle of linguistic expression: "Nixon was the medium of a sporadically incontinent candor. Sometimes his resentments burst through the enveloping veneer of his unction, and those accidental ruptures made him a kind of honest man."[129]

The "kind of" qualifier is a hallmark of disavowal, and so we might conclude that for Black Nixon was perverse, but in a nonmoral sense. The Wizard of Oz Rule is still in effect.

Accepting our posthumanist druthers, however, means that there is no essence behind the curtains—*but the curtains still matter.* Whatever elusive singularity remains "after the subject," moral critique must rest on a responsi-bility—a response-*ability*—that Diane Davis has shown us is not grounded in a juridical subject but in a rhetoricity, or "an affect*ability* or persuade*ability*" that is the condition of the act.[130] In the backdrop of the steady and knowing destruction of the world, directly felt in environmental disasters and dramatic changes of the weather right outside our windows, with urgency Davis enlists Jean-Luc Nancy to argue that it is "more necessary than ever today, still today, to embrace a responsibility that does not duck and roll into anthropocentric safety zones, that resists both a panicked 'return to the subject' as if only a Subject can save us, and the obscene, chest-beating, 'posthumanist' presump-tion of the subject's 'simple liquidation,' which itself amounts to a grotesque display of said hubris."[131] To proclaim Donald Trump is perverse in the easy sense of dismissal, to describe him as a "psycho" or "fascist," retreats to a para-doxically dangerous safety zone. To proclaim Donald Trump is nothing more than a perverse phantasmagoria produced in the simulacra of culture rehearses much of the same, denying that these hands and body are mine.[132] To assert, as I do, that Donald Trump is perverse is to say something about an actually ex-isting human, but such an observation doesn't lodge at the level of his essence any more than it would diagnose a medical condition. Perversion is ultimately a label for a habituated manner of relating to others discernable in gestures sustained over time and retrospectively perceived. To say that Donald Trump is perverse is to say that the technique of disavowal and demand is dominant in his discourse and that there is a profound failure by Mr. Trump to take respon-sibility for his speech, but *also* that the identification of the perverse structure should not foreclose the possibility of his ever doing so. Futurity is key and its embrace affords the responsibility of respect due to the living (and dead). In other words, "Yes, but . . ."

CONCLUSION

Don't Play (with) That

If the pervert looks for legal authorities to bear witness to obscene acts and thus to review their complicity in the very scenes that would seduce them from their virtue . . . this is not to mortify the law simply, but through this mortification to purify the law of the arbitrary and contingent, to purge it of flesh.

JOAN COPJEC[1]

By the time you finish this book, there will have been another mass shooting. In the introduction I fashioned a similar sentence: by the time readers started chapter 1, the president would have said something more abhorrent than when they began the introduction. The point of these sentences is less one of prophecy than of discursive parallels, that the generic templates for political impropriety and targeted violence share a predictable logic that I have been describing as structural perversion.[2]

The arbitrary character of the law writ large—not just the penal but also the sexual and racial contracts, class inequities, and language itself—is often the mainspring of symbolic and targeted violence, especially when we are caused to reckon with ourselves as playthings of social media, social structures, the unconscious, and so on. Contingency also reminds us that we are much less in control of our affective and speech-based lives than we like to believe, and accepting this limitation is part of what it means to be a "grown-up." A lack of control or agency is an almost unbearable reckoning for the structural pervert, however, often inciting tantrums and meanness.

I will work to close this study (for now) by describing how the perverse logic of contemporary politics—of political perversion—is homologous to that of targeted violence: both are attempts to stabilize the law by purging it of flesh and feeling, by blowing stuff up. Both evince a strong paring of disavowal and demand, and both oblige us to make some contingent ethical and legal judgments. I argue that the key to understanding the relationship between electoral and targeted violence is a universal practice that I've been toying with from the beginning: *play.*

We tend to think about play and playfulness as positive practices closely linked to humor, sex, sport, and youth; however, it is perhaps better to imagine the practices of play in various permutations of creativity and destructiveness, bound by context and the players concerned. Many psychoanalytic theorists, sometimes unwittingly, advance a binary with good play and creativity and bad play and maliciousness,[3] which I hope to avoid or at least navigate carefully, because such a binary is premised on a singular understanding of perversion that I have sought to undo throughout this study. For example, one reporter writes that, "even at his most outrageous during the primaries, there was often a playfulness to Mr. Trump's bantering stump style."[4] Yet such playfulness is certainly contingent on who is listening to and affected by such banter, as many others regard his rhetoric as malicious too. Both perspectives are about perversion, and both are faithful to peoples' experiences. Nevertheless, I think that our understanding of perversion can help us shake out the different patterns of play in a way that gives us another angle from which to detangle common perversion from the obscene. Inasmuch as I argue for celebrating our common perversity and the joy of playfulness, I must also underscore how playing dirty has also become a harmful and increasingly pervasive pastime. As I warned in the preface, this story does not end well.

PLAYING DIRTY IN PUBLIC

The leader can be loved only if he himself does not love.

THEODOR W. ADORNO[5]

In the second chapter on cultural psychosis I examined a number of examples of acting out in public (climate change denial, sexting, and so on) to show how these words and deeds are goaded by speed and the lack of a sense of oversight (the Third Thing or big Other). The perception of an erosion of authority is what Žižek and Dean dub the "decline of symbolic efficiency," and collectively I selected illustrations that suggested a compulsive lack of self-awareness. Most of the subsequent examples of structural perversion in later chapters have, however, come from the words and deeds of Donald Trump, but his discourse is, in the end, a production of culture (he'd like to think this book is about him, but to echo Carly Simon, it's not). Once we start noticing presumably "playful" rhetoric that features disavowal and demand, political perversion becomes easier to see without the presidential decree. For example, consider another screened scene from the White House—which means it's about playing dirty, just only by degrees, because the victim of foul play here is not a person. In a memorable 2018 segment from NBC's *Meet the Press* hosted by Chuck Todd, Trump's personal lawyer, Rudy Giuliani, wrestled with a peculiar word. While the FBI was concluding a years-long investigation of possible campaign collusion with Russia, Giuliani explained why he tried to keep Trump from testifying:

CHUCK TODD (HOST): You believe this [discord] is on [the Special Counsel investigation]? That you would've, that you guys have not delayed the interviewing, ah, delayed the negotia—

GIULIANI: No!

TODD: —tions with Mr. Mueller?

GIULIANI: Yes! Each time by three or four days so we can write a letter in response. They have taken two to three weeks to get back to us. So, uh, what I have to tell you is, look, I'm not gonna be rushed into having him testify so that he gets trapped into perjury, and when you tell me that, you know, he should testify because he's gonna tell the truth and he shouldn't worry, well, that's so silly because it's somebody's version of the truth, not the truth, he didn't have a, a conversation about—

TODD: Truth is truth, I don't mean to go, like, I—

GIULIANI: No, it isn't truth. Truth isn't truth! The president of the United States says, I didn't, I—

TODD: *[fist to forehead, laughing]* Truth isn't truth? Mr. Mayor, do you realize what, I, I, I—

GIULIANI: No!

TODD: —this is going to become a bad meme![6]

Or it's going to become an excellent example of political perversion. Here Rudy Giuliani bumbles through an argument familiar to many humanities scholars, that truth is perspectival, at best a cognitive coordination of Venn diagrams, especially in a legal system premised on an adversarial process. Although many of us understand what Giuliani meant, his remarks were taken up as an astonishing statement and kind of motto for so-called fake news, political disinformation, and the "truthful hyperbole" of the Trump administration.

Indecision about where to locate the place of truth in our contemporary moment overlaps with the ethical issue of responsibility that we engaged in the previous chapter: Without an anchor in truth or fact, to what or whom are people responsible? I've argued, of course, "You are your rhetoric"—that there is no essential self "behind the curtain," which, following the work of Diane Davis, entails a relentless, ceaseless disposition of response-ability toward others.[7] So we can and should make judgments about Trump as a political figure; indeed, we cannot avoid doing so if we are to remember that politics is about power and concerns the legitimate use of force. But we should keep relating to others and keep the way we relate dynamic. This is not simply a matter of saying, "Donald Trump is a pervert," washing one's hands, and then not having to rethink the statement again.

Taken out of a legal context, Giuliani's declaration points to a kind of non-foundational sense of authority that symbolic efficiency denotes: at some level we know that our social and political institutions, our system of checks and balances, our sense of community—the big Other—can only function if we agree that they do. Truth can only function as truth if there is a commitment to a continual responsibility toward others, especially strangers. In the broadest sense, in fact, a given society is symbolically efficient only with a collective disavowal of the notion that there is no big Other or Third Thing to begin with (again, we are *all* perverse). Giuliani's acknowledgment is doubly perverse because he disavows the responsibility of participating in the various symbolic regimes that make communication efficient.

Of course, for most people the convention is to project a Third Thing to stabilize claims—very few folks are walking around thinking about the demise of the big Other, at least in such terms. Instead, and understandably so, many would suggest responsibility concerns a fidelity to civility or common decency, a respect for our governing institutions and offices, a commitment to scientific expertise, or perhaps humility before the all-seeing eye of deity. Giuliani's unwitting acknowledgment of the fragility of the big Other and the decline of symbolic efficiency implicates an ethical pickle: (1) pragmatically, the US political world longs to function on the assumption of an authority as an external anchor, which the Trump regime was elected to destroy; appeals to some Third Thing seem necessary for social change, as well as to avoid the kind of unproductive fragmentation of our communities today. But (2) the ethic I would prefer seeks the kind of nonessentialist or nonfoundational authority that entails a ceaseless rethinking of judgments and relating and re-relating to others. While I do not think (1) and (2) are incompatible, I am also not quite sure how these can be reconciled explicitly in our current cultural conjuncture. Would it be possible to rethink pragmatic politics from the position of nonfoundational authority? That remains one of the many tasks for me and other scholars to take up as structural perversion has become more consciously pronounced in public discourse. If we cannot coordinate the tension between these two dimensions of politics and responsibility, at the very least, we can keep them both in mind and leave the squaring of a nonfoundational ethics and politics as a productive, open question. Working to continually keep the question open may be our best answer.

I think we wrestle with the tension between political pragmatism and ethical responsibility especially when attending to one of the most structurally perverse twists of our time: the return to public bigotry as (political) *humor* and the disavowal of any responsibility for hatred. Explicit racism, misogyny, bigotry, and hatred are expressions that we have developed many tools for confronting because these are conspicuous (and because these have, so to speak, an investment in symbolic efficiency). A more structurally perverse bigotry, understood as harmless "play," is much harder to address. For example, in November, 2018, a racist preprom photo was posted anonymously on Twitter and circulated widely. It featured a number of young men from Baraboo High School in Wisconsin, smiling and standing in front of a county courthouse and giving the Nazi salute.[8] Despite popular outrage, the students were not punished. The superintendent said, first, that the students have First Amendment rights and, second, "We cannot know the intentions in the hearts of those who were involved."[9] With nods to Hannah Arendt, apparently evil is still banal. News of publicly racist behavior among young people has become particularly pronounced after Trump assumed the throne—indeed, incidents of hate are on the rise across the country among all generations.[10] What most troubles the director of California State San Bernardino's Center on Hate and Extremism, however, is that "many of these people who are engaging in hate speech are not hardcore hatemongers. . . . We have this middle group of people who think bigotry is funny."[11] In a sense, bigoted humor, understood as playfulness, is structural perversion on a stick: harm is done *precisely* because one can deny any intention to harm others. Assuredly such humor is irresponsible and requires us to think hard about the conditions of our culture, beyond the present political regime, that make it possible today; newly permitted bigotry also requires pragmatic solutions and strategic appeals to something like a respect for human dignity, as problematic (i.e., essentialist) as this may seem.

Our contemporary culture of speed and phatic gratification plays a structural role in public bigotry too, as it constrains the space and time for reflection. As I argued in chapter 2, if what appears to matter the most in the public square of screens and speakers is acting right now and achieving immediate notoriety, coupling presentism with bigoted humor has created a kind of *fast hate*, the dirty disposition of the drive-by "troll." For example, in a segment from a 2016 episode of ABC's *Nightline* on Internet trolling, journalist Terry Moran interviewed the right-wing polemicist Milo Yiannopoulous. Yiannopoulous became an Internet celebrity after a series of sexist, racist tweets about actor and comedian Leslie Jones:

MORAN: Are you a troll?

YIANNOPOULOUS: Of course!

MORAN: What is trolling? How do you look at it?

YIANNOPOULOUS: I like to think of myself as a virtuous troll, you know, I'm doing god's work.

MORAN: *[as voice-over]* Milo Yiannopoulous, also known as Nero online, joined in the tormenting of Jones, calling her a man on Twitter to his 350,000 plus followers.

MORAN: In the Twitter storm, you called her a "dude"—

YIANNOPOULOUS: —Ah, sure, I was mean to—

MORAN: If Leslie Jones were right here—

YIANNOPOULOUS: —I've gone native.

MORAN: —would you say, "You look like a dude?"

YIANNOPOULOUS: Yeah, probably.

MORAN: You would say that to her?

YIANNOPOULOUS: Yeah probably. I probably would.

MORAN: Then you're an idiot. Really.[12]

When a lawyer is set in relationship to something called "truth," or Nazi-saluting snots are set in relationship to genocide, or a social media troll is called on to reckon with his vile tweets, there is the assumption of the absence of some authority that might anchor truth or judge these behaviors as immoral. Yiannopoulous refuses to pretend that the emperor has beautiful new clothes, a precondition of nihilism.

THE VARIETIES OF PLAYFUL EXPERIENCE

I think it is in the presence of horror that we understand the necessity of play in making [reality] bearable.

ANDRÉ GREEN[13]

With these examples of dirty play in mind, I am better ready to describe how "play" plays a role in becoming a self-conscious person in the social world: reckoning with thirdness, the Third Thing, the big Other, or an assumed, outside authority *requires playing*. The Oedipal triangle is just one way of conceptualizing the important formative functions of play and its relationship to the art of substitution that we term, simply, "creativity." One of the most widely read scholars of play—second only, I suspect, to Jean Piaget[14]—is British psychoanalyst Donald Woods Winnicott, who argued that play is a form of creativity that is essential for selfhood.[15] Wed to the Lacanian refiguring of Oedipal thirdness discussed in chapter 2, for children play is crucial for negotiating and achieving alienation and separation. As adults, play is also a route toward reparation, which Melanie Klein described as an orientation toward others as separate people, bound up with some degree of guilt, that strives toward the activities of repairing or restoring relationships.[16]

Before a young person can successfully become alienated from the primary parent and then separated as a self-conscious person, they have to negotiate how this is done by playing with various objects that stand in for the primary caregiver. Winnicott's theory of play provides useful insights about "where" and "when" this occurs: before a child successfully detaches from the primary parent, various objects are played with to ease this transition in a liminal or holding space. These objects represent, in some sense, a kind of primal security. Winnicott calls these objects, simply enough, "transitional objects." Many of us are familiar with transitional objects, especially if we have been involved in raising children in some way: these objects are teddy bears or dolls or blankets—or in my case, a Kermit the Frog—made sleazy over time by encrusted saliva (*and don't you dare wash them!*). In youth, this transitional period of separation and alienation is not easy; a young person must learn that parents do not cease to exist when they disappear, a lesson taught by peekaboo, acquiring what Piaget described as "object permanence."

Winnicott argues that these transitional objects are also subject to aggression, that children will first try to consume them until they learn that, despite those efforts, the object can't be eaten or destroyed. This first and formative form of play, he says, is an imaginative zone, a what-if space in which rules and social codes are negotiated. For Winnicott, successful playing teaches us that objects have an independence of their own, a kind of vitality that eventually gets afforded to other people—a kind of concern or caring for others, not as objects but as subjects in themselves.[17] A failure to "play nice" or "play well with others" thus suggests a kind of structural perversion of play that regards others as mere objects, often in the absence of goodwill.[18] If playing represents the fundamental, creative means of making and maintaining relationships with others as subjects, then the sneaky lawyer or apprentice authoritarian or social media troll is certainly having a kind of "object trouble," and they're not playing by the same rules as everyone else.

How, then, do we describe the rules of everyone else and the cultural playing that these both confine and condone? The answer, of course, is the symbolic efficiency of an assumed authority. Socially sanctioned play, which is most familiar to us as gaming, sex, sporting, and entertainment, operates on the basis of mutually shared rules and often various implied pacts or social contracts. Such a view of neurotic or "normal" playfulness is consistent with research on play across a broad spectrum of humanistic and scientific perspectives.[19] Regardless of one's theoretical commitments, there is a widespread consensus that play is central to the brain, body, and overall social being of many animals, not just humans.[20] Currently, much of the play research in the social sciences takes aim at video games,[21] which is constrained by widely known media effects scholarship that can discern a connection to aggression (which is true of most forms of play) but no direct causal relationship between violent media and social violence.[22] The critical and social scientific work on play in rhetoric and communication does, however, track a perception of a shift in modes of play, the most conspicuous of which are mean.[23] In this respect the tricky lawyer, the bigoted young buck, and conniving troll seem to understand cultural norms and expectations but violate them anyway, as if to say, "I'm going to issue racist and sexist attacks because I can." A key difference between psychotic and perverse rhetoric is self-awareness; in these three examples symbolic authority is *knowingly* disavowed, suggesting a structurally perverse form of cultural play is afoot.

Whether or not Lacan's refiguring of Freud's Oedipal triangle is persuasive, the motto of structural perversion derived from it is helpful: "I know what I'm doing is wrong, but I'm doing it anyway." The neurotic feels guilt, recognizes her abilities, and uses play as a creative way to negotiate limitation. The psychotic can't really play at all. And the pervert understands the rules but thinks only suckers and losers follow them; this is because the pervert is the enforcer of the rules. We can now argue that disavowal actually represents a perversion of play and a fundamental *lack of creativity*. Destructive play, or what Janine Chasseguet-Smirgel describes as regression to anal sadism,[24] is almost always scripted and rigidly rule bound—harmful play is, in fact, often by the book. Although, strictly speaking, play is often an alloy of creativity and aggression, a genre or pattern of structurally perverse play is typified by a series of demands that the rules must be followed, only that these rules are from a law book that many of us like to pretend doesn't exist.

FLAGGING PERVERSION BETWEEN
A BAND AND A BURIAL

Although the film originally repulsed spectators,[25] Hal Ashby's deliciously perverse 1971 romantic black comedy *Harold and Maude* is an excellent example of common perversion, permissible play, and ethical reparation. A brief analysis of the film also provides a useful counterpoint to the foul play of bigotry previously discussed and the targeted violence I will soon take up. The narrative is about a rich and fatherless twenty-year-old, Harold Chasen (played by Bud Cort), who regulates his fetish for finitude by staging suicides, ultimately for the love of his self-obsessed mother. In a manner similar to pornographic films, the plot is punctuated periodically with creatively gruesome, mock money shots—a hanging, a drowning, a gun to the head, an immolation, and so on—but Harold cannot seem get a rise (from or) out of his mother. Harold's creatively staged deaths suggest a form of liminal transition, each weapon a transitional object, as well as a structurally perverse desire to control the rules of maternal recognition. The film is funny because his mother will not play, something that Harold gradually comes to accept by the film's end, thereby achieving separation.

While attending the funeral of a stranger for kicks, he first meets seventy-nine-year-old Dame Marjorie "Maude" Chardin (played by Ruth Gordon) doing the same, foretasting more taboos yet to come by offering him candy. They fall in love, of course, and Harold declares that they will marry. The overdetermined denouement is the suggestion of a premarital consummation: after visions of fireworks, on the morning after Harold blissfully blows soap bubbles in bed while Maude sleeps. The film ends with Maude's deliberate overdose on sleeping pills, as she had decided her eightieth birthday was a good time to go on her own terms. Harold mourns by staging a concluding suicide, driving his hearse off a cliff.[26] Harold could neither control his mother nor his lover, a neurotic lesson that unfolds, in playfully dark humor, for the character and the spectator alike.

The film's current popularity and cult status contrasts coolly with its fiery popular reception in early 1970s. Producer Charles Mulvehill lamented: "The idea of a 20-year-old boy with an 80-year-old woman just made people want to vomit. If you asked people what it was about, ultimately it became a boy who was fucking his grandmother."[27] In other words, the film was originally received as obscenely perverse in the popular parlance. In our less prudish present, however, many would suggest that the film is about how Maude's generous, vibrant life force is spent redirecting Harold's demanding death drive toward the desiring of self-acceptance, signified by his learning to play the banjo. Others might argue that the film's narrative is also a rehearsal of the pre-Oedipal, "good breast / bad breast" or good mother / bad mother struggle of infancy described by psychoanalyst Melanie Klein.[28] Either way, the film also serves as an excellent condensation of the conceptual coordinates of this study, directing us toward a more playful and common iteration of perversion instead of the increasingly pervasive and perilous alternative.

As an illustration, *Harold and Maude*'s simultaneously jubilant and jeremiadic mood reflects that of *Political Perversion*, as I have tried to write from the deliberately playful to the increasingly sober. The film reminds us of both the humor, creativity, and playfulness of common perversion and the potentially suicidal consequences of the more structural sort. The triangular character system in *Harold and Maude* can certainly be read as a functional illustration of Kleinian or Freudian dramas: it is as much a commentary on the role of primary caregiver (a pre-Oedipal struggle between the bad mother and the joyful surrogate) as it is on the absence or impotence of a paternal figure (the death of the father and a "castrated" uncle). The work of psychosis and perversion as stylistic signatures and generic structures in (film) art is easier to notice when we compare *Harold and Maude* to its shadow, Alfred Hitchcock's 1960 classic, *Psycho*. The pre-Oedipal dyad between mother and son in both films is almost cartoonish: Norman Bates's failure to recognize a father or to separate from "Mother" results in the foreclosure of psychosis, or an inability to connect with new love objects outside of the smothering omnipotence of the matriarch.[29] Norman plays dirty by enforcing the rules of the only game in town: killing women who represent a threat to the all-consuming mother. Harold's contrast to Norman, then, is that he is alienated from the mother and resorts to repeatedly and creatively staging his demise as a demand for recognition. Harold *might have seemed structurally perverse*, but his relationship with Maude illustrates otherwise. Although outside of the narrative *Harold and Maude* announces itself as perverse film from the opening scene (Harold hangs himself and his mother responds, "I suppose you think that's very funny, Harold"), any sense of revulsion is *not* in response to the recognition of a perverse structure: as Christopher Beach observes, Harold displays "a striking degree of neurosis."[30] The film does too, reminding the spectator at each plot point, whether with scenes that contrast with the gentle, folk crooning of Cat Stevens, a marching band, blood spatter, or fireworks, that death can be confronted comically. Unlike Norman, Harold is repeatedly alienated from a controlling mother. Indeed, the ham-handed, cultural critique advanced by

Harold and Maude is directed at the puritanical and religious condemnations of a perversity we all share, reflecting what Joan Copjec describes as Freud's "exact, if too concise" understanding of neurosis as "the *negative* of perversion."[31] Concisely or not, the film is a neurotic answer to *Psycho*'s psychosis, abounding with commonly perverse behaviors and themes but advancing quite the opposite of their critique. Such a reading depends on the very important distinction between perverse behaviors or traits and dispositions or structures with which we began.

Like both Freud and Lacan, *Harold and Maude* seems to project an argument for embracing sexuality in (almost) whatever form it takes, but only *after mutual agreement*: despite their difference in age, Maude and Harold's bond is consensual and not manipulative, their courtship teases but does not enact a juridical perversion ("Would you like some licorice?"), and their love is an affront to patriarchal propriety.[32] Their "dates" are playfully creative too, whether they concern stealing a tree or a trip to the carnival or making love in Maude's boxcar home.

GUNPLAY

In various ways, *Harold and Maude* demonstrates the both/and character of common perversion as a playful endeavor in a way that also resonates as a commentary on contemporary political parallels; that the film debuted during the postassassination, Nixon-and-Vietnam zeitgeist tracks a perverse cultural tone particular to the early 1970s in narrative, aesthetics, music, and editing. Today a similar tone has rebounded, as if there has been some popular return of the repressed, a return to the tonic or a regression to the primal note of a sordid, political scale. One early scene from *Harold and Maude* is particularly prescient, echoing a tonal recurrence of our time: shortly after meeting at their funeral crashing, Harold and Maude exit the church with the procession. The camera cuts to the blaring sound of triumphantly cheerful music; an over-the-shoulder shot shows pallbearers carrying a casket and feeding it into a hearse. As the casket is loaded, in the visual field a high school band appears from behind the hearse, marching by and brandishing US flags. Such an obnoxious juxtaposition captures a *presumed* deviance from what is appropriately mournful, all the while arguing in sound and scene that life is strange, rarely conforms, and marches on after we're gone. In so doing *Harold and Maude* is demonstrative of how dark comedy as a genre is commonly perverse and thoroughly neurotic, even ethically playful in its creativity and regard for the spectator (despite the initial misguided reception).

The contrast between the marching band and the hearse, between patriotism and pallbearing, also captures the life-or-death "mood" of publics represented in the media in the wake of the 2016 presidential election. For many commentators, the aftermath of the election was funerary, both a wake and a call from beyond by interred sisters and ancestors of color to "get out"—like, to Canada—or to "get woke."[33] The scene captures the attempts of many—especially those considered politically left of center—to play the part of resilient marchers while pallbearing the political, motivating our comrades to push back the darkness despite a mournful mood that something, both a promise and a pretense, has died, or that long-established norms of propriety have been warped.[34] Of course, insofar as the Electoral College is a vestige of slavery and a reminder that elites are often fearful of demotic stupidity, one might argue that our elections have been perverted at least since 1804.[35] Still, as I have suggested throughout, political discourse has always been perverse, only it's becoming more so—or perhaps more structurally entrenched, less contingent, and more machinic. The electile dysfunction of Trump is a symptom of an increasingly psychotic, techno-mediated public and the perverse political rhetoric it promulgates. Attending to a public's modes of pathological play—that is, foul or dirty play, broadly speaking—can produce something like a partially developed Polaroid of contemporary communicative predicaments.

Getting to the pith of political perversion begins by attending to the repetition of relational patterns that many of us would describe as transgressions but that are actually a compulsive repetition of defenses (disavowals and demands). What appears as playfulness is actually a form dirty work, an acknowledgment of consensus reality and a denial of it at the same time. Once again, for an all-too-fitting example let's return to Trump's stump scene in Wilmington, North Carolina, in 2016: "If [Hillary Clinton] gets to pick her [Supreme Court] judges," Trump belched, "there's nothing you can do, folks. Although the Second Amendment people—maybe there is, *I don't know*" (my emphasis).[36] These shots from the stump are particularly demonstrative of playing dirty. What makes disavowal a perverse rhetorical strategy is the relationship implied by such turns of speech in the "I don't know" coda: the speaker is above or beyond or embodies the symbolic order he denies, he takes no responsibility for it—he is, after all, just being playful. His campaign handlers explained the remark was meant to reference the "tremendous power" of Second Amendment fanatics; Trump followed that "there can be no other interpretation. . . . I mean, give me a break."[37] *Harold and Maude* does not tempt violence, even though it is all about violence (or rather, a critique of the symbolic kind). Trump on the stump did and does, moving us now from the harmless perversion of putting ketchup on an overdone steak toward a lust for seemingly playful bloodletting.

Trump's obvious example of Second Amendment obscenity leads us, finally, to playing with guns. In our time, weapons, and particularly guns, have become nontransitional objects that function as a symptom of a larger, harmful cultural perversion. Most of us can regress to the enjoyment of a transitional object like a teddy bear; many of us collect objects that remind us of a happier time in our youth like dolls or action figures or . . . Elvis lamps. Fetishizing functional weapons is a much different story, as guns are not meant to be played with like toys. Given their prevalence in the United States today, mass shootings can also be described as a cultural regression to anal sadism and playful destruction. Gunplay is but one kind of pathological play, as I have already noted examples of many other sorts of dirty play so far (e.g., bigotry), but it is among the most prominent and deadly, and dialectically interlocked with the news media discourse about it.

I conclude with an illustration closer to home, taking the reader with me to Texas.[38] On May 18, 2018, at approximately 7:40 a.m., a seventeen-year-old student entered Santa Fe High School south of Houston and shot dozens of people with a shotgun and a pistol, killing ten and wounding thirteen others. The only school shooting that resulted in more deaths in US history was at Stoneman Douglas High School in Florida just three months earlier. The shootings are horrifying, as are those that have happened since *Political Perversion* went to press. My focus is on how this carnage was covered in the mainstream news media, which both reflects and re-creates the larger, destructive discourse of political perversion.[39]

On the evening of the Santa Fe shooting, ABC ran a *Nightline* program about the killings that was predictably manipulative: against a cloying voiceover recounting facts and describing the grief of the high school community, a montage of aerial shots of the school are shown. Young people are seen running; then the spectator hears emergency dispatch radio recordings. These sounds fade into still photographs of families embracing and so on. The most contrived aspect of this segment, however, is the use of an ominous drone that gradually fades up into the soundtrack.

Although mass shootings seem to be increasing, at the time of my writing their frequency is not; they are getting more coverage in the national news media, and they are getting deadlier.[40] And despite popular rhetoric concerning an epidemic of targeted violence, such perceptions are largely the consequence of media overexposure and a firmly entrenched genre of what we could term "active shooter television." I underscore that the *Nightline* segment foregrounds slow zooms and maudlin drones (the latter less conspicuous but increasingly ubiquitous in media segments on trauma), which have become fixed, generic features that are deliberately designed to double *as traumatic stressors* for viewers. It is not simply that the news is "covering" traumatic events (analog); they are *re-creating* them (digital). The perversity of spectatorship that is so well documented as a quality of cinema has traveled deep into the private home, into living rooms, bedrooms, and home offices, structuring repeated traumas in "private" spaces. And because active shooter television is now produced with such high cinematic production values, we should not be surprised that there is mounting evidence to suggest that the media coverage and framing of targeted violence encourages imitation and fame seeking.[41] A popular infamy previously reserved for movie stars and serial killers (real and imagined) is now central to the coverage of mass violence too.

Teleplaying with affect attempts to collapse a sense of spatial and temporal distance and delay, exacerbating a sensibility of crisis that is phatic and addictive in character.[42] This is to say that the structurally perverse and ossified genre of active shooter television is a mainstream, breaking-news fixation that has veered from the common and consensual fetishes of everyday perversion into the ideological dimensions of a kind of perverse coercion. As a form of repetition compulsion, we should not be surprised that "addiction" can be compared to disavowal: they are both compulsive, and they are both defensive.

If our attention to the media coverage of targeted violence is addictive, we need to also say—in the same breath—that many claim the same about gun ownership too. *These addictions are intimately related, two sides of a shared projection.* Popular discussions of gun violence frequently rehearse the adage that "America is addicted to guns,"[43] with "three-in-ten American adults" claiming to own a gun, "and another 11%" living with someone who does.[44] This so-called addiction is reflected in high gun homicide rates; in the United States gun deaths are 25.2 times higher than in other "high-income" countries. Parts of Central and South America are worse.[45] Although media overexposure has helped to raise awareness and set agendas against targeted violence, public discussion tends to focus on issues of mental health or "commonsense" gun control, routinely missing the opportunity, like a broken record, to understand targeted violence as both systemically cultivated and a systemic *reaction*.

Owing to a US tendency to resign the responsibility of violence to individuals, we appear to have locked ourselves into the "erroneous assumption that prevention requires prediction."[46] Of course, many crucial preventative measures have been taken (active shooter plans, the distribution of casualty response kits, and so on), but my point is that our individualistic ideology leads to well-documented failures like profiling: we know, for example, that weapons and whiteness are linked. But to-the-person profiling doesn't really help. Shooters tend to be white, male, and prone to aggression; however, this is an impressionist portrait of a rather large pond. For empiricists, there are simply "no reliable predictors" for mass shootings.[47]

OF KETCHUP AND BLOOD

This promise, love and all things go
From my love
She said please be kind and
Please be brave and kill for fun.

THE BLACK ANGELS, "Don't Play with Guns"[48]

Except, of course, that there *are* persuasive predictors of mass shootings—they just don't fit the generic requirements of active shooter television. As scholars and citizens alike we need to widen our acceptance of what counts as reliable research beyond behavioral empiricism, thinking more critically and less about the circular straightjacket of lone-wolf deviance, of which Trump is simply another example. Our public addiction to reruns of real-time catastrophe and individually focused pathology, this cycle of control-freakism from left to right might be better dubbed a "structural violence,"[49] which Johan Galtung described as avoidable, nonpersonal violence experienced as social injustice but obscured or hidden in cultural fantasies of the American spirit. Analyst Glen Slater elaborates: "When you look hard enough you come to see that the ethos of the American Dream has a built-in but well camouflaged structural violence, a series of dynamics that promote opportunity but create disenfranchisement."[50] The observation resonates with Robert Merton's argument over sixty years ago: US culture stresses financial success without structural opportunity, leading to massive strains and the relief valve of criminal innovations and quick fixes.[51]

What better represents the quick fix than a gun, a symbol of power and control, an object that functions as a route to mastery much like a transitional object, except the object isn't transitional—it's stuck! The gun is jammed in US culture and appears impervious to substitution, to creativity.[52] "The Swiss are armed to the teeth," reports Helena Bachmann, but targeted violence in Switzerland is rare, which is a point the National Rifle Association likes to emphasize. In the United States, and in *no small part* because of the NRA,[53] the gun persists as a constant object, something that rhetoricians term synecdoche but that we can more generally describe as a fetish.[54] We hardly need to detail the fetishism of the gun; John Lennon did that already on the *White Album* in 1968. What I do want to stress here is the way in which the gun has become *an object of play*, a synecdoche celebrated first in childhood as a toy and later on screens as a great equalizer of power. Rhetorically speaking, the gun is a part that stands in for whole fantasies of Western expansionism and self-made men of action.[55]

Consequently, gunplay is shorthand for a ubiquitous fantasy of leveling the playing field—first in war and cinema, then television, then video games, now mass shootings, full circle. Notably, gunplay is tied as much to the camera as it is to the bullet. First, there is the fame-seeking component, which consists of circulation in multiple media, an aspect of targeted violence as a route to celebrity. Moreover, as Rosa A. Eberly has argued, the fantasy of shooting up a school "is not very mysterious. Half a century of gun violence in schools and other public spaces has provided copious examples for imitation."[56] And if your violence "goes viral," *you've made it in America*. Second, there is an epistemic symmetry to gunplay and mass media too: both are kinds of shooting that depend on what the late Paul Virilio described as a logic or "aesthetic of disappearance."[57] A logic of disappearance is another way of describing motion and action: unless something disappears from the scope or the frame, nothing happens, no one is moved. Reflection and thinking are perhaps better reserved for stilettos and still photography, which is a curious way to say that disappearance is the peekaboo of gunplay, an addiction to *action*.[58] Shoot first, think later.

Consider, for example, my state governor shooting off his mouth at a press conference shortly after the massacre at Santa Fe High School: "We also know, uh, information already, uh, that there, that the shooter has information contained in journals on his computer and cell phone, that, that, he said, that, uh, not only did he want to commit the shooting, but he wanted to commit suicide, uh, after the shooting. As you probably know, uh, he gave himself up, and admitted at the time that he didn't have the courage, uh, to commit the suicide that he wanted to, uh, take his own life earlier."[59] The governor did not wear his customary suit and tie but an official state governor shirt that resembled a police uniform. Is the violence of or at this scene reducible to one troubled teen, when those who are most responsible for framing it evoke the fantasy of masculine resolve? That the trench-coat-wearing shooter and others partake in the same Columbine script should be obvious: *cowards don't shoot straight*. Again, I repeat that playing dirty is not creative; it is a structurally perverse, prefab game, and the rules must be ruthlessly enforced. Governor

Abbott played along, as did Education Secretary Betsy DeVos, who revived the national discussion for arming teachers.[60] This is a rather uncreative solution that mistakes prevention with prediction, based not on research but on Hollywood shoot-'em-ups.

Orwellian fantasy brings me back to the reality of electoral politics with which I began, but now in a slightly different light: many of us who study culture and politics have been asking ourselves, in the wake of the 2016 election, how did Trump secure the presidency despite all the predictors and polling and conventional logic? One answer, of course, is that Trump put conventions—this is to say, both politics as usual and the RNC rally at Nuremburg—on amphetamines. But another is to understand the "Fuck it" electorate as a perverse and almost scripted response to an ideological promise that—like disavowal—dismantles the means to achieve that very same promise.

So many revered public figures, from Susan B. Anthony to Malcolm X to the students from Marjory Stoneman Douglas High School, have publicly decried this disjunction, each in their own way pointing out the ideological perversion of trying to dream "American," each in their own way pointing out how the restful dream for a few is a nightmare for everyone else. Some have suggested that the sentiment that people of color are prevented from dreaming was quelled during the Obama presidency, perpetuating what Jordan Peele terms the postracial lie.[61] Some have argued that the unprecedented number of women running for office in 2018 marks it as the "Year of the Women,"[62] and yet we keep hearing the echoes of "#MeToo" everywhere at an increasing volume.[63] Regardless of one's political convictions, many recent national and local elections reflect a resurgent racism and misogyny, a structurally perverse and criminal innovation or demand to *blow it all up*—and not just figuratively. The remarks of one Florida voter on *PBS NewsHour* sum up a willfully destructive disavowal of human subjectivity and a demand for violence: "I believe [Trump] is a force for positive. I don't think we needed just a nice, normal politician. I think our country was in such a state that we needed a wrecking ball to go into Washington and wreck it."[64] This is no mere metaphor. In yet another voter's remorse story in the *New York Times*, ostensibly covering a community recovering from a hurricane and struggling with the 2019 partial government shutdown, a prison employee repents, "I voted for him, and he's the one who's doing this. . . . I thought he was going to do good things. He's not hurting the people he needs to be hurting."[65]

The demands for hurting people and wrecking our institutions of government are not reducible to the remarks of two voters; these voters are as much a part of "the system" as you and I and, especially, so are the mainstream news and social media journalists who fail, time and time again, to focus on systemic and cultural ills (e.g., interviewing one voter as the representative of a group of people and implying that they constitute either a problem public or one deserving of maudlin pity). A commitment to reducing our public problems to individual responsibility, to the wall-demanding tantrums of a structurally perverse figure or to mentally ill "lone wolves," entails the *avoidable and foreseen*, dehumanizing consequences of a willful explosion. People deserve compassion and charity, not exploitation or reduction. Blowing things and people up isn't a revolution; it's an amplification of what we've already got.[66]

In what sense has voting been reduced to quick-fix action? Is voting the outcome of a considered and reflective process? Is pulling the lever for Clinton or Trump or anyone akin to the control-freakism of shooting? It could be that electoral politics is no longer a liminal space of transition and play, a moment of pure contingency and "What if?" but rather a cruel game; it could be that voting obscures the violent structure underwriting it, that the Electoral College and voting suppression—vestiges of antisuffrage and slavery—give lie to the pipe dream of "liberty for all."[67]

Some have said that playing politics is war by other means.[68] Insofar as elections can result in the dismantling of welfare writ large, such as ending human services or separating families at the border[69] or describing anyone of color as a criminal or animal[70] or refusing to provide enough aid to a Puerto Rico devastated by a hurricane[71] or supporting dictators and fascists who kill reporters[72] or goading anti-Semitic shooting sprees[73] or making fun of women who were sexually assaulted[74] or trying to repeal health care coverage for those who need it[75] or rolling back protections for LGBTQAI persons[76] or inspiring the rise of "nationalism" and Nazism[77] or in responding to mass shootings by saying we need more guns, including armed teachers,[78] in what sense can we say that US elections are *structurally* perverse and that electoral politics has become mass shooting by other means?

ACKNOWLEDGMENTS

Seventeen years ago an editor wrote to me that my author note for an essay in production was too "obsequious." I had to look up the word. Sitting down to write the acknowledgments, as my gratitude grows, I *still* worry about failing to mention someone who was important to the book's completion. Owing to the unconscious, an oversight is inevitable, so my first thank you goes out to my basket of unmentionables.

The completion of this study was made possible by leave time provided by a 2018 Faculty Research Assignment from the Graduate School at the University of Texas at Austin. Funds to lower the book cost, as well as to purchase licenses to reprint copyrighted art, were secured with a University of Texas at Austin Book Subvention Grant and funding from the Department of Communication Studies. I praise and thank my home department's Senior Dragon Slayer, Jennifer Betancourt, for cleverly conquering the bureaucracy of my grant grubbing and lovingly shielding me from the fire. I thank my friend Brian Sharkey Vaught for help with the figures and Mitch O'Connell for his permission to use his *Alien Trump* artwork. I also must thank the tireless librarians at UT's Perry-Castaneda Library, particularly those working with interlibrary loan scanning, who have provided me with gigabytes of digital resources; I know you're not allowed to sign your name when fulfilling my requests, but whoever you are, thank you. The intellectual and moral support of my colleagues at UT helped me tremendously—the topic is not, in the end, very cheerful—especially Diane Davis and Johanna "Red Pen" Hartelius. The feedback and friendship of my colleagues Karma Chávez, Rick Cherwtiz, Rod Hart, Hana Masri, Trish Roberts-Miller, and Karin Wilkins were invaluable.

138 *Acknowledgments*

My friends and colleagues in the wider world of academia, in one way or another, provided valuable feedback and commentary on the arguments shared here, formally and informally, and at least once in a stairwell. My thanks to Andrea Alden, David Beard, Carole Blair, Karlyn Kohrs Campbell, Jim Catano, Devika Chawla, Dana Cloud, James Darsey, Rosa Eberly (our time together and long talk about this book in New Orleans for Derek Smalls's tour was invaluable, gums and all), Kendall Gerdes, Chuck Goehring, Ron Greene, Mirko Hall, Atilla Hallsby, Susan Jarratt, Paul Johnson, Martin Law, Steve Llano, John Lucaites, Christian Lundberg, Ashley Mack, Michelle Massé, Brian McCann, Marty Medhurst, Jen Mercieca, Jaishikha Nautiyal, Angela Ray, Valerie Regenar, Kayla Rhidenhour, Marnie Ritchie, Brad Serber, Ryan Skinnell, Christopher Swift, Mary Anne Taylor, Shaun Treat, and Kristine Weglarz. I have shared many "talks" based on different arguments in *Political Perversion* across the United States for many years, mostly at universities, and am thankful for the invitations to share and the generous feedback my work received. A large portion of the book was completed at my favorite writing retreat in Vancouver; my thanks to my crew there for talking with me as I wrote: Graham and Marsha Rennie, Sandra Ackermann, Michael Kleinman, and Jayne Dixon.

Clinical insights from members of the Austin Society for Psychoanalytic Psychology were especially helpful for getting a perspective outside of the academy. And speaking of therapy, I have spent many sessions with my own therapist, Catherine "Katie" Rees, discussing political affects, and I appreciate our time spent "working through" what I can only describe as political depression. In this respect, I should also recognize the support of my constant companion (and comfort, most of the time) of thirteen years, a twelve-pound Xoloitzcuintli named Jesús, also known as Sir Barks-a-Lot or Shakey Mc-Jones, who often sat behind me in my writing chair as I banged out the book.

At the University of Chicago Press, my first editor, the late, great, Doug Mitchell, initially had to make a double take with this manuscript but with kindness and a wicked sense of humor helped to shepherd the project into production. After Doug retired, my second editor, Kyle Wagner, escorted me the rest of the way, generously offering advice and ensuring I didn't fall off a cliff. His assistant, Dylan Joseph Montanari, has also been invaluable. My father died while I was completing the book, and Kyle and Dylan's patience and care during a difficult time was and remains a great comfort. Major props also to my gracious copy editor, George Roupe, for enduring my puns and helping to make this manuscript appear competent (all the remaining gaffes are, of course, my own). Much gratitude also goes to the production team at Chicago, who successfully pushed *Political Perversion* to the end of the line and tried to make it look pretty: Skye Agnew (production controller), Tamara Ghattas (production editor), Adrienne Meyers (promotions manager), and Kevin Quach (book designer).

I started this book in 2015 as a series of short essays that I tried to publish in the popular press (the *Atlantic*, the *New Republic*, the *Huffington Post*, and so on); I realized after almost twenty rejections during a three-month period that no one was ready yet to entertain an argument about perversion and politics. I coauthored a piece on Trump's inaugural address (the "American Carnage" speech) with Christian Lundberg, but I never succeeded with a popular press piece on my own. I then tried to publish some of the arguments as academic articles; what eventually evolved into chapters 3 and 4 was an essay that was reviewed and rejected once and desk-rejected twice. Still, because of a sense of urgency, like her, I persisted, and did get some of the arguments out in chunks, which I acknowledge here: parts of chapter 2 appear in "On Social Networking and Psychosis," *Communication Theory* 28.1 (2018): 69–88 (used by courtesy of Oxford University Press); and in "Tears of Refusal: Crying with Collins (and Lundberg), with Reference to Pee-wee Herman," *Rhetoric & Public Affairs* 18.2 (2015): 347–58 (used by courtesy of Michigan State University Press); and parts of chapters 3 and 4 appear in "On Political Perversion," *Rhetoric Society Quarterly* 48.2 (2018): 161–86 (used by courtesy of Routledge). With a popular readership in mind, a much simplified version of my claims about political perversion appears in Ryan Skinnell's edited volume *Faking the News: What Rhetoric Can Teach Us about Donald J. Trump* (Exeter: Imprint Academic, 2018). The argument I advance in the conclusion regarding gun violence was originally shared as the Carroll C. Arnold Distinguished Lecture at the National Communication Association Convention in November 2018 in Salt Lake City.

Finally, I dedicate this study to four of my mentors, all of whom played a larger role in the completion of *this* book (some were readers, some were pushers). Barbara Biesecker has mentored me and taught me much and has become a trusted confidant; Barb tried her best to keep me from making totalizing claims, but sometimes my passion for polemic still got in the way. Barry Brummett has advised me like a big brother, in both senses (he was my department chair for fifteen years), and has been on me (gently) to finish a book for years. Edward Schiappa continues providing professional and intellectual guidance from afar—often with lightning-speed email responses. Ed also vetted the book proposal for *Political Perversion* and suggested revisions. Tom Frentz routinely reads and edits my work (oh, and tells me inappropriate jokes) and has been a trusted colleague, friend, and confidant for decades; Tom has read this book through many drafts, and his advice is threaded throughout. These four friends have donated to me an exceptional amount of their time, wisdom, and care, and I am grateful to and for them.

NOTES

PREAMBLE

1. With all due respect to Morrissey, vocalist, "That Joke Isn't Funny Anymore," by the Smiths, track 5 on *Meat Is Murder*, Sire Records, 1985.

2. Even though many of her pleasing policy highlights were, as my friend Mary Anne objected that night, in significant tension with the party platform.

3. See David Held, *Introduction to Critical Theory: Horkheimer to Habermas* (Berkeley: University of California Press), 142–143. These conclusions were drawn from Theodore W. Adorno, Else Frenkel-Brunswik, Daniel J. Levinson, and R. Nevitt Sanford, *The Authoritarian Personality*, abridged ed. (New York: W. W. Norton, 1993).

4. Theodor W. Adorno, "Freudian Theory and the Pattern of Fascist Propaganda," in *The Essential Frankfurt School Reader*, ed. Andrew Arato and Eike Gebhardt (New York: Continuum, 2002), 119.

5. For a remarkably lucid and short explanation of demagoguery, see Patricia Roberts-Miller, *Demagoguery and Democracy* (New York: The Experiment, 2017).

6. See Sigmund Freud, *Civilization and Its Discontents*, trans. James Strachey (New York: W. W. Norton, 1961), 108.

7. Freud, *Civilization*, 64–74.

8. Mark Edmundson, "Freud and the Fundamentalist Urge," *New York Times Magazine*, April 30, 2006, https://www.nytimes.com/2006/04/30/magazine/freud-and-the-fundamentalist-urge.html, para. 7.

9. Edmundson, "Freud and the Fundamentalist Urge," para. 8.

10. George Orwell, "As I Please (28)," *Tribune* (UK), March 24, 1944, in George Orwell, *Essays, Journalism & Letters*, ed. Sonia Orwell and Ian Angus (Boston: Pareil Books, 2000), 3:135–138.

11. Gianni Riotta, "I Know Fascists; Donald Trump Is No Fascist," *Atlantic*, January 16, 2016, https://www.theatlantic.com/international/archive/2016/01/donald-trump-fascist/424449/.

INTRODUCTION

1. Jacques Derrida, "'Eating Well,' or the Calculation of the Subject: An Interview with Jacques Derrida," in *Who Comes after the Subject?*, ed. Eduardo Cadava, Peter Connor, and Jean-Luc Nancy (New York: Routledge, 1991), 114.

2. Lizzie O'Leary, "In the World of Ketchup, Heinz Is the Most Iconic," *Marketplace*, July 4, 2017, https://www.marketplace.org/2017/06/29/business/world-ketchup-heinz-most-iconic.

3. Mercy Ingraham, "The History of Ketchup," *Early American Life* 46.5 (2015): 60–65.

4. Quoted in Jane Tibbetts Schulenburg, *Forgetful of Their Sex: Female Sanctity and Society, ca. 500–1100* (Chicago: University of Chicago Press, 1998), 213.

5. James Joyce, *Finnegans Wake* (New York: Penguin Books, 1976), 628, 3; Dave Boyer, "Trump Dubs His Mar-a-Lago Resort 'The Southern White House,'" *Washington Times*, February 18, 2017, https://www.washingtontimes.com/news/2017/feb/18/trump-calls-mar-lago -resort-southern-white-house.

6. Lawrence Donegan, "Trump: Making Golf Horrible Again," *New York Review of Books*, February 9, 2018, http://www.nybooks.com/daily/2018/02/09/trump-making-golf-horrible -again/. To understand better how the term "Southern White House" is coded for many as a gesture to the Confederacy, see Ian Haney López, *Dog Whistle Politics: How Coded Racial Appeals Have Reinvented Racism and Wrecked the Middle Class* (New York: Oxford University Press, 2015).

7. Jan Reid, "C. W. Post: The Cerial [*sic*] King Made His Fortune with Grape-Nuts, but He Saw His Salvation in Texas," *Texas Monthly*, March 1987, https://www.texasmonthly.com /the-culture/c-w-post/.

8. Frances Bellamy, ed., *Effective Magazine Advertising* (New York: Mitchell Kennerly, 1909), 235.

9. Alexandra Petri, "The Day Donald Trump First Became a Stable Genius," *Washington Post*, January 12, 2018, https://www.washingtonpost.com/blogs/compost/wp/2018/01/12/the -day-donald-trump-first-became-a-stable-genius/.

10. Brenna Houck, "Trump's Weird Junk Food Habits Revealed by Former Campaign Manager," *Eater*, December 4, 2017, https://www.eater.com/2017/12/4/16733356/trump -fast-food-diet-mcdonalds-campaign-corey-lewandowski.

11. Cindy Boren and Des Bieler, "President Trump Serves Up a Fast-Food Feast for Clemson Tigers during Their White House Visit: 'Everything That I Like,'" *Chicago Tribune*, January 15, 2019, https://www.chicagotribune.com/sports/college/ct-spt-clemson-national-cham pionship-trump-white-house-20190114-story.html.

12. Tim Marcin, "Trump Eats McDonald's Because He's Afraid of Being Poisoned Elsewhere," *Newsweek*, January 3, 2018, http://www.newsweek.com/trump-eats-mcdonalds-because -afraid-poison-donald-fast-food-obsession-769796.

13. One of my favorites features an image of Gollum from the *Lord of the Rings* films with the text, "WHEN YOU PUT KETCHUP ON YOUR STEAK YOU RUINS IT!"

14. Helen Rosner, "Actually, How Donald Trump Eats His Steak Matters," *Eater*, February 28, 2017, https://www.eater.com/2017/2/28/14753248/trump-steak-well-done-ketchup-personality.

15. Rosner, "Actually," para. 16.

16. Jason Hanna, Kaylee Hartung, Devon M. Sayers, and Steve Almasy, "Virginia Governor to White Nationalists: 'Go Home . . . Shame on You,'" CNN.com, August 13, 2017, https://www.cnn.com/2017/08/12/us/charlottesville-white-nationalists-rally/index.html. For HBO, *Vice News* produced a remarkable documentary on the march and ensuing violence; see *Vice News*, "Charlottesville: Race and Terror," August 21, 2017, https://news.vice.com/en_us/article/qvzn8p/vice-news-tonight-full-episode-charlottesville-race-and-terror.

17. Michael D. Shear and Maggie Haberman, "Trump Defends Initial Remarks on Charlottesville; Again Blames 'Both Sides,'" *New York Times*, August 15, 2017, https://www.nytimes.com/2017/08/15/us/politics/trump-press-conference-charlottesville.html.

18. Lawrence D. Bobo, "Racism in Trump's America: Reflections on Culture, Sociology, and the 2016 US Presidential Election," *British Journal of Sociology* 68.S1 (2017): S90.

19. "perverse, n.1." *Oxford English Dictionary*, 2nd ed., 20 vols. (Oxford: Oxford University Press, 1989).

20. Sally Kohn, *The Opposite of Hate: A Field Guide to Repairing Our Humanity* (Chapel Hill, NC: Algonquin Books, 2018), 7.

21. James Penney, *After Queer Theory: The Limits of Sexual Politics* (London: Pluto, 2014), 54. Also see Judith Butler, Ernesto Laclau, and Slavoj Žižek, *Contingency, Hegemony, Universality: Contemporary Dialogues on the Left* (New York: Verso, 2000), esp. Žižek's conclusion, 308–329.

22. Charles W. Mills, *The Racial Contract* (Ithaca, NY: Cornell University Press, 1997), 3.

23. See Carole Pateman, *The Sexual Contract* (Stanford, CA: Stanford University Press, 1988); and bell hooks, "Understanding Patriarchy," Louisville Anarchist Federation Federation [LAFF], n.d., http://imaginenoborders.org/pdf/zines/UnderstandingPatriarchy-imposed.pdf.

24. Slavoj Žižek, *On Belief* (New York: Routledge, 2001), 20. Also see Matthew Sharpe and Geoff Boucher, *Žižek and Politics: A Critical Introduction* (Edinburgh: Edinburgh University Press, 2010), 139–164.

25. See Kirsten Hyldgaard, "The Conformity of Perversion," *Symptom* 5 (Winter 2004): http://www.lacan.com/conformperf.htm.

26. For example, how the slavery system became the prison system: see Lisa M. Corrigan, *Prison Power: How Prison Influenced the Movement for Black Liberation* (Jackson: University Press of Mississippi, 2017); and Bryan J. McCann, *The Mark of Criminality: Rhetoric, Race, and Gangsta Rap in the War-on-Crime Era* (Tuscaloosa: University of Alabama Press, 2017).

27. For a book-length explication of homological analysis, see Barry Brummett, *Rhetorical Homologies: Form, Culture, Experience* (Tuscaloosa: University of Alabama Press, 2004).

28. Rachel Vorona Cote, "Donald Trump Eats His Steak Well Done with Ketchup, Like a Damn Child," *Jezebel*, February 26, 2017, https://jezebel.com/donald-trump-eats-his-steak-well-done-with-ketchup-lik-1792770173. Taking such observations to the underside of levity, like calling out the trauma underwriting a comedic stand-up routine, it is sobering to note that children continue to starve in Africa in alarming numbers, more recently as a consequence of terrorist insurgencies, and this despite ceaseless campaigns for global awareness; see May Bulman, "90,000 Children Are Expected to Die in Nigeria over the Next 12 Months, Unicef Warns," *Independent*, January 25, 2017, http://www.independent.co.uk/news/world/africa/nigerian-children-starve-to-death-2017-nigeria-africa-help-unicef-international-community-aid-a75461

76.html. At the time of this writing the Trump administration has proposed budget cuts to USAID, which is responsible for developmental assistance and health-related programs in Africa. John Campbell, former UN Ambassador to Nigeria, observes that "Africa would be disproportionately affected" by the cuts because "roughly one-third of USAID funds go to the continent"; Armsfree Ajanaku and Gbenga Salau, "US Africa Policy in an Era of Trumpism," *Guardian*, March 11, 2018, https://guardian.ng/saturday-magazine/cover/us-africa-policy-in-an-era-of-trumpism/. Sometimes ketchup on a steak is just ketchup on a steak, except that the point of this introduction is to argue that it's not.

29. Hear Robert B. Sherman and Richard M. Sherman, "A Spoonful of Sugar," *Mary Poppins* (original soundtrack), performed by Julie Andrews, Walt Disney Records, 1964. One can also hear the song in the 1964 Walt Disney film *Mary Poppins*.

30. "That immunity from all the usual laws of politics—the Teflon Factor—is the ultimate mystery of Ronald Reagan's success." "How Good a President?," *Newsweek*, August 27, 1984: 31.

31. By "methodology" I mean the study of, or theories about, method, including making value judgments about methods. Although I very briefly explain my approach to criticism in the next chapter, it is not, strictly speaking, a "method." Rhetorical criticism is a *craft*.

32. Aristotle, *On Rhetoric: A Theory of Civic Virtue*, 2nd ed., trans. George A. Kennedy (New York: Oxford University Press, 2007), 37.

33. For example, see Jamelle Bouie, "Meaningless: President Trump's Rhetoric Means Nothing, Even to His Own Administration," *Slate*, March 2, 2018, https://slate.com/news-and-politics/2018/03/president-trumps-rhetoric-means-nothing-even-to-his-own-administration.html.

34. Edward Schiappa, "Did Plato Coin *Rhêtorikê*?," *American Journal of Philology* 111.4 (1990): 457–470.

35. Plato, *Phaedrus*, trans. Alexander Nehamas and Paul Woodruff (Indianapolis: Hackett, 1995), 32–39.

36. My personal working definition—which is a composite of many I have come across in my career—is this: *rhetoric* is the study of how representation influences people to do or think what they otherwise would not ordinarily do or think. Such a view is complicated, of course, by recent work on "rhetoricity," which denotes a *capacity* for rhetoric prior to representation; see Diane Davis, *Inessential Solidarity: Rhetoric and Foreigner Relations* (Pittsburgh: University of Pittsburgh Press, 2010).

37. See Plato, *Gorgias*, trans. Robin Waterfield (New York: Oxford University Press, 2008).

38. Many posthumanist assumptions underwrite this study (e.g., a critique of the idea of autonomy, the centrality of the human to the world, and so on). I discuss them most explicitly in chapter 4. Readers interested in my own elaborations should see Joshua Gunn, "Mourning Humanism, or, the Idiom of Haunting," *Quarterly Journal of Speech* 92.1 (2006): 77–102; and Christian Lundberg and Joshua Gunn, " 'Ouija Board, Are There Any Communications?': Agency, Ontotheology, and the Death of the Humanist Subject," *Rhetoric Society Quarterly* 35.4 (Fall 2005): 83–105. For a nice elaboration of the-US-based understanding of posthumanism vis-à-vis media ecology, see Casey Boyle, *Rhetoric as a Posthuman Practice* (Columbus: Ohio State University Press, 2018).

39. I will revisit and elaborate this claim in respect to "posthumanism" in chapter 4.

40. Harold Bloom, "Foreword: Northrop Frye in Retrospect," in Northrop Frye, *Anatomy of Criticism* (Princeton, NJ: Princeton University Press, 1990), xi.

41. See Carl R. Burgchardt and Hillary A. Jones, eds., *Readings in Rhetorical Criticism*, 5th ed. (State College, PA: Strata, 2017), esp. 1–128.

42. A milestone for this switcheroo is Edwin Black, *Rhetorical Criticism: A Study in Method* (New York: Macmillan, 1965).

43. See Jordynn Jack and L. Gregory Appelbaum, "'This is Your Brain on Rhetoric': Research Directions for Neurorhetorics," *Rhetoric Society Quarterly* 40.5 (2010): 411–437. For a discussion about the widening domain of rhetorical objects of study, see Joshua Gunn and Diane Davis, eds., *Fifty Years of "Rhetoric Society Quarterly": Selected Readings, 1968–2018* (New York: Routledge, 2018), esp. 243–245; also see Brian L. Ott and Greg Dickinson, *The Routledge Reader in Rhetorical Criticism* (New York: Routledge, 2013).

44. My position here is not necessarily or widely shared. Differing viewpoints on the proper object domain of rhetorical study are most easily gleaned from the so-called Big Rhetoric debate. For an overview, see Edward Schiappa, "Second Thoughts on the Critiques of Big Rhetoric," *Philosophy & Rhetoric* 34.3 (2001): 260–274.

45. Herbert A. Wichelns, "The Literary Criticism of Oratory," *Readings in Rhetorical Criticism*, 5th ed., ed. Carl R. Burgchardt and Hillary A. Jones (State College, PA: Strata, 2017), 3–27.

46. Bordwell's aesthetic approach to film theory and criticism is best represented by his and Kristin Thompson's famous film studies textbook, *Film Art*, first published in 1979. See David Bordwell, Kristin Thompson, and Jeff Smith, *Film Art: An Introduction*, 11th ed. (New York: McGraw Hill, 2016).

47. Will Brooker, *Cultural Studies* (Lincolnwood, IL: NTC/Contemporary, 1999), 23. Also see Patrick Brantlinger, *Crusoe's Footprints: Cultural Studies in Britain and America* (New York: Routledge, 1990).

48. Richard Hoggart, *The Uses of Literacy* (New Brunswick, NJ: Transaction, 1992).

49. Lawrence Grossberg, *Bringing It All Back Home: Essays on Cultural Studies* (Durham, NC: Duke University Press, 1997), 246.

50. Lawrence Grossberg, *Cultural Studies in the Future Tense* (Durham, NC: Duke University Press, 2010), 25.

51. Grossberg, *Bringing It All Back Home*, 246.

52. See Lance Strate, *Media Ecology: An Approach to Understanding the Human Condition* (Bern: Peter Lang, 2017).

53. Grossberg has been particularly vocal about the tensions between communication and cultural studies and has argued that historical narratives such as mine are "illusory" for blunting the radical contextualization central to the Birmingham School project. My point, however, is to show how communication studies—and by extension, rhetorical studies—and cultural studies *both began* with a commitment to the "industrial classes" and the underprivileged student, or a certain shared set of values expressed in similar scholarly and pedagogical practices. See Lawrence Grossberg, "Can Cultural Studies Find True Happiness in Communication?," *Journal of Communication* 43.4 (1993): 89–97.

54. See Frank Donoghue, *The Last Professors: The Corporate University and the Fate of the Humanities* (New York: Fordham University Press, 2008).

55. See Ronald Walter Greene, "Rhetoric (Dis)Appearing," *Communication and Critical/ Cultural Studies* 10.2–3 (2013): 259–264.

56. See, for example, Lawrence Grossberg, "Marxist Dialectics and Rhetorical Criticism," *Quarterly Journal of Speech* 65.3 (1979): 235–249. The dis-ease between cultural studies and the rhetorical tradition first openly discussed by Grossberg is palpable in the first volume of *Communication and Critical/Cultural Studies* under the brief editorship of James Hay: most scholars from the speech or rhetorical tradition are excluded. Perhaps foreseeing the exclusion, cultural studies *and* rhetorical scholar Ronald Water Greene opens his invited essay for an issue on the topic of "critique": "One cannot do justice to the key words of this journal without taking into account the word rhetoric. . . . The claim I wish to pursue here is that the future of the journal's key terms—communication, critical, and cultural studies—cannot be easily extracted from the institutional histories of rhetoric." Greene, "Rhetoric (Dis)Appearing," 259.

57. Mark Mothersbaugh and Gerald Casale, "Peek-a-Boo!," by Devo, track 2 on *Oh, No! It's Devo*, Warner Brothers, 1982.

58. Gabriella M. Petrick, " 'Purity as Life': H. J. Heinz, Religious Sentiment, and the Beginning of the Industrial Diet," *History and Technology* 27.1 (2011): 38.

59. Text from a Grape-Nuts cereal box circa 1900–1920, *New-York Historical Society*, n.d., http://www.nyhistory.org/exhibit/box-food-6.

60. Petrick, " 'Purity as Life,' " 43, 41.

61. See Theresa R. Richardson, *The Century of the Child: The Mental Hygiene Movement and Social Policy in the United States and Canada* (Albany: State University of New York Press, 1989); and Claudia Wannamaker, "The Meaning and Significance of Social Adjustment," *Journal of Health and Physical Education* 10.1 (1939): 12–54.

62. "80s Ads: Heinz Tomato Ketchup 1984," *YouTube*, March 5, 2016, https://www.youtube .com/watch?v=xxWwUQ8FEUE.

63. For example, see Matt Richtel and Andrew Jacobs, "American Adults Just Keep Getting Fatter," *New York Times*, March 23, 2018, https://www.nytimes.com/2018/03/23/health /obesity-us-adults.html. "Biopolitics" references the productive power of life promotion central to modern modes of governance described by Michel Foucault, while "necropolitics" is Achille Mbembe's contrapuntal concept for the use of power to determine who lives or dies. Michel Foucault, *The History of Sexuality*, vol. 1, *An Introduction* (New York: Vintage Books, 1990); Achille Mbembe, "Necropolitics," *Public Culture* 15.1 (2003): 11–40.

64. "Revenue of the Quick Service Restaurant (QSR) Industry in the United States from 2002 to 2020 (in Billion US Dollars)," *Statistica* (2018), https://www.statista.com/statistics /196614/revenue-of-the-us-fast-food-restaurant-industry-since-2002/.

65. Jillian Kramer, "The Fast Food Industry Is Growing Faster than the U.S. Economy," *Food & Wine*, August 10, 2017, http://www.foodandwine.com/news/fast-food-industry-growing -us-economy.

66. See Francis Bacon, "From *The Advancement of Learning*," in *The Rhetorical Tradition: Readings from Classical Times to Present*, 2nd ed., ed. Patricia Bizzell and Bruce Herzberg (New York: Bedford / St. Martin's, 2001), 740–745; Jacques Lacan, *The Seminar of Jacques Lacan*, book 11, *The Four Fundamental Concepts of Psychoanalysis, 1959–1960*, trans. Alan Sheridan (New York: W. W. Norton, 1998), 161–186.

67. When discussing persuasion, English philosopher Francis Bacon contrasted the appetites or "affections," short-term impulses for gratification, with the will, a rational self-interest in long-term gains. Later I will suggest that what is described as the appetites in rhetorical theory becomes the drives in psychoanalytic theory. See Bacon, "From *The Advancement*," 743.

68. I reference a 2004 documentary in which the director, Morgan Spurlock, eats only food from McDonald's for thirty days, to harmful effect. Michael Pollan has also brought much attention to the harmful effects of industrial diets. See Michael Pollan, *In Defense of Food: An Eater's Manifesto* (New York: Penguin Books, 2009).

69. "As Lacan emphasised again and again, the essential content of the superego's injunction is 'Enjoy!'" Slavoj Žižek, "'You May!'" *London Review of Books* 21.6 (18 March 1999), https://www.lrb.co.uk/v21/n06/slavoj-zizek/you-may, para. 16.

70. The catchphrase "treat yo self" was popularized by the successful sitcom *Parks and Recreation* in an episode that aired on October 13, 2011. The televisual holiday, made up by the character Donna Meagle, is one in which a person indulges consumerist extravagance. See Cady Lang, "Here's How Donna from 'Parks and Recreation' Would Celebrate 'Treat Yo' Self' Day in 2017," *Time*, October 12, 2017, http://time.com/4976614/donna-on-parks-and-recreation-would-celebrate-treat-yo-self-day-interview/.

71. Victoria Moran, "Devour's Racy Launch Campaign Pushes 'Food You Want to Fork,'" *Advertising Age*, August 1, 2016, http://adage.com/article/cmo-strategy/devour-aims-heat-things-frozen-food-aisle/305249/.

72. Sigmund Freud, *The Standard Edition of the Complete Psychological Works of Sigmund Freud*, (1901–1905), trans. James Strachey (London: The Hogarth Press, 1953), 7:171.

73. Freud, *Standard Edition*, 7:145n.

74. See Jeremy G. Gordon, Katherine D. Lind, and Saul Kutnicki, eds., "A Rhetorical Bestiary," special issue of *Rhetoric Society Quarterly* 47.3 (2017): 222–228.

75. See Diane Davis and Michelle Baliff, eds., "Extrahuman Rhetorical Relations: Addressing the Animal, the Object, the Dead, and the Divine," special issue of *Philosophy & Rhetoric* 47.4 (2014).

76. Freud, *Standard Edition*, 7:123–245.

77. Tim Dean and Christopher Lane, "Homosexuality and Psychoanalysis: An Introduction," in *Homosexuality & Psychoanalysis*, ed. Tim Dean and Christopher Lane (Chicago: University of Chicago Press, 2001), 5.

78. Astrid Gessert, "Exploring Transgression from a Lacanian Perspective," in *Perversion Now!*, ed. Diana Caine and Colin Wright (New York: Palgrave, 2017), 38.

79. Jack Drescher, "Out of DSM: Depathologizing Homosexuality," *Behavioral Sciences* 5.4 (2015): 565–575, available at https://www.ncbi.nlm.nih.gov/pmc/articles/PMC4695779/.

80. See Joshua Gunn, "*Maranatha*," *Quarterly Journal of Speech* 98.4 (2012): 359–385.

81. Gessert, "Exploring," 39.

82. Gessert, "Exploring," 39.

83. James Penney, *The World of Perversion: Psychoanalysis and the Impossible Absolute of Desire* (Albany: State University of New York Press, 2006), 15.

84. Penney, *The World*, 15; also see Paul Verhaeghe, *On Being Normal and Other Disorders: A Manual for Clinical Psychodiagnostics*, trans. Sigi Jottkandt (New York: Other Press, 2004).

85. Verhaeghe, *On Being Normal*, 398–399.

86. Verhaeghe, *On Being Normal*, 399–400.

87. See Alex Horton, "Something Bill Cosby Admitted Years Ago Convinced One Juror He Was Guilty," *Washington Post*, April 30, 2018, https://www.washingtonpost.com/news/arts -and-entertainment/wp/2018/04/30/something-bill-cosby-admitted-years-ago-convinced-one -juror-he-was-guilty/?utm_term=.fc3ac1b818c0.

88. See Roxane Gay, ed., *Not That Bad: Dispatches from Rape Culture* (New York: Harper Perennial, 2018).

89. Pateman, *The Sexual Contract*, esp. 1–18.

90. Gayle Rubin, "The Traffic in Women: Notes on the 'Political Economy' of Sex," in *Toward an Anthropology of Women*, ed. Rayna R. Reiter (New York: Monthly View Press, 1975), 173.

91. Rubin, "The Traffic in Women," 175–176.

92. For an elaboration of how a "woman" is present in a screened scene in which women are physically absent, see Claire Sisco King and Joshua Gunn, "On a Violence Unseen: The Womanly Object and Sacrificed Man," *Quarterly Journal of Speech* 99.2 (2013): 200–208.

93. For example, see Northrop Frye, *Anatomy of Criticism* (Princeton, NJ: Princeton University Press, 1990 [1957]), esp. 243–237.

94. See Joshua Gunn and Dana L. Cloud, "Agentic Orientation as Magical Voluntarism," *Communication Theory* 20.1 (2010): 50–78.

CHAPTER ONE

1. Edwin Black, *Rhetorical Questions: Studies of Public Discourse* (Chicago: University of Chicago Press, 1992), 4–5.

2. Mary Shelley, *Frankenstein*, 3rd ed., ed. Johanna M. Smith (New York: Bedford / St. Martin's, 2016), 45.

3. Friedrich Nietzsche, "Lecture Notes on Rhetoric," trans. Carole Blair, *Philosophy & Rhetoric* 16.2 (1983): 94–129. Also see Debra Hawhee, *Moving Bodies: Kenneth Burke at the Edges of Language* (Columbia: University of South Carolina Press, 2009).

4. Steven Connor, *Dumbstruck: A Cultural History of Ventriloquism* (New York: Oxford University Press, 2000), 3–43.

5. See Diane Davis, *Breaking Up [at] Totality: A Rhetoric of Laughter* (Carbondale: University of Southern Illinois Press, 2000); and Catherine Liu, *Copying Machines: Taking Notes for the Automaton* (Minneapolis: University of Minnesota Press, 2000).

6. See Christian Lundberg, *Lacan in Public: Psychoanalysis and the Science of Rhetoric* (Tuscaloosa: University of Alabama Press, 2012), esp. 44–72; and John P. Muller and William J. Richardson, *The Purloined Poe: Lacan, Derrida, and Psychoanalytic Reading* (Baltimore: Johns Hopkins University Press, 1988).

7. John 1:14 (NRSV).

8. Roland Barthes, "The Grain of the Voice," in *Image, Music, Text*, ed. and trans. Stephen Heath (New York: Hill and Wang, 1977), 179–189.

9. See Larry Gross, "Modes of Communication and the Acquisition of Symbolic Competence," in *Communications Technology and Social Policy: Understanding the New "Cultural*

Revolution," ed. George Gerbner, Larry P. Gross, and William H. Melody (New York: John Wiley and Sons), 189–208.

10. Friedrich Nietzsche, "On Truth and Lies in a Nonmoral Sense," trans. Daniel Breazeale, in *The Rhetorical Tradition: Readings from Classical Times to the Present*, ed. Patricia Bizzell and Bruce Herzberg (Boston: Bedford / St. Martin's, 1990), 888–896.

11. This is also an oblique reference to the great sophist of antiquity, Gorgias. Channeling his teacher Empedocles, Gorgias famously asserted that nothing exists, and if it did it could not be known, and if it could be known it could not be communicated, and if it could be communicated it could not be understood. Just when we figure out a way to translate, we must abandon the original and leave understanding to projection. See Rosamond Kent Sprague, ed., *The Older Sophists* (Columbia: University of South Carolina Press, 1972), 42–46.

12. Isocrates insisted on the centrality of role models, not rulebooks, and Plato on the erotic charge of interpersonal encounter. See Isocrates, "Against the Sophists," trans. George Norlin, in *The Rhetorical Tradition: Readings from Classical Times to the Present*, ed. Patricia Bizzell and Bruce Herzberg (Boston: Bedford / St. Martin's, 1990), 46–49; and Plato, *Phaedrus*, trans. Alexander Nehamas and Paul Woodruff (Indianapolis: Hackett, 1995).

13. Johnny Marr and Steven Morrissey, "Hand in Glove," by the Smiths (single), Rough Trade, 1983.

14. Morrissey's incest joke is based on the controversy of Shelley's novel, in which a histrionic Victor Frankenstein marries a childhood friend raised as his cousin, Elizabeth Lavenza. Mary Shelley and her husband Percy revised a number of editions of *Frankenstein* to avoid the taboo connotations. For an obsessively exhaustive account of these changes, see Mary Shelley, *The New Annotated Frankenstein*, ed. Leslie S. Klinger (New York: W. W. Norton, 2017).

15. See G. W. F. Hegel, "Phenomenology of Spirit: Self-Consciousness," in *Hegel: Selections*, ed. M. J. Inwood (New York: Macmillan, 1989), 168–180.

16. As do many; he was played by the long-haired queer culture icon Joe Dallesandro.

17. Maurice Yacowar, *The Films of Paul Morrissey* (New York: Cambridge University Press, 1993), 77.

18. See Carole Pateman, *The Sexual Contract* (Stanford, CA: Stanford University Press, 1988).

19. The signature piece here, of course, is Hélène Cixous, "The Laugh of the Medusa," trans. Keith Cohen and Paula Cohen, *Signs: A Journal of Women in Culture and Society* 1.4 (1976): 875–893, but certainly also Julia Kristeva, *Revolution in Poetic Language*, trans. Margaret Waller (New York: Columbia University Press, 1984). Also see Dilip Gaonkar, "Object and Method in Rhetorical Criticism: From Wichelns to Leff and McGee," *Western Journal of Speech Communication* 54 (1990): 290–316; Leslie Hill, "Barthes' Body," *Paragraph* 11.2 (1988): 107–126; and John Mowitt, *Text: The Genealogy of an Antidisciplinary Object* (Durham, NC: Duke University Press, 1992), esp. 83–138. The comparison of texts to bodies is an old one (we still have "headers" and "footers" in our digital documents); the practice of binding books in human skin was a thing called anthropodermic bibliopegy too: see Carolyn Marvin, "The Body of the Text: Literacy's Corporeal Constant," *Quarterly Journal of Speech* 80.2 (1994): 129–149.

20. See André Green, "Thirdness and Psychoanalytic Concepts," *Psychoanalytic Quarterly* 73.1 (2004): 99–135.

21. Plato, *Phaedrus*, 63–65 (sec. 265–266).

22. For a marvelous argument for critical listening, see Lisbeth Limpari, *Listening, Thinking, Being* (University Park: Pennsylvania State University Press, 2014).

23. Edwin Black, *Rhetorical Criticism: A Study in Method* (New York: Macmillan, 1965), 7.

24. For example, Aristotle's inventory of emotions is useful to orators; see Aristotle, *On Rhetoric: A Theory of Civic Virtue*, trans. George Kennedy (New York: Oxford University Press, 1991), 113–147.

25. There are exceptions, of course, such as Mark A. Smith's argument that we should attend to the language of conservatives to discern the direction politics is going; ultimately Smith is critiqued for nevertheless ignoring affect and emotion by recentering the rational choice model in Aristotle's *Rhetoric*. See Mark A. Smith, *The Right Talk: How Conservatives Transformed the Great Society into the Economic Society* (Princeton, NJ: Princeton University Press, 2007); and Joshua Gunn, "Holes, God-Shaped and Otherwise: A Response to *Right Talk* and Philip C. Wanter," *Rhetoric Review* 27.2 (2008): 212–215. Also See Bruce Fink, *Lacan to the Letter: Reading "Écrits" Closely* (Minneapolis: University of Minnesota Press, 2004), 141–153. For my account of the disappearance of emotion from study in communication and rhetorical studies, see Joshua Gunn, "Speech's Sanatorium," *Quarterly Journal of Speech* 101.1 (2015): 18–33.

26. For an account of the appeal of humorlessness, as well as the projective identification of accusing others of it, see Lauren Berlant, "Genre Flailing," *Capacious: Journal of Emerging Affect Inquiry* 1.2 (2018): 156–162, http://capaciousjournal.com/cms/wp-content /uploads/2018/06/capacious-berlant-genre-flailing.pdf.

27. For example, see Peggy Phalen, *Unmarked: The Politics of Performance* (New York: Routledge, 1993); Della Pollock, *Telling Bodies Performing Birth* (New York: Columbia University Press, 1999); Aimee Carrillo Rowe, *Power Lines: On the Subject of Feminist Alliances* (Durham, NC: Duke University Press, 2008); and Diana Taylor, *The Archive and the Repertoire: Performing Cultural Memory in the Americas* (Durham, NC: Duke University Press, 2003).

28. See Melissa Gregg and Gregory J. Seigworth, eds., *The Affect Theory Reader* (Durham, NC: Duke University Press, 2010); and Brian Massumi, *Parables for the Virtual: Movement, Affect, Sensation* (Durham, NC: Duke University Press, 2002).

29. See Lauren Berlant, *Cruel Optimism* (Durham, NC: Duke University Press, 2011); Ann Cvetkovich, *An Archive of Public Feelings: Trauma, Sexuality, and Lesbian Public Cultures* (Durham, NC: Duke University Press, 2003); and Kathleen Stewart, *Ordinary Affects* (Durham, NC: Duke University Press, 2007).

30. See Jane Bennett, *Vibrant Matter: A Political Ecology of Things* (Durham, NC: Duke University Press, 2010); Barbara A. Biesecker and John Lucaites, eds., *Rhetoric, Materiality, and Politics* (Bern: Peter Lang, 2009); Diane Davis, "Rhetoricity at the End of the World," *Philosophy & Rhetoric* 50.4 (2017): 431–451; and Rick Dolphijn and Iris van der Tuin, eds., *New Materialism: Interviews and Cartographies* (Ann Arbor, MI: Open Humanities, 2012).

31. Chuck E. Morris III's career-long effort to queer rhetorical criticism is particularly notable here; see Charles E. Morris III, "(Self)portrait of Prof. R.C.: A Retrospective," *Western Journal of Communication* 74.1 (2010): 4–42.

32. Barbara A. Biesecker revived interest in psychoanalysis because of a powerful review essay: "Rhetorical Studies and the 'New' Psychoanalysis: What's the Real Problem? Or Fram-

ing the Problem of the Real," *Quarterly Journal of Speech* 84.2 (1998): 222–240. Two recent books do an exemplary job of reimagining psychoanalysis in rhetorical studies, largely though a Lacanian lens: Christian Lundberg, *Lacan in Public*; and Calum L. Matheson, *Desiring the Bomb: Communication, Psychoanalysis, and the Atomic Age* (Tuscaloosa: University of Alabama Press, 2018).

33. My perspective on the critique of mastery is informed loosely by Bruce Fink, "Against Understanding: Why Understanding Should Not Be Viewed as an Essential Aim of Psychoanalytic Treatment," in *Against Understanding*, vol. 1, *Commentary and Critique in a Lacanian Key* (New York: Routledge, 2014), 5–26.

34. Michel Foucault, *Discipline and Punish: The Birth of the Prison*, trans. Alan Sheridan (New York: Vintage Books, 1995), 138.

35. The "speech sciences" tended to dominate the field of communication, and rhetorical criticism was seen as something of a subfield and practice; see Pat J. Gehrke, *The Ethics and Politics of Speech: Communication and Rhetoric in the Twentieth Century* (Carbondale: Southern Illinois University Press, 2009), esp. 60–87. For my take on the abandonment of feelings in pursuit of "reason" in criticism, see Joshua Gunn, "Speech's Sanatorium," 2–17.

36. Lester Thonssen and A. Craig Baird, *Speech Criticism: The Development of Standards for Rhetorical Appraisal* (New York: Ronald, 1948), 20.

37. Thonssen and Baird, *Speech Criticism*, 16. Also see James Jasinski, "The Status of Theory and Method in Rhetorical Criticism," *Western Journal of Communication* 65.3 (2001): 249–270.

38. Black, *Rhetorical Criticism*, 9.

39. I teach this four-step process as I was taught, and it is more or less the same in most textbooks on rhetorical criticism. See Karlyn Kohrs Campbell, *Critiques of Contemporary Rhetoric*, 2nd ed. (Belmont, CA: Wadsworth, 1997); and Roderick P. Hart, Suzanne Daughton, and Rebecca LaVally, *Modern Rhetorical Criticism*, 4th ed. (New York: Routledge, 2018).

40. "precision, n.1." *Oxford English Dictionary*, 2nd ed., 20 vols. (Oxford: Oxford University Press, 1989).

41. Walter Benjamin, "The Work of Art in the Age of Reproducibility [Third Version]," trans. Harry Zohn and Edmund Jephcott, in *Walter Benjamin: Selected Writings*, vol. 4, *1938–1940*, ed. Howard Eiland and Michael W. Jennings (Cambridge, MA: Belknap Press of Harvard University Press, 2003), 263.

42. "Our destination is nowhere / Our feelings are destroyed / . . . are you receiving?" Killing Joke, "Are You Receiving?," by Killing Joke, side B, track 1 on *Almost Red*, Island Records, 1979.

43. For two excellent book-length projects that explain both how and why we have a tendency to make monsters of things or people that or whom we do not understand, see Edward J. Ingebretsen, *At Stake: Monsters and the Rhetoric of Fear in Public Culture* (Chicago: University of Chicago Press, 2001); and Richard Kearney, *Strangers, Gods, and Monsters: Interpreting Otherness* (New York: Routledge, 2003).

44. Aristotle, *Nicomachean Ethics*, trans. James E. C. Welldon, in *On Man in the Universe*, ed. Louise Ropes Loomis (New York: Grammercy Books / Random House, 1971), 87–88.

45. Psychoanalysis was taken up largely in the "ego-psychology" inflection in the United States, which unfortunately radically transformed Freud's suspicious protocol into the certitude

of a master psychoanalyst. This is *not* the brand of psychoanalysis with which I am concerned, about which more below. See Bruce Fink, "A Lacanian Response to Foucault's Critique of Psychoanalysis," in *Against Understanding*, 1:47.

46. For example, see Jonathan Gottschall, *Literature, Science, and a New Humanities* (New York: Palgrave Macmillan, 2008).

47. Black, *Rhetorical Criticism*, 1, 2.

48. One of the most provocative accounts refigures "science" as a failed machine or economy to make the claim that psychoanalysis is a science work; see Lundberg, *Lacan in Public*, esp. 44–72.

49. Henry James, *The Turn of the Screw*, 2nd Norton Critical Edition, ed. Deborah Esch and Jonathan Warren (New York: W. W. Norton, 1999 [1966]).

50. Edna Kenton, "Henry James to the Ruminant Reader: *The Turn of the Screw*," *Arts* 6 (November 1924): 245–255.

51. Shoshana Felman, "Henry James: Madness and the Risks of Practice (Turning the Screw of Interpretation)," in James, *The Turn of the Screw*, 2nd Norton Critical Edition, 199.

52. See Gehrke, *The Ethics and Politics of Speech*, esp. 16.

53. Sigmund Freud, *The Interpretation of Dreams*, trans. Joyce Crick (New York: Oxford University Press, 1999), 211–329.

54. Freud, *The Interpretation of Dreams*, 9.

55. Paul Ricoeur, *Freud and Philosophy: An Essay on Interpretation* (New Haven, CT: Yale University Press, 1977).

56. See Frederick Crews, *The Memory Wars: Freud's Legacy in Dispute* (New York: New York Review of Books, 1990); and K. B. MacDonald, "Freud's Follies: Psychoanalysis as Religion, Cult, and Political Movement," *Skeptic* 4.3 (1996): 94–99.

57. Sigmund Freud, *Group Psychology and the Analysis of the Ego*, trans. James Strachey (New York: W. W. Norton, 1990).

58. Sigmund Freud, *The Future of an Illusion*, trans. James Strachey (New York: W. W. Norton, 1989); Sigmund Freud, *Civilization and Its Discontents*, trans. James Strachey (New York: W. W. Norton, 2005).

59. Mark Edmundson, "Freud and the Fundamentalist Urge," *New York Times Magazine*, April 30, 2006, https://www.nytimes.com/2006/04/30/magazine/freud-and-the-fundamentalist-urge.html.

60. See Mark C. Long, "Tending to the Imagination: Perspective by Incongruity in Williams Carlos Williams and Kenneth Burke," paper presented at the Modern Language Association Conference, Toronto, December 1997, *K.B. Journal*, http://kbjournal.org/long_tending. Also see Kenneth Burke, *Counter-Statement*, 2nd ed. (Berkeley: University of California Press, 1968), 216; and Kenneth Burke, *Permanence and Change: An Anatomy of Purpose*, 3rd ed. (Berkeley: University of California Press, 1984 [1935]).

61. I reference Benjamin's conception of "aura"; see Walter Benjamin, "The Work of Art in the Age of Its Technological Reproducibility," trans. Edmund Jephcott and Harry Zohn, in *Walter Benjamin: Selected Writings*, vol. 3, *1935–1938*, ed. Marcus Bullock, Howard Eiland, and Gary Smith (Cambridge, MA: Belknap Press of Harvard University Press, 2002), 101–133.

62. This is most popularly in his critiques of astrology and popular music, but more meticulously in his writings on philosophy and musicology. Respectively, see Theodor W. Adorno,

The Stars Down to Earth and Other Essays on the Irrational in Culture (New York: Routledge, 1994); and Theodor W. Adorno, *Essays on Music*, trans. Susan H. Gillespie, ed. Richard Leppert (Berkeley: University of California Press, 2002).

63. Michael W. Jennings, *Dialectical Images: Walter Benjamin's Theory of Literary Criticism* (Ithaca, NY: Cornell University Press, 1987), esp. 164–211.

64. Walter Benjamin, "The Concept of Criticism in German Romanticism," trans. David Lachterman, Howard Eiland, and Ian Balfour, in *Walter Benjamin: Selected Writings*, vol. 1, *1913–1926*, ed. Marcus Bullock and Michael W. Jennings (Cambridge, MA: Belknap Press of Harvard University Press, 1999): 116–185.

65. Michael C. Leff, "Interpretation and the Art of the Rhetorical Critic," *Western Journal of Speech Communication* 44.4 (1980): 345.

66. See Hans-Georg Gadamer, *Truth and Method* (New York: Bloomsbury Revelations, 2013). For a more elaborate discussion of the power dynamics of "close reading," see Joshua Gunn, *Modern Occult Rhetoric: Mass Media and the Drama of Secrecy in the Twentieth Century* (Tuscaloosa: University of Alabama Press, 2005), esp. 79–105.

67. Fink, "A Lacanian Response," 1:47.

68. For an account of the dominance of ego psychology in North America, see Antonio Viego, *Dead Subjects: Towards a Politics of Loss in Latino Studies* (Durham, NC: Duke University Press, 2007).

69. Maud Ellmann, introduction to *Psychoanalytic Literary Criticism* (New York: Longman, 1994), 10.

70. Sigmund Freud, "A Difficulty in the Path of Psychoanalysis," trans. Joan Riviere, in *Sigmund Freud: Psychological Writings and Letters*, ed. Sander L. Gilman (New York: Continuum, 1995), 275.

71. See Davis, *Breaking Up*. Some ado has been made about Northrop Frye after his "notebooks" for preparing his landmark *Anatomy of Criticism* were published. Found there was a "statement for the day of my death," which read in part, "I have genius. No one else in the field known to me had quite that." Similarly, Edwin Black's landmark *Rhetorical Criticism* opens with the preface "Of all the responses a book can evoke, none is so obituary as silence. A treatise is, after all, nothing if not a statement, and even the humblest statement implicitly courts its counterstatement. Yet, no books seem to inspire a deathlike hush so dependably as those on the subject of rhetoric. Aristotle's *Rhetoric*, for the supreme example . . . was followed—with pitifully two exceptions—by two millennia of feeble echoes and the babbling murmur of second-rate minds." Such charity! See Thomas Willard, "The Genius of Northrop Frye," in *Northrop Frye: New Directions from Old*, ed. David Rampton (Ottawa: University of Ottawa Press, 2009), 36–49; and Black, *Rhetorical Criticism*, vii.

72. Bert Oliver, "Lacan's Theory of Discourse," *Thought Leader*, May 9, 2010, http://thoughtleader.co.za/bertolivier/2010/05/09/lacan%E2%80%99s-theory-of-discourse/, para. 6.

73. For an overview, see Bruce Fink, *The Lacanian Subject: Between Language and Jouissance* (Princeton, NJ: Princeton University Press, 1995), 129–137.

74. The problem of the universal is as unavoidable as it is a big fat problem; see Judith Butler, "Restaging the Universal: Hegemony and the Limits of Formalism," in Judith Butler, Ernesto Laclau, and Slavoj Žižek, *Contingency, Hegemony, Universality: Contemporary Dialogues on the Left* (New York: Verso, 2000), 11–43.

75. Fredric Jameson, *The Political Unconscious: Narrative as a Socially Symbolic Act* (Ithaca, NY: Cornell University Press, 1971), 60–83. For more on Benjamin's notion of "magic" criticism, see Joshua Gunn, "Benjamin's Magic," *Telos* 119 (2001): 58–74.

76. John McCole, *Walter Benjamin and the Antinomies of Tradition* (Ithaca, NY: Cornell University Press, 1993), 98–99.

77. McCole, *Walter Benjamin*, 98–99.

78. See Sarah Ley Roff, "Benjamin and Psychoanalysis," in *The Cambridge Companion to Walter Benjamin*, ed. Davis S. Ferris (New York: Cambridge University Press, 2004), 115–133; and Elizabeth Stewart, *Catastrophe and Survival: Walter Benjamin and Psychoanalysis* (New York: Bloomsbury Academic, 2009).

79. "Psychoanalytic literary criticism has always been something of an embarrassment," writes Peter Brooks. "One resists labeling as a 'psychoanalytic critic' because the kind of criticism evoked by the term mostly deserves the bad name it largely has made for itself." Peter Brooks, "The Idea of Psychoanalytic Literary Criticism," *Critical Inquiry* 13 (Winter 1987): 334.

80. "There is nothing like Freudian theory to elicit sniggers of embarrassment or snorts of disbelief," writes Maud Ellmann, "and even the abstrusities of Lacan can reduce a classroom to cascades of giggles." Ellmann, introduction, 1.

81. Black, *Rhetorical Criticism*, 26–27. Notably, by 1992 Black changed his chew: "Rhetorical criticism shares with psychoanalysis at least one fundamental conviction: For its purposes, no one ever lies. People can, of course, say things they do not understand, or what they believe only temporarily, or even that they actively disbelieve at the moment of utterance. But those sorts of statements and misstatements are all material to the truths that rhetorical criticism seeks." Black, *Rhetorical Questions*, 9.

82. I reference, in particular, the work of scholars published in the journal *Screen*, such as Jean-Louis Baudry, Christian Metz, and Laura Mulvey. See Mark Nash, *Screen Theory Culture* (New York: Palgrave, 2008).

83. See Slavoj Žižek, *The Sublime Object of Ideology* (New York: Verso, 1989).

84. Tim Dean, "Art as Symptom: Žižek and the Ethics of Psychoanalytic Criticism," *diacritics* 32.2 (2002): 21–41.

85. Ellman, introduction, 2.

86. Ellman, introduction, 3. Also see Shoshana Felman, ed., *Literature and Psychoanalysis: The Question of Reading: Otherwise* (Baltimore: Johns Hopkins University Press, 1980); Lundberg, *Lacan in Public*; and Elizabeth Wright, *Psychoanalytic Criticism: A Reappraisal*, 2nd ed. (New York: Polity, 1998).

87. Green insists, pace Lacan, that the unconscious is *not* structured like a language but, following Freud, "thing presentations." See André Green, "The Greening of Psychoanalysis: André Green in Dialogues with Gregorio Kohon," in *The Dead Mother: The Work of André Green*, ed. Gregorio Kohon (New York: Routledge, 1999), 23–25.

88. Jacques Lacan, *The Seminar of Jacques Lacan*, book 3, *The Psychoses, 1955–1956*, trans. Russell Grigg (New York: W. W. Norton, 1993), 167.

89. Gilbert D. Chaitin, *Rhetoric & Culture in Lacan* (New York: Cambridge University Press, 1996), 4.

90. Lundberg, *Lacan in Public*, 38.

91. See especially Freud, *The Interpretation of Dreams*, 211–329.

92. Anna Freud, *The Ego and the Mechanisms of Defense* (New York: International Universities Press, 1966 [1936]).

93. Edwin Black, "A Note on Theory and Practice in Rhetorical Criticism," *Western Journal of Speech Communication* 44 (1980): 334.

CHAPTER TWO

1. Ray Bradbury, *Fahrenheit 451* (London: Folio Society, 2011), 77.

2. James Popniewozik, "Review: 'Fahrenheit 451' Has Fire and Fury but Sheds Little Light," *New York Times*, May 16, 2018, https://www.nytimes.com/2018/05/16/arts/television/fahrenheit -451-review-hbo.html.

3. For one of many examples, see Amy Glynn, "How Did HBO's Adaptation of *Fahrenheit 451* Go So Wrong?," *Paste*, May 18, 2018, https://www.pastemagazine.com/articles/2018/05 /how-did-hbos-adaptation-of-fahrenheit-451-go-so-wr.html.

4. Paul Virilio, *The Vision Machine*, trans. Julie Rose (Bloomington: Indiana University Press, 1994), 14.

5. Sylvère Lotringer makes a similar observation introducing the work of Virilio vis-à-vis the theorist of spectacle, Guy Debord, who "hadn't really grasped what was so powerful about the pictures he denounced. It wasn't their sheer accumulation that mattered most in the spectacle, but their *motion*." Paul Virilio and Sylvère Lotringer, *Crepuscular Dawn* (New York: Semiotext[e], 2002), 15–16. Also see Guy Debord, *Society of Spectacle*, trans. Donald Nicholson-Smith (New York: Zone Books, 1995).

6. Bradbury, *Fahrenheit 451,* 77.

7. At the time of my writing, Snapchat is a messaging application that enables users to send messages or images to others for a short period of time before the messages disappear. By the time this manuscript is printed, the application could be replaced by something else; the argument advanced in this chapter *does* attempt to account for the inevitable obsolescence of software and hardware.

8. See Paul Virilio, *The Information Bomb*, trans. Chris Turner (New York: Verso, 2008), 7–18.

9. Hint: it makes possible the emergence of perverse public figures, of course, the topic of succeeding chapters.

10. Slavoj Žižek, *The Ticklish Subject: The Absent Centre of Political Ontology* (New York: Verso, 1999), 322–334; Jodi Dean, *Blog Theory: Feedback and Capture in the Circuits of Drive* (Malden, MA: Polity, 2010), 5–9.

11. The section title is a play on what Virilio once dubbed "cathode democracy" and his later characterization of the same as a "democracy of emotion." See Paul Virilio, *Desert Screen: War at the Speed of Light*, trans. Michael Degener (London: Continuum, 2005), 32; and Paul Virilio, *The Administration of Fear*, trans. Ames Hodges (Los Angeles: Semiotext[e], 2012), 46.

12. ABC News, "Colorado High School Sexting Scandal Highlights Challenges for Schools, Prosecutors," *Nightline*, November 9, 2015, http://abcnews.go.com/Nightline/video /colorado-high-school-sexting-scandal-hightlights-challenges-schools-35090862.

13. Tamar Lewin, "Rethinking Sex Offender Laws for Youth Texting," *New York Times*, March 20, 2010, https://www.nytimes.com/2010/03/21/us/21sexting.html.

14. See Joel Best and Kathleen A. Bogle, *Kids Gone Wild: From Rainbow Parties to Sexting, Understanding the Hype over Teen Sex* (New York: New York University Press, 2014); and Jessica Sabbah-Mani, "Sexting Education: An Educational Approach to Solving the Media Fueled Sexting Dilemma," *Southern California Interdisciplinary Law Journal* 24.2 (2015): 529–560.

15. See Charles R. Acland, *Youth, Murder, Spectacle: The Cultural Politics of Youth in Crisis* (Boulder, CO: Westview, 1995); and John Sloop and Joshua Gunn, "Status Control: An Admonition Concerning the Publicized Privacy of Social Networking," *Communication Review* 13.4 (2010): 289–308.

16. See Y. Hayashi, C. T. Russo, and O. Wirth, "Texting While Driving as Impulsive Choice: A Behavioral Economic Analysis," *Accident Analysis & Prevention* 83 (2015): 182–189; and S. Tucker, P. Simon, J. Morrish, and M. Ruf, "Prevalence of Texting While Driving and Other Risky Driving Behaviors among Young People in Ontario, Canada: Evidence from 2012–2014," *Accident Analysis & Prevention* 84 (2015): 144–152.

17. "Masturbation: From Myth to Sexual Health," *Contemporary Sexuality* 37.3 (2003): i–viii.

18. See Bill Zeiser, "[Insert Pun Here]: On the Trail with Weiner and Spitzer," *American Spectator* 46.7 (2013): 38–40; and JoAnn Wypijewski, "Weiner in a Box," *Nation* 293.1–2 (April 7, 2011): 6–8.

19. Ron Dicker, "Teacher Accused of Sending Racy Photos to Students Is Fired," *Huffington Post*, February 11, 2016, https://www.huffingtonpost.com/entry/teacher-accused-of-sending-racy-photos-to-students-is-fired_us_56bca297e4b0c3c550502cd0.

20. See David Bateman, "High School Teacher Fired after Investigation into 'Racist' Tweets," *Star* (Toronto), September 9, 2015, https://www.thestar.com/yourtoronto/education/2015/09/09/high-school-teacher-fired-after-investigation-into-racist-tweets.html.

21. Susan Edelman, "'I Hate Their Guts—They Are All Devil's Spawn,'" *New York Post*, February 5, 2012, https://nypost.com/2012/02/05/i-hate-their-guts-they-are-all-devils-spawn/.

22. See Susan Herbst, *Rude Democracy: Civility and Incivility in American Politics* (Philadelphia: Temple University Press, 2010); and Diana Mutz, *In-Your-Face Politics: The Consequences of Uncivil Media* (Princeton, NJ: Princeton University Press, 2015).

23. Brian Beutler, "Trump the Disrupter," *New Republic* 247.5 (2016): 38–41; Andrew Sullivan, "America Has Never Been So Ripe for Tyranny," *New York*, May 2, 2016, http://nymag.com/daily/intelligencer/2016/04/america-tyranny-donald-trump.html.

24. Cable News Network, "Donald Trump on Trade, Healthcare and More (CNN Interview with Jake Tapper)," *YouTube*, June 28, 2015, https://www.youtube.com/watch?v=8fT7Np6PFao&feature=youtu.be.

25. Eric Holthaus, "'America Is Not a Planet': The Only Thing Marco Rubio Got Right on Climate Change," *Slate*, September 17, 2015, http://www.slate.com/blogs/the_slatest/2015/09/17/gop_debate_marco_rubio_s_terrible_answer_on_climate_change.html.

26. "Acceptance of Global Warming among Americans Reaches Highest Level Since 2008," *Issues in Energy and Environmental Policy* 25 (October 2015), http://closup.umich.edu/issues-in-energy-and-environmental-policy/25/acceptance-of-global-warming-among-americans-reaches-highest-level-since-2008/.

27. For an admittedly absurd example, see Ileana Johnson Paugh, *U.N. Agenda 21: Environmental Piracy* (self-published, 2012), available on Amazon.com.

28. See James Fallows, "'There's No Such Thing Anymore, Unfortunately, as Facts,'" *Atlantic*, November 30, 2016, https://www.theatlantic.com/notes/2016/11/theres-no-such-thing-any-more-unfortunately-as-facts/509276/.

29. "social network," *Oxford English Dictionary Online*, 3rd. ed., www.oed.com; Avery Holton, "Negating Nodes of Liquid Fragmentation: Extending Conversations of Diffusion, Social Networks, and Fragmentation," *Communication Theory* 22.3 (2012): 279–298.

30. For example, see David L. Altheide, "Media Logic, Social Control, and Fear," *Communication Theory* 23.3 (2013): 223–238.

31. danah m. boyd and Nicole B. Ellison, "Social Network Sites: Definition, History, and Scholarship," *Journal of Computer-Mediated Communication* 13 (2008): 211.

32. John Armitage, "From Discourse Networks to Cultural Mathematics: An Interview with Friedrich A. Kittler," *Theory, Culture & Society* 23.7–8 (2006): 17–38; Friedrich A. Kittler, *Discourse Networks, 1800/1900*, trans. Michael Metteer and Chris Cullens (Stanford, CA: Stanford University Press, 1992); Daniel Silver and Monica Lee, "Self-Relations in Social Relations," *Sociological Theory* 30.4 (2012): 207–237.

33. See Joseph Bayer, Nicole B. Ellison, Sarita Schoenebeck, and Emily Faulk, "Sharing the Small Moments: Ephemeral Social Interaction on Snapchat," *Information, Communication & Society* 19.7 (2016): 956–977.

34. See Jacques Lacan, *The Seminar of Jacques Lacan*, book 3, *The Psychoses, 1955–1966*, trans. Russell Grigg (New York: W. W. Norton, 1993), 37–38; and Christian Lundberg, *Lacan in Public: Psychoanalysis and the Science of Rhetoric* (Tuscaloosa: University of Alabama Press, 2012), 44–72.

35. Lundberg, *Lacan in Public*, 130.

36. Žižek, *The Ticklish Subject*, 322–334.

37. Jodi Dean, *Publicity's Secret: How Technoculture Capitalizes on Democracy* (Ithaca, NY: Cornell University Press, 2002), 130; Claude Lévi-Strauss, "The Effectiveness of Symbols," in *Structural Anthropology*, trans. C. Jacobson and B. G. Schoepf (New York: Basic Books, 1963), 186–205.

38. Dean, *Blog Theory*, 63.

39. Such as Mark Andrejevic, *Infoglut: How Too Much Information Is Changing the Way We Think and Know* (New York: Routledge, 2013).

40. See Mikkel Borch-Jacobsen, *Lacan: The Absolute Master*, trans. Douglas Brick (Stanford, CA: Stanford University Press, 1991), esp. 1–20.

41. Jacques Lacan, *The Seminar of Jacques Lacan*, book 2, *The Ego in Freud's Theory and the Technique of Psychoanalysis*, trans. Jacques-Alain Miller (New York: W. W. Norton, 1988), 235–247.

42. Mark Andrejevic, "The Body, Torture, and the Decline of Symbolic Efficiency," *Politics and Culture* 1 (2007), https://politicsandculture.org/2009/10/02/mark-andrejevic-on-symbolic-efficiency/.

43. Dean, *Publicity's Secret*, 132.

44. Žižek, *The Ticklish Subject*, 334.

45. The Lacanian coming-out party was a 1977 special issue of *Yale French Studies* edited by Shoshana Felman, later reprinted as a book; see Shoshana Felman, ed., *Literature and Psychoanalysis: The Question of Reading: Otherwise* (Baltimore: Johns Hopkins University Press, 1982). Also see Elizabeth Wright, "Another Look at Lacan in Literary Criticism," *New Literary History* 19.3 (1988): 617–627.

46. The impetus for Lacan's influence, however, was initially British. Much of the theory was pioneered in the British film studies journal *Screen*; for an overview, see Mark Nash, *Screen Theory Culture* (Boston: Palgrave Macmillan, 2007). For the feminist case, see Juliet Mitchell, "Introduction I," in Jacques Lacan, *Feminine Sexuality: Jacques Lacan and the École Freudienne*, 2nd rev. ed., ed. Juliet Mitchell and Jacqueline Rose (New York: Basic Books, 2000), 1–26; and Jacqueline Rose, "Introduction II," Lacan, *Feminine Sexuality*, 27–58.

47. See Borch-Jacobsen, *Lacan*.

48. Dana Birksted-Breen and Sara Flanders, "General Introduction," in *Reading French Psychoanalysis*, ed. Dana Birksted-Breen, Sara Flanders, and Alain Gibeault (New York: Routledge, 2010), 2.

49. See Bruce Fink, *A Clinical Introduction to Lacanian Psychoanalysis: Theory and Technique* (Cambridge, MA: Harvard University Press, 1999).

50. Jacques Lacan, "Seminar on 'The Purloined Letter,'" in *Écrits, trans. Bruce Fink* (New York: W. W. Norton), 6–48.

51. *The Diagnostic and Statistical Manual of Mental Disorders*, 5th ed. (Washington, DC: American Psychiatric Association, 2013).

52. *DSM*-V, s.v. "psychosis," 87.

53. Stephanie S. Swales, *Perversion: A Lacanian Psychoanalytic Approach to the Subject* (New York: Routledge, 2012), xiii; also see Fink, *A Clinical Introduction*, 75–78.

54. See Jean Laplanche and Jean-Bertrand Pontalis, *The Language of Psycho-Analysis*, trans. Donald Nicholson-Smith (New York: W. W. Norton, 1973), 314–319.

55. For a useful discussion, see Slavoj Žižek, *The Plague of Fantasies* (New York: Verso, 1997), esp. 3–44.

56. Paul Verhaeghe, *On Being Normal and Other Disorders*, trans. Sigi Jottkandt (New York: Other Press, 2004), 155.

57. Verhaeghe, *On Being Normal*, 155.

58. See Lacan, *Écrits*, 532.

59. Fink, *A Clinical Introduction*, 64–65.

60. Jacques Lacan, *The Seminar of Jacques Lacan*, book 11, *The Four Fundamental Concepts of Psychoanalysis*, trans. Alan Sheridan (New York: W. W. Norton, 1998), 273–274.

61. Fink, *A Clinical Introduction*, 70–71.

62. See Verhaeghe, *On Being Normal*, 19–36.

63. For an insightfully lucid elaboration of Lacan's formal "revision" of Freud's Oedipal scheme, see Charles Shepherdson, *Vital Signs: Nature, Culture, Psychoanalysis* (New York: Routledge, 2000), 115–151.

64. See D. W. Winnicott, *Playing and Reality* (New York: Routledge, 2005), 1–34.

65. Fink, *A Clinical Introduction*, 113.

66. See Gilles Deleuze and Félix Guattari, *Anti-Oedipus: Capitalism and Schizophrenia*,

trans. Robert Hurley, Mark Seem, and Helen R. Lane (Minneapolis: University of Minnesota Press, 1983); Luce Irigaray, *Speculum of the Other Woman*, trans. Gillian C. Gill (Ithaca, NY: Cornell University Press, 1985); and Juliet Mitchell, *Psychoanalysis and Feminism: A Radical Reassessment of Freudian Psychoanalysis*, 2nd ed. (New York: Basic Books, 2000).

67. Shepherdson, *Vital Signs*, 115–151.

68. Lacan, *Écrits*, 464.

69. See Diane Davis, *Inessential Solidarity: Rhetoric and Foreigner Relations* (Pittsburgh: University of Pittsburgh Press, 2010), 18–36.

70. Fink, *A Clinical Introduction*, 113; also see Lacan, *Seminar*, book 3, esp. 10–11.

71. See Melissa Ames, "Where Have All the Good Men Gone? A Psychoanalytic Reading of the Absent Fathers and Damaged Dads on ABC's *Lost*," *Journal of Popular Culture* 47.3 (2014): 430–450; and K. A. Razzano, "In Light of This Demonstration of Crisis in Our Nation: Paternity, Responsibility, and Welfare," *Cultural Studies* 28.5–6 (2014): 947–975.

72. Lacan distinguishes between "aggression" and "aggressivity"; the former references a continuum of violence, the latter an intense engagement in general (one's nonviolent passion for cooking, for example, is a mode of aggressivity).

73. Lacan, *Seminar*, book 3, 250.

74. Lacan, *Seminar*, book 3, 250.

75. Fink, *A Clinical Introduction*, 84.

76. Žižek, *The Ticklish Subject*, 362.

77. Žižek, *The Ticklish Subject*, 362.

78. Sharpe and Boucher, *Žižek and Politics*, 149.

79. Blue Oyster Cult, "Burnin' for You," by Blue Öyster Cult, track 2 on *Fire of Unknown Origin*, CBS (1981).

80. Louis Althusser, "Ideology and Ideological State Apparatuses (Notes Towards an Investigation)," in Louis Althusser, *Lenin and Philosophy and Other Essays*, trans. Ben Brewster (New York: Monthly Review Press, 1971), 127–186.

81. My gratitude to colleagues at San Diego State University's Communication Department, with whom I shared this research in the winter of 2017, for these helpful questions.

82. Regarding civility, perhaps the best-known conceptions are Habermas's "public sphere" and "communicative rationality," which he has maintained are emergent ideals of public debate and civility. Most critiques of these "ideals" center on the exclusion and oppression of those who cannot assume or assert equal participation. For the broad strokes, see Jürgen Habermas, *The Structural Transformation of the Public Sphere: An Inquiry into a Category of Bourgeois Society*, trans. Thomas Burger and Frederick Lawrence (Cambridge, MA: MIT Press, 1991); and Nancy Fraser, "Rethinking the Public Sphere: A Contribution to the Critique of Actually Existing Democracy," *Social Text* 25–26 (1990): 56–80. Critiques of civility as an ideology that is both helpful and oppressive are well known; see Thomas W. Benson, "The Rhetoric of Civility: Power, Authenticity, and Democracy," *Journal of Contemporary Rhetoric* 1.1 (2011): 22–30; Nina M. Lozano-Reich and Dana L. Cloud, "The Uncivil Tongue: Invitational Rhetoric and the Problem of Inequality," *Western Journal of Communication* 73.2 (2009): 220–226; and Christopher F. Zurn, "Political Civility: Another Illusionistic Ideal," *Public Affairs Quarterly* 27.4 (2013): 341–368. That nasty reportage and "fake news" are nothing new has also been well

documented; see Marcus Daniel, *Scandal and Civility: Journalism and the Birth of American Democracy* (New York: Oxford University Press, 2009); Julien Gorbach, "Not Your Grandpa's Hoax: A Comparative History of Fake News," *American Journalism* 35.2 (2018): 236–249; Robert Mejia, Kay Beckermann, and Curtis Sullivan, "White Lies: A Racial History of the (Post) truth," *Communication and Critical/Cultural Studies* 15.2 (2018): 109–126; and Daniel M. Shea and Alex Sproveri, "The Rise and Fall of Nasty Politics in America," *PS: Political Science and Politics* 45.3 (2012): 416–421.

83. Walter Benjamin, "The Concept of History," trans. Harry Zohn, in *Walter Benjamin: Selected Writings*, vol. 4, *1938–1940*, ed. Marcus Bullock, Howard Eiland, and Gary Smith (Cambridge, MA: Belknap Press of Harvard University Press, 2003), 389–411.

84. Bertell Ollman, *Dance of the Dialectic: Steps in Marx's Method* (Urbana: University of Illinois Press, 2003), 11.

85. To suggest there is a privileged epistemology may be strategically or politically necessary and useful, *but to believe so is the hallmark of ideology.* See Slavoj Žižek, "The Spectre of Ideology," in *The Žižek Reader*, ed. Elizbeth Wright and Edmund Wright (Malden, MA: Blackwell, 1999), 53–86.

86. From a psychoanalytic perspective, such an addition can be described as the "death drive" in Freud's terms. See Sigmund Freud, *Beyond the Pleasure Principle*, trans. James Strachey (New York: W. W. Norton, 1961).

87. Joe Walsh, "Life in the Fast Lane," by the Eagles, track on 1 on *Hotel California*, Asylum Records, 1977.

88. Mark C. Taylor, "Speed Kills: Fast Is Never Fast Enough," *Chronicle of Higher Education*, October 20, 2014, https://www.chronicle.com/article/Speed-Kills/149401, para. 2. His book-length rumination is Mark C. Taylor, *Speed Limits: Where Time Went and Why We Have So Little Left* (New Haven, CT: Yale University Press, 2014).

89. See Paul Virilio, *War and Cinema: The Logistics of Perception*, trans. Patrick Camiller (New York: Verso, 2009).

90. For example, see Jeremy Packer and Stephen B. Crofts Wiley, ed., *Communication Matters: Materialist Approaches to Media, Mobility and Networks* (New York: Routledge, 2011).

91. Nigel Dodd and Judy Wajcman, "Simmel and Benjamin: Early Theorists of the Acceleration Society," in *The Sociology of Speed: Digital, Organizational, and Social Temporalities*, ed. Judy Wajcman and Nigel Dodd (New York: Oxford University Press, 2016), 13–24; Georg Simmel, *The Philosophy of Money* (New York: Routledge, 2011); Walter Benjamin, "The Work of Art in the Age of Its Technological Reproducibility," trans. Edmund Jephcott and Harry Zohn, in *Walter Benjamin: Selected Writings*, vol. 3, *1935–1938*, ed. Howard Eiland and Michael W. Jennings (Cambridge, MA: Belknap Press of Harvard University Press, 2002), 101–133.

92. Filip Vostal, "Thematizing Speed: Between Critical Theory and Cultural Analysis," *European Journal of Social Theory* 17.1 (2014): 99. In this essay Vostal provides an excellent overview of Rosa's work.

93. Vostal, "Thematizing Speed," 99. Also see Hartmut Rosa, *Alienation and Acceleration: Towards a Critical Theory of Late-Modern Temporality* (Aarhus, Denmark: Aarhus University Press, 2010); and Hartmut Rosa, *Social Acceleration: A New Theory of Modernity* (New York: Columbia University Press, 2015).

94. For an excellent sampling of primary texts, see Paul Virilio, *The Virilio Reader*, ed. James Der Derian (Malden, MA: Blackwell, 1998). For a superb overview of Virilio's project, see Peter Zhang, "Media Ecology and Techno-Ethics in Paul Virilio," *Explorations in Media Ecology* 12.3–4 (2013): 241–257. For an overview of Virilio's work keyed to rhetorical scholars of media, see David Beard and Joshua Gunn, "Paul Virilio and the Mediation of Perception and Technology," *Enculturation* 4.2 (Fall 2002), http://enculturation.net/4_2/beard-gunn/.

95. Paul Virilio, *Speed and Politics: An Essay on Dromology*, trans. Mark Polizzotti (South Pasadena, CA: Semiotext[e], 2006 [1977]).

96. Virilio, *Speed and Politics*, 70.

97. Paul Virilio, *The Great Accelerator*, trans. Julie Rose (Malden, MA: Polity, 2012), 26, 29.

98. Jason Michael Adams, "The Speeds of Ambiguity: An Interview with Paul Virilio," *boundary 2* 37.1 (2010): 169.

99. Zhang, "Media Ecology," 245–246.

100. Paul Virilio, *City of Panic*, trans. Julie Rose (New York: Berg, 2005), 32, quoted in Zhang, "Media Ecology," 246.

101. The distinction comes from Brian Massumi, *Parables of the Virtual: Movement, Affect, Sensation* (Durham, NC: Duke University Press, 2002). Elsewhere, following Bruce Fink, I have argued such a distinction is homologous to the "subject of jouissance" or affect and the "subject of speech." See Joshua Gunn, "Speech's Sanitorium," *Quarterly Journal of Speech* 101.1 (2015) 18–33.

102. Marina Denischik, "Temporality in Psychosis: Loss of Lived Time in an Alien World," *Humanistic Psychologist* 43 (2015): 148–159. When considering the subjectivity in principal, the Lacanian approach to understanding psychical structures posits a sort of mythical temporality during that the insertion of the paternal metaphor, or castration, has already occurred in the past because our reckoning with representation is on *this* side of meaning, here signified as so many words on a page. The unconscious, as Freud famously maintained, has no temporality as such. Insofar as one might argue that the psychotic *has no unconscious*, the bewildering effect of a world without continuous time is unrelentingly nonsensical.

103. See Stephen Schneider, "Good, Clean, Fair: The Rhetoric of the Slow Food Movement," *College English* 70.4 (2008): 384–402.

104. The appeal, then, of Benjamin's "dialectical image" of the Angel of History is not *nostalgic*, because he proffers an alternative temporality that makes space for the intimacy of interpersonal relation in spite of the End of the World. See Benjamin, "The Concept of History."

105. Peter Holley, "'She Got Caught Up in the Likes': Teen Accused of Live-Streaming Friend's Rape for Attention," *Washington Post*, April 19, 2016, https://www.washingtonpost.com/news/morning-mix/wp/2016/04/19/she-got-caught-up-in-the-likes-teen-accused-of-live-streaming-friends-rape-for-attention/?utm_term=.499867074420; Aarti Shahani, "Live-Streaming of Alleged Rape Shows Challenges of Flagging Video in Real Time," NPR, April 19, 2016, https://www.npr.org/sections/alltechconsidered/2016/04/19/474783485/live-streaming-of-alleged-rape-shows-challenges-of-flagging-video-in-real-time.

106. Holley, "'She Got Caught Up,'" para. 13.

107. Max Greenwood, "Trump's Lies Aren't Lies Because 'There's No Such Thing' as Facts Anymore, His Surrogate Says," *Huffington Post*, December 1, 2016, https://www.huffingtonpost.com/entry/trump-surrogate-claims-no-facts_us_58408f8ee4b0c68e047fd952.

108. Michael C. McGee, "Text, Context, and the Fragmentation of Contemporary Culture," *Western Journal of Speech Communication* 54.3 (1990): 274–289.

CHAPTER THREE

1. Michael Wolff, *Fire and Fury: Inside the White House* (New York: Henry Holt, 2017), 250.

2. Examples of similar expressions by journalists are voluminous. See Katy Tur, *Unbelievable: My Front-Row Seat to the Craziest Campaign in American History* (New York: De Street Books, 2017).

3. For example [sigh], Ann Coulter, *Godless: The Church of Liberalism* (New York: Three Rivers, 2007); and Mark Taylor, *The Trump Prophecies: The Astonishing True Story of the Man Who Saw Tomorrow . . . and What He Says Is Coming Next* (Crane, MO: Defender, 2017).

4. "The president of the United States currently," political commentator John Heilemann ranted on *Real Time with Bill Maher*, "does not give a flying fuck about an independent judiciary, about an independent FBI, about a Justice Department. All he cares about is self-preservation, and that for me is the degradation of the entire administration." *Real Time with Bill Maher*, June 8, 2018, HBO; excerpt available at https://youtu.be/QUAtHdTTH2w.

5. See Jonathan Lemire, "Trump Caught on Video Making Lewd, Crude Remarks about Women," *Seattle Times*, October 7, 2016, https://www.seattletimes.com/nation-world/nation-politics/trump-caught-on-video-making-lewd-crude-remarks-about-women; and "The Republican Crisis," *National Review*, October 10, 2016, https://www.nationalreview.com/2016/10/donald-trump-access-hollywood-tape-republican-party-crisis/.

6. The sentiment is global. The cover of the April 2, 2017, issue of Germany's *Der Spiegel* features a cartoon Trump wielding a machete in his left hand and holding the bloodied head of the Statue of Liberty in his right. See "America First," *Der Spiegel*, April 2, 2017, http://magazin.spiegel.de/SP/2017/6/index.html.

7. Jeremy Diamond, "Trump: I Could 'Shoot Somebody and I Wouldn't Lose Voters,'" CNN Politics, January 24, 2016, http://www.cnn.com/2016/01/23/politics/donald-trump-shoot-somebody-support/, para. 2; Jesse Byrnes, "Trump Calls Cruz a 'Pussy,'" *Hill*, February 8, 2016, http://thehill.com/blogs/blog-briefing-room/news/268714-trump-calls-cruz-a-puy; Gregory Krieg, "Donald Trump Defends Size of His Penis," CNN Politics, March 4, 2016, http://www.cnn.com/2016/03/03/politics/donald-trump-small-hands-marco-rubio/.

8. The official report found no evidence for collusion, largely because many of Trump's administration would not carry out his orders; whether or not Trump obstructed justice, however, is still an open question at the time of my writing.

9. Michael Kimmage, "The Surprising Promise of the Trump-Putin Summit," *Foreign Affairs*, July 11, 2018, https://www.foreignaffairs.com/articles/russian-federation/2018-07-11/surprising-promise-trump-putin-summit.

10. "Here's What Trump and Putin Actually Said in Helsinki," *Foreign Policy*, July 18, 2018, https://foreignpolicy.com/2018/07/18/heres-what-trump-and-putin-actually-said-in-helsinki/.

11. See, for example, Cristina Maza, "Donald Trump Tells His Own Intelligence Chiefs to 'Go Back to School' over 'Naive' Assessment of 'Dangers of Iran,'" *Newsweek*, January 20, 2019, https://www.newsweek.com/donald-trump-intelligence-twitter-iran-school-1311429.

12. Kevin Liptak and Jeff Zeleny, "Trump, Facing Fury, Says He Misspoke with Putin," CNN Politics, July 18, 2018, https://www.cnn.com/2018/07/17/politics/white-house-mood-donald -trump-vladimir-putin-news-conference/index.html.

13. John Brennan, Twitter post, July 16, 2018, 8:52 a.m., https://twitter.com/johnbren nan/status/1018885971104985093; Ellis Clopton, "Anderson Cooper Slams Trump-Putin Presser as 'Disgraceful,'" *Variety*, July 16, 2018, https://variety.com/2018/tv/news/anderson -cooper-slams-trump-disgraceful-1202874190/.

14. See Steve Inskeep, "Trump's Secret? Channeling Andrew Jackson," *New York Times*, February 17, 2016, http://www.nytimes.com/2016/02/17/opinion/campaign-stops/donald-trumps -secret-channelling-andrew-jackson.html?_r=0; Brian Rosenwald, "Donald Trump Isn't Ronald Reagan—He's Barry Goldwater," *Daily Beast*, July 4, 2016, http://www.thedailybeast.com /articles/2016/07/05/donald-trump-isn-t-ronald-reagan-he-s-barry-goldwater.html; and "Can History Prepare Us for the Trump Presidency?," *Politico*, January 22, 2017, https://www.po litico.com/magazine/story/2017/01/can-history-prepare-us-for-the-trump-presidency-214676.

15. Eun Kyung Kim, "I've 'Never Seen Anything Like' Donald Trump's Campaign, Analyst Says," *Today.com*, December 22, 2015, http://www.today.com/news/i-ve-never-seen-anything-donald -trump-s-campaign-analyst-t63331.

16. Julian E. Zelizer, "What Is Really Unprecedented about Trump?" *Atlantic*, October 27, 2017, https://www.theatlantic.com/politics/archive/2017/10/what-is-really-unprecedented -about-trump/544179/.

17. In this context, by "speech" I do *not include writing*, as analyses of Trump's discourse reveal very different linguistic "styles" in his speaking and writing voice. See Jacques Savoy, "Trump and Clinton's Style and Rhetoric during the 2016 Presidential Election," *Journal of Quantitative Linguistics* 25.2 (2018): 168–189.

18. Richard A. Lanham, "Occultatio," in *A Handlist of Rhetorical Terms*, 2nd ed. (Berkeley: University of California Press, 1991), 105.

19. Jennifer Mercieca, "How Donald Trump Gets Away with Saying Things Other Candidates Can't," *Washington Post*, March 9, 2016, https://www.washingtonpost.com/posteverything /wp/2016/03/09/how-donald-trump-gets-away-with-saying-things-other-candidates-cant/?utm _term=.1347142c2c42; also see Jennifer Mercieca, "The Rhetorical Brilliance of Trump the Demagogue," *Huffington Post*, December 12, 2015, http://www.huffingtonpost.com/the-conversation-us /the-rhetorical-brilliance_b_8792452.html. Mercieca's recent book more meticulously analyzes Trump's rhetoric with the lens of tropes; see Jennifer Mercieca, *Demagogue for President: The Rhetorical Genius of Donald Trump* (College Station: Texas A&M University Press, 2020).

20. AFP (Agence France Presse), "Trump's Tics: Making Hyperbole Great Again," *Yahoo! Finance*, August 16, 2016, http://finance.yahoo.com/news/trump-tics-making-hyperbole-great -again-035009272.html.

21. Igor Bobic, "He Would Never Say It, But This Is Donald Trump's Favorite Rhetorical Device," *Huffington Post*, February 16, 2016, http://www.huffingtonpost.com/entry/donald -trump-rhetorical-device_us_56c358cbe4b0c3c55052b32b.

22. Donald Trump, Twitter post, January 27, 2016, 3:44 a.m., https://twitter.com/realdonald trump/status/692312112115380224?lang=en.

23. *Occultatio* is mentioned here as the master trope of Trump's discourse, but I would be remiss not to mention that the term has been used and elaborated as a particular *style* of rhetorical mystification crafted by the George W. Bush administration: see Donovan Conley and William O. Saas, "*Occultatio*: The Bush Administration's Rhetorical War," *Western Journal of Communication* 74 (2010): 329–350.

24. Roderick P. Hart, review of *The Rhetoric of Heroic Expectations: Establishing the Obama Presidency*, ed. Justin S. Vaughn and Jennifer R. Mercieca, *Perspectives on Politics* 13 (2015), 874; Hart detailed the "problem," although not in name, in Roderick P. Hart, "The Wondering Imperative: Better Criticism through Science," paper presented at the NCA Summer Conference on Teaching Rhetorical Criticism and Critical Inquiry, Tacoma, WA, July 2010. Also see Diane J. Heith, "Evaluating Presidential Leadership Styles in Campaigning and Governing," in *Communication and Language Analysis in the Public Sphere*, ed. Roderick P. Hart (Hershey, PA: Information Science Reference, 2014), 140. For an early discussion, see Roderick P. Hart, "Doing Criticism My Way: A Reply to Darsey," *Western Journal of Communication* 58 (1994): 308–312.

25. Quoted in AFP, "Trump's Tics," para. 2.

26. See Douglas Walton, *Ad Hominem Arguments* (Tuscaloosa: University of Alabama Press, 2009).

27. The switchboard metaphor has been borrowed from Avital Ronell as "walking" and modified here to "rhetorical." See Avital Ronell, "The Walking Switchboard," *SubStance* 19.1 (1990): 75–94.

28. For an elaboration of the ecstasy of online and stream-savvy engagement, see Sandy Baldwin, "On Speed and Ecstasy: Paul Virilio's 'Aesthetics of Disappearance' and the Rhetoric of Media," *Configurations* 10 (2002): 129–148.

29. This doesn't mean, however, there are no consequences. Trump's tweets were investigated as an obstruction of justice. See Michael S. Schmidt and Maggie Haberman, "Mueller Examining Trump's Tweets in Wide-Ranging Obstruction Inquiry," *New York Times*, July 26, 2018, https://www.nytimes.com/2018/07/26/us/politics/trump-tweets-mueller-obstruction .html. Also see John Sloop and Joshua Gunn, "Status Control: An Admonition Concerning the Publicized Privacy of Social Networking," *Communication Review* 13.4 (2010): 289–308.

30. Sigmund Freud, *The Standard Edition of the Complete Psychological Works of Sigmund Freud*, vol. 7, *A Case of Hysteria, Three Essays on Sexuality, and Other Works (1901–1905)*, trans. James Strachey (London: Hogarth, 1953), 171.

31. Freud, *Standard*, 7:135.

32. Freud, *Standard*, 7:191.

33. Dylan Evans, *An Introductory Dictionary of Lacanian Psychoanalysis* (New York: Routledge, 1996), 138.

34. This point is discussed in more depth in the introduction; see pp. 15–18.

35. Richard von Krafft-Ebing, *Psychopathia Sexualis: The Classic Study of Deviant Sex*, trans. Franklin S. Klaf (New York: Arcade, 2011).

36. Freud, *Standard*, 7:171.

37. Tim Dean and Christopher Lane, eds., *Homosexuality & Psychoanalysis* (Chicago: University of Chicago Press, 2001), 5.

38. Dany Nobus and Lisa Downing, eds., *Perversion: Psychoanalytic Perspective/Perspectives on Psychoanalysis* (New York: Karnac, 2006), 3.

39. Paul Verhaeghe, *On Being Normal and Other Disorders: A Manual for Clinical Psychodiagnostics*, trans. Sigi Jottkandt (New York: Other Press, 2004), 399.

40. William Burroughs, *Cities of the Red Night* (New York: Henry Holt), xviii. Although the phrase has a dubious origin, it is frequently associated with *Naked Lunch*, such as in the scene at "Hassan's Rumpus Room," where the host declares, *"Let it be! And no holes barred!!!"* (New York: Grove Weidenfeld, 1990), 79. David Cronenberg uses the phrase as an epigraph to his 1991 filmic interpretation of *Naked Lunch*.

41. Andy Partridge, vocalist, "Garden of Earthly Delights," by XTC, track 1 on *Oranges & Lemons*, Geffen, 1989.

42. Stephanie S. Swales, *Perversion: A Lacanian Psychoanalytic Approach to the Subject* (New York: Routledge, 2012), 86–87.

43. Cormac McCarthy, *No Country for Old Men* (New York: Alfred A. Knopf, 2005), 259–260.

44. Evil is often more banal. See Hannah Arendt, *Eichmann in Jerusalem: A Report on the Banality of Evil* (New York: Viking, 1963).

45. "Perverts suffer from an excess of jouissance," and thus usually seek to limit it in perverse acts, sublimation, desire, or drugs. Swales, *Perversion*, 128–129.

46. Verhaeghe, *On Being Normal*, 406.

47. Verhaeghe, *On Being Normal*, 410–412.

48. Michael Finnegan, " 'It's Going to Be a Big, Fat, Beautiful Wall': Trump's Words Make His California Climb an Even Steeper Trek," *Los Angeles Times*, June 3, 2016, http://www.latimes.com/politics/la-na-pol-trump-california-campaign-20160602-snap-story.html.

49. Clemence Michallon, " 'Perverts Never Change': Donald Trump's Own Words Come Back to Haunt Him as Twitter Sleuths Comment He Once Made about Anthony Weiner," *DailyMail.com*, October 9, 2016, http://www.dailymail.co.uk/news/article-3829953/Donald-Trump-s-tweet-against-Anthony-Weiner-comes-haunt-him.html. Trump's comment was "tweeted" after New York politician Antony Weiner was repeatedly exposed for exposing himself online to a number of women, destroying his political ambitions on many occasions. For an overview, see Amy Chozick and Patrick Healy, "Anthony Weiner and Huma Abedin to Separate after His Latest Sexting Scandal," *New York Times*, August 29, 2016, http://www.nytimes.com/2016/08/30/nyregion/anthony-weiner-sexting-huma-abedin.html?_r=0.

50. My apologies, but this is an oblique Plato joke about one-night stands: "You understand my situation [condition]. I've told you how good it would be for us, in my opinion, if this worked out." Plato, *Phaedrus*, 7.

51. Donald J. Trump, Twitter post, May 8, 2013, 6:37 p.m., https://twitter.com/realdonaldtrump/status/332308211321425920?lang=en

52. Donald J. Trump, Twitter post, December 31, 2016, 5:17 a.m., https://twitter.com/realdonaldtrump/status/815185071317676033?lang=en

53. Donald J. Trump, Twitter post, November 11, 2017, 4:48 p.m., https://twitter.com/realdonaldtrump/status/929511061954297857?lang=en

54. See David Folkenflik, "Analysis: In Trump's Twitter Feed, a Tale of Sound and Fury," NPR, April 7 2018, https://www.npr.org/2018/04/07/600138358/analysis-in-trumps-twitter-feed-a-tale-of-sound-and-fury.

55. Nick Corasaniti, "Donald Trump Calls Obama 'Founder of ISIS' and Says It Honors Him," *New York Times*, August 10, 2016, http://www.nytimes.com/2016/08/11/us/politics/trump-rally.html, para. 2.

56. Sean Sullivan, "Trump Shifts His Tone, Calls 'Founder of ISIS' Comment 'Sarcastic, but 'Not that Sarcastic,'" *Washington Post*, August 12, 2016, https://www.washingtonpost.com/news/post-politics/wp/2016/08/12/trump-shifts-his-tone-calls-founder-of-isis-comment-sarcastic-but-not-that-sarcastic/, para. 4.

57. Robert Hariman, *Political Style: The Artistry of Power* (Chicago: University of Chicago Press, 1995), 4.

58. This approach has been critiqued as instrumental. See Marie Lund, *An Argument on Rhetorical Style* (Aarhus, Denmark: Aarhus University Press, 2017), 101; and Bradford Vivian, "Style, Rhetoric, and Postmodern Culture," *Philosophy and Rhetoric* 35.3 (2002): 223–243.

59. My thanks to Barry Brummett for pointing out that Trump's appearance suggests a homology with his speech; homologies or formal parallels between multiple dimensions of self-presentation are hallmarks of style. Notably, Javier Bardem's chilling portrayal of Anton Chigurh in the Cohen brothers' film adaptation of *No Country for Old Men* sports a deliberately strange and anachronistic "mop-top," bowl-style haircut.

60. Aside from sketch comedies on television that portray Trump (such as Alec Baldwin's caricature on NBC's *Saturday Night Live*), examples are easily found. See, for example, Nigel M. Smith, "Barbara Streisand on Donald Trump: 'He Looks like a Raccoon in a Tanning Bed," *Guardian*, September 22, 2016, https://www.theguardian.com/culture/2016/sep/22/barbra-streisand-donald-trump-hillary-clinton.

61. For one, see Naomi Wolf, *The Beauty Myth: How Images of Beauty Are Used against Women* (New York: Harper Perennial, 2002).

62. See Dick Hebdige, *Subculture: The Meaning of Style* (New York: Routledge, 1979), esp. 113–127.

63. Barry Brummett, *A Rhetoric of Style* (Carbondale: Southern Illinois University Press), xi. Brummett has also developed an approach to the analysis of homologies; see Barry Brummett, *Rhetorical Homologies: Form, Culture, Experience* (Tuscaloosa: University of Alabama Press, 2004).

64. Brummett, *Style*, 36–41.

65. Brummett, *Style*, 3.

66. Hariman, *Political Style*.

67. The villain, often lovable, is the perfect figure of perversion because they often appear as "evil" in comical ways and are thus not as threatening as the psychotic. For example, Snidely Whiplash is such a figure and foil for the neurotically clueless Dudley Do-Right of *The Rocky and Bullwinkle Show*.

68. Richard Hofstadter, *The Paranoid Style in American Politics and Other Essays* (Cambridge, MA: Harvard University Press, 1996), 4.

69. Benjy Sarlin, "Donald Trump Imagines Shadowy 'Conspiracy' behind Women Ac-

cusing Him of Misdeeds," NBC News.com, October 14, 2015, http://www.nbcnews.com
/politics/2016-election/donald-trump-imagines-shadowy-conspiracy-behind-women-accusing
-him-misdeeds-n666091, pars. 4–9.

70. "Why the Trump Allegations Are Consuming Campaign Coverage," *PBS NewsHour*,
October 13, 2016, http://www.pbs.org/newshour/bb/trump-allegations-consuming-campaign
-coverage/.

71. See Harmon Leon, "I Tried to Lie My Way onto 'The Jerry Springer Show,'" *Vice*, January 29, 2015, http://www.vice.com/read/i-tried-to-lie-my-way-on-to-the-jerry-springer-show-126.

72. This is the conclusion of Matthew Sharpe and Geoff Boucher in their insightful analysis
of Slavoj Žižek's somewhat contradictory theories of cultural psychosis and perversion. Matthew Sharpe and Geoff Boucher, *Žižek and Politics: A Critical Introduction* (Edinburgh: Edinburgh University Press, 2010), esp. 139–164. I should mention, however, that for Lacanians an
individual can express a psychotic structure without the signature psychotic style and can conduct a life without ever having a psychotic break. The rare diagnosis of psychosis is not inher-
ently pathological; that much is resigned to violence and criminal violations of juridical norms.

73. Roger Waters, David Gilmour, Nick Mason, and Richard Wright, "Mother," by Pink
Floyd, track 6 on *The Wall*, Columbia, 1979.

74. For a view of the scene, see Jeanne Moos's hilarious CNN report, "And the Most Famous
Escalator Is . . . ," CNN.com, September 3, 2015, http://www.cnn.com/videos/us/2015/09/03
/donald-trump-escalator-moos-erin-dnt.cnn.

75. "Immigration Reform That Will Make America Great Again," DonaldJTrump.com, n.d.,
accessed September 17, 2016, https://www.donaldjtrump.com/positions/immigration-reform.

76. Donald J. Trump, "Here's Donald Trump's Presidential Announcement Speech," *Time
.com*, June 16, 2015, http://time.com/3923128/donald-trump-announcement-speech/, para. 159.

77. Trump, "Here's Donald Trump's," para. 9.

78. See William Axford, "High School Students Chant 'Build the Wall' at Football Game,"
Houston Chronicle, October 3 2017, https://www.chron.com/national/article/build-the-wall
-Trump-high-school-football-Utah-12249288.php; James David Dickson and Candice Wilson, "Royal Oak Middle School Students Chant 'Build That Wall,'" *Detroit News*, November 10, 2016, https://www.detroitnews.com/story/news/local/oakland-county/2016/11/10/royal
-oak-students-chant-build-wall-cafeteria/93581592/; and Mary Papenfuss, "Mexican News
paper Blasts U.S. Spring Breakers for Chanting 'Build the Wall,'" *Huffington Post*, March 21,
2018, https://www.huffingtonpost.ca/entry/mexico-wall-spring-break-cancun_us_58d0b1f6e4
b0ec9d29decb44.

79. Hilary Weaver, "London's Trump Baby Blimp Has Made the President Feel 'Unwelcome,'" *Vanity Fair*, July 13, 2018, https://www.vanityfair.com/style/2018/07/trump-baby
-blimp-in-london.

80. See Ann Applebaum, "Trump's Disastrous UK Visit Could Feed Anti-American Views
for Years to Come," *Independent*, July 16, 2018, https://www.independent.co.uk/voices/trump
-uk-visit-anti-us-protests-brexit-theresa-may-president-queen-a8448976.html.

81. Allison Tate, "Trump Baby Blimp to Fly in U.S.," *Advocate*, July 16, 2018, https://www
.advocate.com/politics/2018/7/16/trump-baby-blimp-fly-us; Naaman Zhou, "Trump Baby
Blimp Expected to Fly over Australia during US Presidential Visit," *Guardian*, July 24, 2018,

https://www.theguardian.com/us-news/2018/jul/24/trump-baby-blimp-expected-to-fly-over
-australia-during-us-presidential-visit.

82. Chantal Da Silva and Chiara Brambilla, "'Trump Baby': Meet the Mind Behind the Inflatable Infant Set to Greet Trump on London Trip," *Newsweek*, July 10, 2018, https://www.newsweek
.com/trump-baby-balloon-make-surprise-appearance-during-presidents-visit-and-go-1015575.

83. See Jen Mills, "San Francisco's 'Trump Chicken' Balloon Is Way Better Than Trump Baby," *Metro*, July 23, 2018, https://metro.co.uk/2018/07/23/san-fransciscos-trump-chicken
-balloon-way-better-trump-baby-7747598/.

84. Sigmund Freud, *The Future of an Illusion*, trans. James Strachey, in *The Freud Reader*, ed. Peter Gay (New York: W. W. Norton, 1989), 685–722. I would contrast what I mean by "rhetoric" here—discourse *after* the signifier—with what Diane Davis terms "rhetoricity," an "affect*ability* or persuade*ability* . . . that is the condition for symbolic action." Diane Davis, *Inessential Solidarity: Rhetoric and Foreigner Relations* (Pittsburgh: University of Pittsburgh Press, 2010), 2.

85. Jacques Lacan, quoted in Evans, *Dictionary*, 34.

86. See Joan Copjec, *Read My Desire: Lacan against the Historicists* (Cambridge, MA: MIT Press, 1994), 148–149; and Ed Pluth, *Signifiers and Acts: Freedom in Lacan's Theory of the Subject* (Albany: State University of New York Press, 2007), 60–64.

87. Ernesto Laclau, *On Populist Reason* (New York: Verso, 2005), 73.

88. Christian Lundberg, "On Being Bound to Equivalential Chains," *Cultural Studies* 26.2 (2012): 299–318.

89. Slavoj Žižek, "Cyberspace, or How to Traverse the Fantasy in the Age of the Retreat of the Big Other," *Public Culture* 10.3 (1998): 483–513.

90. Astrid Gessert, "Exploring Transgression from a Lacanian Perspective," in *Perversion Now!*, ed. Diana Caine and Colin Wright (New York: Palgrave, 2017), 42.

91. See Michelle Cottle, "Newt Broke Politics—Now He Wants Back In," *Atlantic*, July 14 2016, https://www.theatlantic.com/politics/archive/2016/07/newt-broke-politicsnow-he-wants
-back-in/491390/.

92. Simon Gallup, Robert Smith, Porl Thompson, and Boris Williams, "Never Enough," by the Cure, track 11 on *Mixed Up*, Elektra, 1990.

93. Laura J. Collins, "The Second Amendment as Demanding Subject: Figuring the Marginalized Subject in Demands for an Unbridled Second Amendment," *Rhetoric & Public Affairs* 17.4 (2014): 737–756.

94. Strangely, "There is a tendency for the demanding subject to be satisfied by the fact of performance rather than [the] material satisfaction of its demands," as Lundberg explains. Lundberg also describes demand politics as "addictive." Lundberg, "On Being Bound," 300.

95. Oliver Laughland and Lois Beckett, "March for Our Lives: Thousands Join Anti-Gun Protests around the World," *Guardian*, March 25, 2018, https://www.theguardian.com
/us-news/2018/mar/24/washington-march-for-our-lives-gun-violence.

96. Dick Metcalf, "Target: Me," *Politico*, January 14, 2014, https://www.politico.com/maga
zine/story/2014/01/guns-second-amendment-target-me-102133#.UtV4T2RDtcQ.

97. See Lundberg, "On Being Bound," for useful elaboration of the demand and *jouissance*.

98. For Lacan, "*Jouissance* is suffering." See Evans, *Dictionary*, 91–92.

99. For a rather bald rehearsal of the "talking points," have a listen to Acumen Nation, "Gun Lover," track 1 on *Transmissions from Eville*, Fifth Column Records, 1995.

100. Lundberg suggests the "three primary classes of subjects" excluded from political are "those who are overcome with emotion; children; and madmen." Christian Lundberg, "Agreeing to Perpetually Disagree—Stasis, Enjoyment and Democratic Authority," paper presented at the biannual Public Address Conference, Atlanta, GA, October 18, 2014.

101. Nancy Fraser, "Rethinking the Public Sphere: A Contribution to the Critique of Actually Existing Democracy," *Social Text* 25–26 (1990): 56–80; Michael Warner, "Publics and Counterpublics (Abbreviated Version)," *Quarterly Journal of Speech* 88 (2002): 413–425.

102. See Nina M. Lozano-Reich and Dana L. Cloud, "The Uncivil Tongue: Invitational Rhetoric and the Problem of Inequality," *Western Journal of Communication* 73 (2009): 220–226; Pat J. Gehrke, *The Ethics and Politics of Speech: Communication and Rhetoric in the Twentieth Century* (Carbondale: Southern Illinois University Press, 2009); Ronald Walter Green and Darrin Hicks, "Lost Convictions: Debating Both Sides and the Ethical Self-Fashioning of Liberal Citizens," *Cultural Studies* 19 (2005): 100–126; and Darrin Hicks, "The New Citizen," *Quarterly Journal of Speech* 93 (2007): 358–360.

103. Alternately, we can describe the exchange as the failure of what Marcel Mauss identified as the function of "the gift," and in a cognate context, of what Gayle Rubin describes as the "traffic in women" (as object): whatever the object of argument or barter, it is merely a ruse for communication about identity.

104. Gene Loves Jezebel, "Desire," track 6 on *Discover*, Beggars Banquet, 1986.

105. The relationship between "desire" and "love" in Lacanian theory is complex. As Dylan Evans explains, on one level the two are opposed insofar as desire only desires more desire (no ending), while love is premised on a fantasy of wholeness or unity (an ending). On another level, however, desire and love are similarly structured because neither can be satisfied. See Evans, *Dictionary*, 103–104.

106. Lundberg, "Agreeing to Perpetually Disagree."

107. Slavoj Žižek, *Looking Awry: An Introduction to Jacques Lacan through Popular Culture* (Cambridge, MA: MIT Press, 1992): 83–84.

108. Lundberg, "Agreeing to Perpetually Disagree."

109. Miller Williams, "Compassion," performed by Lucinda Williams, track 1 on *Down Where the Spirit Meets the Bone*, Highway 20 Music / BMI, 2014.

110. Herbert Marcuse, *Five Lectures: Psychoanalysis, Politics, and Utopia*, trans. Jeremy J. Shapiro and Shierry M. Weber (Boston: Beacon, 1970): 52.

111. Marcuse, *Five Lectures*, 52.

112. Marcuse, *Five Lectures*, 53–54; see Michel Foucault, "Governmentality," trans. Pasquale Pasquino, in *The Foucault Effect: Studies in Governmentality, with Two Lectures by and an Interview with Michel Foucault*, ed. Graham Burchell, Colin Gorgon, and Peter Miller (Chicago: University of Chicago Press, 1991): 87–104.

113. The phrase is my modification of "*vaterlose Gesslschaft*." See Marcuse, *Five Lectures*, 53.

114. Sigmund Freud, *Civilization and Its Discontents*, trans. James Strachey (New York: W. W. Norton, 1961), 43–44n4.

115. Abby Ohlheiser, "Urban Outfitters Apologizes for Its Blood-Red-Stained Kent State Sweatshirt," *Washington Post*, September 15, 2014, http://www.washingtonpost.com/news /morning-mix/wp/2014/09/15/urban-outfitters-red-stained-vintage-kent-state-sweatshirt-is-not -a-smart-look-this-fall/.

116. See Craig Saper, "Sublimation as Media: *Inter Urinas et Faeces Nascimur*," *Discourse* 31 (2009): 51–71.

117. Jodi Dean, *Blog Theory: Feedback and Capture in the Circuits of Drive* (Malden, MA: Polity, 2010), esp. 4–9.

CHAPTER FOUR

1. Friedrich Nietzsche, *On the Genealogy of Morality*, trans. Maudemarie Clark and Alan J. Swensen (Indianapolis: Hackett, 1998), 69–70.

2. Michelle Goldberg, "Lordy, Is There a Tape?," *New York Times*, April 16, 2018, https:// www.nytimes.com/2018/04/16/opinion/comey-book-steele-dossier.html.

3. Glen R. Simpson and Peter Fritsch, "The Republicans' Fake Investigations," *New York Times*, January 2, 2018, https://www.nytimes.com/2018/01/02/opinion/republicans-investiga tion-fusion-gps.html.

4. See Hilary Krieger, "An Introduction to the Dark Arts of Opposition Research," *FiveThirtyEight*, October 31, 2017, https://fivethirtyeight.com/features/an-introduction-to-the -dark-arts-of-opposition-research/.

5. Mark Hensch, "Biden: Intel Officials Warned Us of Trump Dossier," *Hill*, January 12, 2017, http://thehill.com/policy/national-security/intelligence/313999-biden-intel-officials-warned -us-of-trump-dossier.

6. See Jeff Donn, "Some Questions in Trump-Russia Dossier Now Finding Answers," CBS News, June 29, 2018, https://www.cbsnews.com/news/some-questions-in-trump-russia -dossier-now-finding-answers/.

7. Scott Shane, Adam Goldman, and Matthew Rosenberg, "Trump Received Unsubstanti-ated Report That Russia Had Damaging Information about Him," *New York Times*, January 10, 2017, https://www.nytimes.com/2017/01/10/us/politics/donald-trump-russia-intelligence.html.

8. Evan Perez, Jim Sciutto, and Jake Tapper, "Intel Chiefs Presented Trump with Claims of Russian Efforts to Compromise Him," CNN Politics, January 12, 2017, https://edition.cnn .com/2017/01/10/politics/donald-trump-intelligence-report-russia/index.html.

9. Ken Bensigner, Miriam Elder, and Mark Schoofs, "These Reports Allege Trump Has Deep Ties to Russia," *BuzzFeed News*, January 10, 2017, https://www.buzzfeednews.com/article /kenbensinger/these-reports-allege-trump-has-deep-ties-to-russia#.dhAlQBD97.

10. For example, see Erik Wemple, "BuzzFeed's Ridiculous Rational for Publishing the Trump-Russia Dossier," *Washington Post*, January 10, 2017, https://www.washingtonpost.com /blogs/erik-wemple/wp/2017/01/10/buzzfeeds-ridiculous-rationale-for-publishing-the-trump -russia-dossier/?utm_term=.aa4fdc51f789.

11. Michael S. Schmidt and Maggie Haberman, "Trump Humiliated Jeff Sessions after Muel-ler Appointment," *New York Times*, September 14, 2017, https://www.nytimes.com/2017/09/14 /us/politics/jeff-sessions-trump.html.

12. Jessica Taylor, "President Trump Fires FBI Director James Comey," NPR, May 9, 2017, https://www.npr.org/2017/05/09/527663050/president-trump-fires-fbi-director-james-comey.

13. See Andrew Buncombe, "Comey: 'I Don't Know If Trump Was with Prostitutes Peeing on Each Other in Moscow,'" *Independent*, April 13, 2018, https://www.independent.co.uk/news/world/americas/us-politics/donald-trump-pee-tape-golden-showers-prostitutes-moscow-james-comey-cnn-a8303056.html.

14. James Comey, *A Higher Loyalty: Truth, Lies, and Leadership* (New York: Flatiron Books, 2018).

15. Late night talk-show host Stephen Colbert, for example, repeatedly references the "pee tape" as a critique of the president's fitness for office. See "Stephen Rents the Trump 'Pee Pee Tape' Hotel Room for a Night," *The Late Show with Steven Colbert*, July 21, 2017, https://youtu.be/LkluBMZOaXc.

16. See Jim Newell, "Pelosi and Schumer Move Closer to a 'Kompromat' Theory of Donald Trump," *Slate*, July 16, 2018, https://slate.com/news-and-politics/2018/07/pelosi-schumer-suggest-putin-has-dirt-on-president-trump-after-helsinki-press-conference.html.

17. Sophie Tatum and Kara Scannell, "Tom Arnold Says He Has Tapes of the President That Have Yet to Be Heard by the Public," CNN Politics, June 22, 2018, https://www.cnn.com/2018/06/22/politics/tom-arnold-tapes-michael-cohen-donald-trump/index.html.

18. Maureen O'Conner, "The Sheer Perfection of Donald Trump's Golden Shower," *Cut*, January 11, 2017, https://www.thecut.com/2017/01/the-sheer-perfection-of-donald-trumps-golden-shower.html.

19. Goldberg, "Lordy, Is There a Tape?"

20. O'Conner, "The Sheer Perfection."

21. Goldberg, "Lordy, Is There a Tape?"

22. See Caitlin Flanagan, "The First Porn President," *Atlantic*, May 3, 2018, https://www.theatlantic.com/politics/archive/2018/05/the-porn-president/559523/.

23. Paul Verhaeghe, *On Being Normal and Other Disorders: A Manual for Clinical Psychodiagnostics*, trans. Sigi Jottkandt (New York: Other Press, 2004), 400.

24. See Astrid Gessert, "Exploring Transgression from a Lacanian Perspective," in *Perversion Now!*, ed. Diana Caine and Colin Wright (New York: Palgrave, 2017), 35–44.

25. A note of qualification: reading a genre *as* a psychical structure is not to claim it *is* one. Rather, I will suggest that like style, genres are expressions of psychical structures that inhere in culture and that help to forge the scaffolding of neurotic, psychotic, or perverse selfhood.

26. Julian Zelizer, "Trump Sounds Normal in Private. It's All an Act," CNN Opinion, July 25, 2018, https://www.cnn.com/2018/07/25/opinions/michael-cohen-donald-trump-tape-strategy-zelizer/index.html.

27. See Ian Haney López, *Dog Whistle Politics: How Coded Racial Appeals Have Reinvented Racism and Wrecked the Middle Class* (New York: Oxford University Press, 2015).

28. See Emily Nussbaum, "The TV That Created Donald Trump," *New Yorker*, July 31, 2017, https://www.newyorker.com/magazine/2017/07/31/the-tv-that-created-donald-trump.

29. For an overview, see Zachary Shucklin, "A Chronological List of Trump's 8 Known Mistresses," *Advocate*, May 24, 2018, https://www.advocate.com/politicians/2018/5/24/chronological-list-trumps-8-known-mistresses#media-gallery-media-0.

30. See, for example, Nussbaum, "The TV That Created Donald Trump."

31. Sigmund Freud, *The Standard Edition of the Complete Psychological Works of Sigmund Freud*, vol. 13, : *Totem and Taboo and Other Works (1913–1914)*, trans. James Strachey (London: Vintage, 1955), 159.

32. E. L. James, *Fifty Shades of Grey* (New York: Vintage Books, 2011).

33. Tanya Sweeney, "The 'Kink-Shaming' of Donald Trump Reeks of Hypocrisy," *Irish Times*, January 11, 2017, https://www.irishtimes.com/life-and-style/people/the-kink-shaming -of-donald-trump-reeks-of-hypocrisy-1.2933217. Also see Olivia Blair, "How Our Culture of Kink-Shaming Is Making Us Much Less Sexually Liberated Than We Think," *Independent*, February 15, 2017, https://www.independent.co.uk/life-style/love-sex/sex-kink-shaming-porn -preferences-society-not-as-sexually-liberated-as-it-thinks-a7579496.html.

34. See Roland Chemama, "A Few Questions about the Idea of Ordinary Perversion," in *Perversion Now!*, ed. Diana Caine and Colin Wright (New York: Palgrave, 2017), 87–91.

35. See Adam Withnail, "Donald Trump's Unsettling Record of Comments about His Daughter Ivanka," *Independent*, October 10, 2016, https://www.independent.co.uk/news/world /americas/us-elections/donald-trump-ivanka-trump-creepiest-most-unsettling-comments-a -roundup-a7353876.html.

36. The term "truthful hyperbole" was coined by Trump's ghostwriter for *The Art of the Deal*, Tony Schwartz, which he later denounced as a "contradiction in terms. It's a way of saying, 'It's a lie, but who cares?' " Jane Mayer, "Donald Trump's Ghostwriter Tells All," *New Yorker*, July 25, 2016, http://www.newyorker.com/magazine/2016/07/25/donald-trumps-ghostwriter-tells-all.

37. To my knowledge, I was among the first to point out Trump's perversity on my blog, *The Rosewater Chronicles* (and *Medium*) in the spring of 2016, which I subsequently removed a year later so as not to scoop my own book! The first public intellectual to do so was Andrew Sullivan, "The Perverse Presidency of Donald Trump," *New York*, June 23, 2017, http://nymag.com/daily /intelligencer/2017/06/andrew-sullivan-the-perverse-presidency-of-donald-trump.html.

38. Annie Lowrey, "Hearing Donald Trump Refer to Ted Cruz as a 'Pussy' Told Me Everything I Need to Know About His Campaign," *New York*, February 8, 2016, http://nymag .com/daily/intelligencer/2016/02/trump-sums-up-candidacy-with-vulgar-cruz-slam.html, para. 3.

39. Gianni Riotta, "I Know Fascists; Donald Trump Is No Fascist," *Atlantic*, January 16, 2016, http://www.theatlantic.com/international/archive/2016/01/donald-trump-fascist/424449/, para. 3.

40. Many commentators compared the 2016 Republican National Convention to the Nuremberg rallies, such as David Brooks: "If we're going to get Trump, we might as well get the Nuremberg rallies to go with it. No, I mean, the number-one trait that associates or correlates with Trump support is authoritarianism." David Brooks, interview by Chuck Todd, *Meet the Press*, March 6, 2016, http://www.nbcnews.com/meet-the-press/meet-press-march-6–2016-n532881.

41. See Jennifer Mercieca, *Demagogue for President: The Rhetorical Genius of Donald Trump* (College Station: Texas A&M University Press, 2020); Greg Sargent, "Donald Trump Is a Highly Skilled Demagogue. This One Chart Shows It's Working," *Washington Post*, January 26, 2016, https://www.washingtonpost.com/blogs/plum-line/wp/2016/01/26/donald-trump-is -a-highly-skilled-demagogue-this-one-chart-proves-it/?utm_term=.2bcbd902087f.

42. The focus of empirical research on political behavior has been widely critiqued; see, for example, Donald Green and Ian Shapiro, *Pathologies of Rational Choice Theory: A Critique of Applications in Political Science* (New Haven, CT: Yale University Press, 1996).

43. Henry Alford, "Is Donald Trump Actually a Narcissist? Therapists Weigh In!," *Vanity Fair*, November 11, 2015, http://www.vanityfair.com/news/2015/11/donald-trump-narcissism -therapists; Dan P. McAdams, "The Mind of Donald Trump," *Atlantic*, June 2016, http://www .theatlantic.com/magazine/archive/2016/06/the-mind-of-donald-trump/480771/.

44. Aaron Blake, "The American Psychiatric Association Issues a Warning: No Psychoan- alyzing Donald Trump," *Washington Post*, August 7, 2016, https://www.washingtonpost.com /news/the-fix/wp/2016/08/07/the-american-psychiatric-association-reminds-its-doctors-no -psychoanalyzing-donald-trump/.

45. Maria A. Oquendo, "The Goldwater Rule: Why Breaking It Is Unethical and Irre- sponsible," *APA Blogs*, August 3, 2016, https://www.psychiatry.org/news-room/apa-blogs/apa -blog/2016/08/the-goldwater-rule, para. 1.

46. What suffering person would want to seek treatment, the reasoning goes, if they are worried about their privacy? For an accessible overview of the issue vis-à-vis presidential cam- paigns, see Stephen M. Soreff and Patricia H. Bazemore, "Mental Health and the Run for the White House," *Behavioral Healthcare* 28 (2008): 22–26.

47. Oquendo, "The Goldwater Rule," para. 2.

48. See Sharon Crowley, *Composition in the University: Historical and Polemical Essays* (Pittsburgh: University of Pittsburgh Press, 1998), 215–227.

49. See Joshua Gunn, "Speech's Sanatorium," *Quarterly Journal of Speech* 101.1 (2015): 18–33.

50. Lester Thonssen and A. Craig Baird, *Speech Criticism: The Development of Standards for Rhetorical Appraisal* (New York: Ronald, 1948), 384–385. Also see Frederick J. Antczak, "Teaching Rhetoric and Teaching Morality: Some Problems and Possibilities of Ethical Criti- cism," *Rhetoric Society Quarterly* 19 (1989): 15–22.

51. Edwin Black, *Rhetorical Criticism: A Study in Method* (New York: Macmillan, 1965), esp. 138–147. I resist dismissing criticism prior to the paradigm shifts in the 1960s as "neo- Aristotelian" because the patsy label mischaracterizes the variety of approaches adopted by communication scholars for criticism since the 1920s, however much it helped to advance theory.

52. William K. Wimsatt and Monroe C. Beardsley, "The Intentional Fallacy," *Sewanee Re- view* 54 (1946): 468–488; also see René Wellek and Austin Warren, *Theory of Literature*, 3rd ed. (San Diego: Harcourt Brace, 1975), 41–43. For an excellent overview of its influence, see Ryan K. Clark, "The Original Problem of Agency: Revisiting the 'Intentional Fallacy,'" paper presented at the National Communication Association Conference, Chicago, November 2007. I would describe the work of Kenneth Burke as party to the "formalist turn."

53. Michael Barbaro and Alexander Burns, "It's Donald Trump's Convention. But the In- spiration? Nixon," *New York Times*, July 18, 2016, http://www.nytimes.com/2016/07/19/us/poli tics/donald-trump-portrayed-as-an-heir-to-richard-nixon.html.

54. Karlyn Kohrs Campbell, "An Exercise in the Rhetoric of Mythical America," in *Critiques of Contemporary Rhetoric* (Belmont, CA: Wadsworth, 1972), 39–58; Forbes Hill, "Conventional

Wisdom—Traditional Form—The President's Message of November 3, 1969," *Quarterly Journal of Speech* 58 (1972): 737–786. The exchange begins with Karlyn Kohrs Campbell, "Conventional Wisdom—Traditional Form: A Rejoinder," *Quarterly Journal of Speech* 58 (1972): 451–454; and Forbes Hill, "Reply to Professor Campbell," *Quarterly Journal of Speech* 58 (1972):454–460.

55. The significance of Nixon's rhetoric—and in my terms, the perversion it introduced to both rhetorical studies and politics—is certainly not lost on Campbell, who has recently published a rigorous, book-length treatment of the Vietnamization speech. See Karlyn Kohrs Campbell, *The Great Silent Majority: Nixon's 1969 Speech on Vietnamization* (College Station: Texas A&M University Press, 2014).

56. See Dana Cloud and Joshua Gunn, "Introduction: W(h)ither Ideology?," *Western Journal of Communication* 75 (2011): 407–420.

57. Edwin Black, "The Second Persona," *Quarterly Journal of Speech* 56 (1970): 111.

58. Black, "Second Persona," 111, 109.

59. Black, "Second Persona," 111.

60. Edwin Black, "Richard Nixon and the Privacy of Public Discourse," *Rhetoric & Public Affairs* 2 (1999): 1–29. For an intriguingly beautiful analysis of the relationship between Black and his persona, see James Darsey, "Edwin Black and the First Persona," *Rhetoric & Public Affairs* 10 (2007): 501–507.

61. Black, "Second Persona," 111–113.

62. Kenneth Burke, *Language as Symbolic Action: Essays on Life, Literature, and Method* (Berkeley: University of California Press, 1996 [1966]), 6.

63. Erving Goffman, *The Presentation of Self in Everyday Life* (New York: Anchor, 1959).

64. Alexandra Petri, "Ben Carson Reveals the Truth—There Are Two Donald Trumps," *Washington Post*, March 11, 2016, https://www.washingtonpost.com/blogs/compost/wp/2016/03/11/ben-carson-reveals-the-truth-there-are-two-donald-trumps/?utm_term=.848f88a36856.

65. Dan Merica, "Clinton Sees 'Similarities' between Day 1 of RNC and 'Wizard of Oz,'" CNN Politics, July 20, 2016, https://www.cnn.com/2016/07/19/politics/hillary-clinton-republican-national-convention/index.html. The comparison of Trump's campaign to Oz's fictional, phantasmagorical feats was common during the 2016 election cycle and began early. For example, until each party nominated a candidate, *The Late Show with Stephen Colbert* regularly featured a segment titled "The Road to the White House" with characters from Baum's Oz mythos, always featuring Trump as Oz.

66. See Diane Davis, *Inessential Solidarity: Rhetoric and Foreigner Relations* (Pittsburgh: University of Pittsburgh Press, 2010), esp. 1–17.

67. Partly in response to the misguided extensions and critiques of her theory of performativity, Judith Butler wrote *Bodies That Matter: On the Discursive Limits of Sex* (New York: Routledge, 2011).

68. See Joshua Gunn, "Agency," in *Encyclopedia of Communication Theory*, ed. Stephen Littlejohn and Karen Foss (Thousand Oaks, CA: Sage, 2009), 27–30; and Christian Lundberg and Joshua Gunn, "'Ouija Board, Are There Any Communications?': Agency, Ontotheology, and the Death of the Humanist Subject," *Rhetoric Society Quarterly* 35.4 (2005): 83–105.

69. "The terminal character of [moral] judgment works to close critical discussion," observed Black, because it is "categorical" and shapes "decisively one's relationship to the object judged." Black, "Second Persona," 109. Even so, I think few would disagree these days with Sharon Crowley's prescient intervention in the discussions about "ideological criticism" over twenty years ago: that as critics, rhetoricians have an obligation to avoid safe retreat into "philosophical idealism" at the expense of "showing people how rhetoric is practice, how language is deployed as a means of coercion, and how they can resist that coercion." Sharon Crowley, "Reflections on an Argument That Won't Go Away: Or, a Turn of the Ideological Screw," *Quarterly Journal of Speech* 78 (1992): 464.

70. For example, in a savvy analysis of personae constellated around the person Joe Biden, the authors show how "circulating personae may neuter roles important to political rhetoric and public culture." Don J. Waisanen and Amy B. Becker, "The Problem with Being Joe Biden: Political Comedy and Circulating Personae," *Critical Studies in Media Communication* 32 (2015): 256–271.

71. "If we could, in a sense," writes Black, "discover for a complex linguistic formulation a corresponding form of character . . . we should then be able to subsume that discourse under a moral order and thus satisfy our obligation to history." Black, "Second Persona," 110.

72. Have you seen *Blade Runner*? Descartes would say it is not science fiction but a horror flick.

73. The phrase is a title from Burroughs; see William S. Burroughs, *The Place of Dead Roads* (New York: Viking, 1983).

74. For an elaboration of subjectivity as an open question, see Caroline Williams, *Contemporary French Philosophy: Modernity and the Persistence of the Subject* (New York: Continuum, 2001), esp. 191–192.

75. Avery Gordon, *Ghostly Matters: Haunting and the Sociological Imagination* (Minneapolis: University of Minnesota Press, 1996), 5.

76. For an excellent explanation of this dis-ease in regard to "style," see Bradford Vivian, "Style, Rhetoric, and Postmodern Culture," *Philosophy & Rhetoric* 35 (2001): 223–243.

77. Black, "The Second Persona," 109.

78. With unnecessary apologies, Kurt Cobain put the point memorably: "What else could I say? Everyone is gay." Kurt Cobain, vocalist, "All Apologies," by Nirvana, track 12 of *In Utero*, DGC, 1993. In this way Cobain proclaimed a cutting of the knot tying perversion to homosexuality. See James Penney, *The World of Perversion: Psychoanalysis and the Impossible Absolute of Desire* (Albany: State University of New York Press, 2006), esp. 11: "It should go without saying that a genuinely antihomophobic engagement with psychoanalysis must object to any a priori connection of the strong sense of perversion with homosexuality."

79. Mark Nash, *Screen Theory Culture* (New York: Palgrave, 2008), 2.

80. Janet Staiger, *Perverse Spectators: The Practices of Film Reception* (New York: New York University Press, 2000), 2. For an extended example, see Joshua Gunn, "MARANATHA," *Quarterly Journal of Speech* 98.4 (2012): 359–385.

81. See Todd McGowan, *The Real Gaze: Theory after Lacan* (Albany: State University of New York Press, 2008).

82. Laura Mulvey, "Visual Pleasure and Narrative Cinema," in *The Sexual Subject: A Screen Reader in Sexuality* (New York: Routledge, 1992), 22–34.

83. Sigmund Freud, *The Standard Edition of the Complete Psychological Works of Sigmund Freud*, vol. 7, *A Case of Hysteria, Three Essays on Sexuality, and Other Works (1901–1905)*, trans. James Strachey (London: Hogarth, 1953), 135.

84. Gessert, "Exploring Transgression," 36.

85. Many argue contractarian thinking as such is coercive (for example, the film *Last Tango in Paris*). See Carole Pateman, *The Sexual Contract* (Stanford, CA: Stanford University Press, 1988); and Charles W. Mills, *The Racial Contract* (Ithaca, NY: Cornell University Press, 1997).

86. See Michelle E. Deming, Eleanor Krassen Covan, Suzanne C. Swan, and Deborah L. Billings, "Exploring Rape Myths, Gendered Norms, Group Processing, and the Social Context of Rape among College Women: A Qualitative Analysis," *Violence against Women* 19 (2013): 465–485; and Joseph S. Fulda, "The Limits of Consent," *Sexuality & Culture* 17 (2013): 659–665.

87. Dylan Evans, *An Introductory Dictionary of Lacanian Psychoanalysis* (New York: Routledge, 1996), 138.

88. Sabrina Siddiqui, "Donald Trump Pleads Ignorance to Megyn Kelly over 'Bimbo' Tweets: 'Did I Say That?,'" *Guardian*, May 18, 2016, https://www.theguardian.com/us-news /2016/may/17/megyn-kelly-trump-interview-bimbo-tweet.

89. "Trump's Surprise Media Event with Bill Clinton Accusers," *Wall Street Journal*, October 10, 2016, https://youtu.be/3jDUBz53hBk.

90. "Trump Invites His Employees to Praise Him," *Huffington Post*, June 12, 2017, https:// youtu.be/YLZNj_9sPgI.

91. Gabriel Sherman, "How Donald Trump Decided to Make Bill Clinton's Accusers a Campaign Issue," *New York*, October 12, 2016, http://nymag.com/daily/intelligencer/2016/10 /how-trump-decided-to-make-clinton-accusers-a-campaign-issue.html.

92. See Gayle Rubin, "The Traffic in Women: Notes on the 'Political Economy' of Sex," in *Toward an Anthropology of Women*, ed. Rayna R. Reiter (New York: Monthly View Press, 1975), 157–210.

93. Dan Merica, "Trump Says Both Sides to Blame amid Charlottesville Backlash," CNN Politics, August 16, 2017, http://www.cnn.com/2017/08/15/politics/trump-charlottesville-delay /index.html.

94. Gunn, "MARANATHA," 364.

95. My viewpoint on genre is heavily influenced by the work of Linda Williams; see Linda Williams, "Film Bodies: Gender, Genre, and Excess," *Film Quarterly* 44 (1991): 2–14.

96. See Karlyn Kohrs Campbell and Kathleen Hall Jamieson, eds., *Form and Genre: Shaping Rhetorical Action* (Falls Church, VA: Speech Communication Association, 1978); and Karlyn Kohrs Campbell and Kathleen Hall Jamieson, *Presidents Creating the Presidency: Deeds Done in Words* (Chicago: University of Chicago Press, 2008).

97. See Jan Jagodozinski, "The Perversity of (Real)ity TV: A Symptom of Our Times," *Journal for the Psychoanalysis of Culture and Society* 8 (2003): 320–329.

98. Which, I confess, is a nod to the groundbreaking work of Bonnie Dow; see Bonnie J. Dow, *Prime-Time Feminism: Television, Media Culture, and the Women's Movement since 1970* (Philadelphia: University of Pennsylvania Press, 1996).

99. See Slavoj Žižek, *The Plague of Fantasies* (New York: Verso, 1997), esp. 3–44.

100. The revolving retitling of the presidential campaign on the weekly HBO comedy tabloid *Last Week with John Oliver* captures the spirit: "Clowntown Fuck-the-World Shitshow 2016," or "Lice on Rats on a Horse Corpse on Fire 2016." Readers can review these weekly "titles" for the presidential campaign by visiting the show's YouTube channel, https://www.youtube.com/user/LastWeekTonight.

101. See Susan Murray and Laurie Ouellette, *Reality TV: Remaking Television Culture*, 2nd ed. (New York: New York University Press, 2008).

102. Hank Stuever, "How Reality TV Gave Us Reality Candidate Donald Trump," *Washington Post*, July 17, 2016, https://www.washingtonpost.com/entertainment/tv/how-reality-tv-gave-us-reality-candidate-donald-trump/2016/07/16/0ebc597e-4454-11e6-8856-f26de2537a9d_story.html.

103. For an "inside account," see Ragan Fox, "'You Are Not Allowed to Talk about Production': Narratization on (and off) the Set of CBS's *Big Brother*," *Critical Studies in Media Communication* 30 (2013): 189–208.

104. For Jameson, the fantasy bribe immerses spectators in a story world that screens, in both senses, "the psyche against the frightening and potentially damaging eruption of powerful archaic desires and wish material." Fredrick Jameson, "Reification and Utopia in Mass Culture," *Social Text* 1 (1979): 141. Also see Dana Cloud, "The Irony Bribe and Reality Television: Investment and Detachment in *The Bachelor*," *Critical Studies in Media Communication* 27 (2010): 415.

105. Cloud, "The Irony Bribe," 415; italics in original.

106. Žižek, *Plague*, 10–13.

107. Cloud, "The Irony Bribe," 415.

108. I reference the sportscasting framing of CNN's broadcasts, which are slugged as "smackdowns" and always cast in terms of winning and losing; see "Who Won the Presidential Debate?," CNN Opinion, September 27, 2016, http://www.cnn.com/2016/09/27/opinions/hillary-clinton-donald-trump-debate-opinion-roundup/. The story is slugged as "Presidential Debate: Who Won Clinton-Trump Smackdown?" for Internet search engines.

109. See Jenna Johnson, "Donald Trump Says the Election is 'Rigged.' Here's What His Supporters Think That Means," *Washington Post*, October 18, 2016, https://www.washingtonpost.com/news/post-politics/wp/2016/10/18/donald-trump-says-the-election-is-rigged-heres-what-his-supporters-think-that-means/.

110. This trend is parodied by a 2006 film by Paul Weitz titled *American Dreamz*, in which a US president becomes involved in a spoof of the vote-by-text talent contest show *American Idol*.

111. I jest about a widely read book; see Thomas Frank, *What's the Matter with Kansas? How Conservatives Won the Heart of America* (New York: Holt Paperbacks, 2005).

112. I say "might" conclude and not "should conclude" because one could also argue Trump support is classically hysteric, a neurotic disposition.

113. See Bluford Adams, *E Pluribus Barnum: The Great Showman and the Making of U.S. Popular Culture* (Minneapolis: University of Minnesota Press, 1997). Arguably, however, politics is the most perverse genre of discourse because of the conditioned affordances of duplicity are central to it: from Plato forward, political rhetoric has often been described as an ironic

and often flattering cosmetic (cynically stated, political discourse is the egg that made the reality TV chicken possible).

114. "Jerry Springer: Trump's Reality TV Speak Made His Rise 'Inevitable,'" *Takeaway*, September 28, 1996, http://www.wnyc.org/story/jerry-springer-knows-about-mixing-politics-entertainment/.

115. See Leon Hunt, "Hell in a Cell and Other Stories: Violence, Endangerment and Authenticity in Professional Wrestling," in *The Spectacle of the Real: From Hollywood to "Reality" TV and Beyond*, ed. Geoff King (Portland, OR: Intellect, 2005), 117–127.

116. "Fuck it, I'm voting for Trump," anonymous message on "The Donald" discussion forum, Reddit.com, March 2016, https://www.reddit.com/r/The_Donald/comments/4bibbw/fuck_it_im_voting_for_trump/.

117. As a political philosophy, "Fuck it!" can be read as a Habermasian public by other means. See Peter Lunt and Paul Stenner, "*The Jerry Springer Show* as Emotional Public Sphere," *Media, Culture & Society* 27 (2005): 58–81. My thanks to Paul Johnson for this reference.

118. Conor Friedersdorf, "A Sanders Supporter Leans toward Supporting Trump," *Atlantic*, June 2, 2015, http://www.theatlantic.com/politics/archive/2016/06/why-bernie-sanders-supporters-should-reject-donald-trump/485258/. Lunt and Stenner argue of shows like *The Jerry Springer Show*: "What emerges is an argument that public deliberation can produce knowledge, testimony and reflection not by attempting a realistic representation of events or by building consensus of opinion, but by setting up a set of circumstances that afford a mixture of emotional expression, argument, reflection and ethical summary." Lunt and Stenner, "*The Jerry Springer Show*," 76.

119. See Laura J. Collins, "The Second Amendment as Demanding Subject: Figuring the Marginalized Subject in Demands for an Unbridled Second Amendment," *Rhetoric & Public Affairs* 17 (2014): 737–756.

120. Slavoj Žižek, *Looking Awry: An Introduction to Jacques Lacan through Popular Culture* (Cambridge, MA: MIT Press, 1992), 102.

121. See Angie Drobnic Holan, "Joe Wilson of South Carolina Said Obama Lied, but He Didn't," Politifact, September 9, 2009, http://www.politifact.com/truth-o-meter/statements/2009/sep/09/joe-wilson/joe-wilson-south-carolina-said-obama-lied-he-didnt/.

122. Slavoj Žižek, *The Ticklish Subject: The Absent Centre of Political Ontology* (New York: Verso, 1999), 315; also see Jodi Dean's insightful elaboration of the consequence in terms of "whatever being." Dean, *Blog Theory: Feedback and Capture in the Circuits of Drive* (Malden, MA: Polity, 2010), 61–90.

123. Žižek, *The Ticklish Subject*, 315.

124. Sigmund Freud, *Group Psychology and the Analysis of the Ego*, trans. James Strachey (New York: W. W. Norton, 1959), 69–77.

125. For an alternative account of a generalized perversion in terms of the "politics of demand," see Christian Lundberg, "On Being Bound to Equivalential Chains," *Cultural Studies* 26 (2012): 299–318.

126. It should be said that Žižek's diagnosis of a generalized perversity is complicated, involving the interplay of the superego (a cultural force that demands everyone to "enjoy!" in a sort of punishing consumerism) and a kind of symbolic figure (the Ego Ideal) that has been removed

in the liberal pursuit of an enlightened society (the "decline of symbolic efficiency" or "authority"). Taking leads from the insightful analysis of Sharpe and Boucher, the gist is something like this: the symbolic order is now the matrix of global capitalism, and its "obscene" underbelly is the relentless injunction to *consume!* In modernity, various authorities functioned to moderate and regulate social order. With the erosion of such figures in postmodernity—or the idea of authority at all—the punishing, superegoic command to enjoy! or consume! is overwhelming, paving the way for a figure like Trump. See Sharpe and Boucher, *Žižek and Politics*, esp. 139–164.

127. See Campbell, *The Great Silent Majority*, esp. 72–96.

128. Thomas W. Benson, "Edwin Black's Cornell University," *Rhetoric & Public Affairs* 10 (2007): 482.

129. Black, "Richard Nixon," 26.

130. Davis, *Inessential Solidarity*, 2–4.

131. Diane Davis, "Rhetoricity at the End of the World," *Philosophy and Rhetoric* 50.4 (2017): 431–451.

132. The phrase is Butler's; see Judith Butler, *Senses of the Subject* (New York: Fordham University Press, 2015), 17–35. "If the body is what inaugurates the process of its own spectralization through writing, then it is and is not determined by the discourse it produces. . . . This body is neither a surface nor a substance, but the linguistic occasion of the body's separation from itself, one that eludes its capture by the figure it compels" (35).

CONCLUSION

1. Joan Copjec, *Imagine There's No Woman: Ethics and Sublimation* (Cambridge, MA: MIT Press, 2002), 229.

2. Bradley Serber has persuasively argued we should use the term "targeted violence" instead of "mass shooting" for a number of reasons, including its precision as well as its more encompassing scope. Bradley A. Serber, "Reaction Rhetorics: Targeted Violence and Public Security" (Ph.D. diss., Pennsylvania State University, 2016), 7–10.

3. For example, see Janine Chasseguet-Smirgel, *Creativity and Perversion* (London: Free Association Books, 1984).

4. James Poniewozik, "A Donald Trump Speech Whose Sunny Spots Came Mostly from the Stage Lights," *New York Times*, July 22, 2016, https://www.nytimes.com/2016/07/23/arts/donald-trump-rnc-speech.html.

5. Theodor W. Adorno, "Freudian Theory and the Pattern of Fascist Propaganda," *The Frankfurt School Reader*, ed. Andrew Arato and Eike Gebhardt (New York: Continuum, 2002), 127.

6. NBC News, "Rudy Giuliani: 'Truth Isn't Truth,'" *Meet the Press*, August 19, 2018, https://www.youtube.com/watch?v=CljsZ7lgbtw.

7. See Diane Davis, "Rhetoricity at the End of the World," *Philosophy and Rhetoric* 30.4 (2017): 431–452; and Diane Davis, *Inessential Solidarity: Rhetoric and Foreigner Relations* (Pittsburgh: University of Pittsburgh Press, 2010).

8. Christina Caron, "Students Who Made Apparent Nazi Salute in Photo Won't Be Punished," *New York Times*, November 24, 2018, https://www.nytimes.com/2018/11/24/us/baraboo-wisconsin-nazi-salute-photo.html.

9. Caron, "Students Who Made," para. 3.

10. Hannah Fry and Colleen Shalby, "Racist 'Promposal' and a Troubling Social Media Trend: 'Bigotry Is Funny,'" *Los Angeles Times*, May 16, 2019, https://www.latimes.com/local /lanow/la-me-racist-promposal-social-media-palos-verdes-20190516-story.html.

11. Fry and Shalby, "Racist 'Promposal,'" para. 4.

12. ABC News, "Milo Yiannopoulos Interview: No Regrets on Leslie Jones Attack, Part 1," *Nightline*, September 2, 2016, https://www.youtube.com/watch?v=jkrY6Ny7pMg. Mr. Yiannopoulos's apparent conviction in his omnipotence led to his firing by the "alt-right" Breitbart News Network and the cancellation of a lucrative book contract with Simon and Schuster, not because of his hate speech or patently racist and sexist remarks but because he joked about one of the few juridical perversions that remains forbidden in Western culture: pedophilia. See Rebecca Hersher, "After Comments on Pedophilia, Breitbart Editor Milo Yiannopoulos Resigns," NPR, February 21, 2017, https://www.npr.org/sections/thetwo-way/2017/02/21/516473521 /after-comments-on-pedophilia-breitbart-editor-milo-yiannopoulos-resigns.

13. André Green, *Play and Reflection in Donald Winnicott's Writings* (London: Karnac, 2005), 8.

14. Jean Piaget, *Play, Dreams and Imitation in Childhood*, trans. G. Gettegno and F. M. Hodgson (New York: W. W. Norton, 1962).

15. D. W. Winnicott, *Playing and Reality* (New York: Routledge, 2005), 72–73.

16. Melanie Klein, *The Writings of Melanie Klein*, vol. 3, *Envy and Gratitude and Other Works*, 146–1963 (New York: Free Press, 1975), 258–259.

17. In her series of lectures titled *Public Things*, Bonnie Honig draws on Winnicott's theory of the transitional object to argue for the profound significance of shared public objects as a kind of social "holding space." See Bonnie Honig, *Public Things: Democracy in Disrepair* (New York: Fordham University Press, 2017); my thanks to Barbara Biesecker for pointing me to this remarkable study.

18. There is a caveat here: in a more common sense, those made to witness a pervert's presumed transgressions *are* objectified, insofar as their humanness or capacity to relate is denied. The inability to regard others as subjects is a common description of perversion and pathological play. I think, however, Sergio Benvenuto makes a compelling case that perverts demand others *as subjects* to witness them while denying any sense of charity. In other words, the pervert cannot treat others as mere objects because one can demand recognition only from subjects. Even so, in a more common sense those made to witness a pervert's presumed transgressions *are* objectified, insofar as their humanness or capacity to relate is denied. See Sergio Benvenuto, "Perversion and Charity: An Ethical Approach," in *Perversion: Psychoanalytic Perspectives/ Perspectives on Psychoanalysis*, ed. Dany Nobus and Lisa Downing (London: Karnac, 2006), 59–78.

19. Much of this research can be traced back to Freud and the case of "Little Hans," a boy who had a phobia of horses. Freud's therapeutic technique with adults depended on free association in speech, something children couldn't quite master. So he discovered that a child's playing with toys could be another way to help them verbalize by-proxy. Freud's daughter, Anna Freud, as well as Melanie Klein, would later help to develop "play therapy" as a childhood technique, leading in turn to the insights of Piaget and Vygotsky on the crucial importance of play for cognitive development. See Anna Freud, *The Ego and the Mechanisms of Defense*, rev. ed.

(New York: International Universities Press, 1966), esp. 83–91; Melanie Klein, *The Psycho-Analysis of Children*, trans. Alix Strachey (New York: Free Press, 1975), esp. 16–34; Piaget, *Play, Dreams and Imitation in Childhood*; and Lev S. Vygotsky, "Play and Its Role in the Mental Development of the Child," trans. Nikolai Veresov and Myra Barrs, *International Research in Early Childhood Education* 7.2 (2016): 3–25.

20. For example, see Robert M. Fagen, *Animal Play Behavior* (New York: Oxford University Press, 1981).

21. Also, much of this work builds on the influential theory of playing and games of Johan Huizinga. See Johan Huizinga, *Homo Ludens: A Study of the Play-Element in Culture* (Kettering, OH: Angelico, 2016).

22. See Robert Busching, Johnie J. Allen, and Craig A. Anderson, "Violent Media Content and Effects," in *Oxford Research Encyclopedia of Communication* (March 2016), http://communication.oxfordre.com/view/10.1093/acrefore/9780190228613.001.0001/acrefore-9780190228613-e-1?print=pdf.

23. The title of Christopher Paul's recently published book pretty much sums it up: *The Toxic Meritocracy of Video Games: Why Gaming Culture Is the Worst* (Minneapolis: University of Minnesota Press, 2018).

24. Chasseguet-Smirgel, *Creativity and Perversion*, 1–12.

25. See Vincent Canby, "Screen: 'Harold and Maude' and Life: Hal Ashby's Comedy Opens at Coronet Ruth Gordon, Bud Cort Star as Odd Couple," *New York Times*, December 21, 1971, https://www.nytimes.com/1971/12/21/archives/screen-harold-and-maude-and-lifehal-ashbys-comedy-opens-at-coronet.html; and Roger Ebert, "Harold and Maude," rogerebert.com, January 1, 1972, https://www.rogerebert.com/reviews/harold-and-maude-1972.

26. Viewers of the film may recall that the closing shot is a pan from the crashed car back to the cliff, where Harold is seen (surprisingly) to be alive, walking away, playing a banjo and doing a jig. This "happy" ending was actually the third shot; the original endings suggest Harold finally went "all the way"—which would have made the film too pointedly perverse from the vantage of the spectator. See Christopher Beach, *The Films of Hal Ashby* (Detroit: Wayne State University Press, 2009), 65–66.

27. Quoted in Alex Godfrey, "Bud Cort: 'Harold and Maude Was a Blessing and a Curse,'" *Guardian*, July 14, 2014, https://www.theguardian.com/film/2014/jul/10/burt-cort-harold-and-maude-blessing-and-curse.

28. Melanie Klein, "A Contribution to the Psychogenesis of Manic-Depressive States," in *The Writings of Melanie Klein*, vol. 1, *Love, Guilt and Reparation and Other Works, 1921–1945* (New York: Free Press, 1975), 262–289. The argument here is that Harold's lesson is one of reparation and gratitude.

29. The mother as abject, monstrous, or smothering has been elaborated and critiqued extensively in psychoanalytic theory; see Julia Kristeva, *Powers of Horror: An Essay on Abjection*, trans. Leon S. Roudiez (New York: Columbia University Press, 1982); and Barbara Creed, "Horror and the Monstrous-Feminine: An Imaginary Abjection," *Screen* 27.1 (1986): 44–54. For a brilliant psychoanalytic contextualization of *Psycho* as a cultural watershed, see Laurence A. Rickels, *The Psycho Records* (New York: Wallflower, 2016).

30. Beach, *The Films of Hal Ashby*, 39.

31. Joan Copjec, *Read My Desire: Lacan against the Historicists* (Cambridge, MA: MIT Press, 1994), 109. Freud admits his understanding may be too concise, so to speak: "Symptoms" of perversion "are formed in part at the cost of *abnormal* sexuality; *neuroses are, so to say, the negative of perversions*" (emphasis in original). Sigmund Freud, "The Sexual Aberrations," in *The Standard Edition of the Complete Psychological Works of Sigmund Freud*, vol. 8, *Jokes and Their Relation to the Unconscious (1905)*, trans. James Strachey (London: Hogarth, 1953), 165.

32. All stereotypical representatives of patriarchal heteronormativity—all paternal figures—are satirized: Uncle Victor's impotence, signified by a missing arm, represents the military; a policeman is duped by the couple; and the clergy is pilloried hilariously. In a pivotal line a priest clearly enjoys saying to Harold, "Now Harold, the church has nothing against the old and the young. . . . But a marital union is concerned with the conjugal rights. I would be remiss in my duties if I did not tell you that the idea of [he swallows] intercourse—the fact of your young, firm [growls] body commingling with the withered flesh, sagging breasts, and flabby buttocks makes me want to vomit!" See Beach, *The Films of Hal Ashby*, 54.

33. I reference what is arguably one of the most significant critiques of racism during Trump's early presidency, Jordan Peele's 2017 horror film, *Get Out*.

34. See Akhil Reed Amar, *The Constitution Today: Timeless Lessons for Issues of Our Era* (New York: Basic Books, 2016), 327–357; and Sanford Levinson, *Our Undemocratic Constitution: Where Our Constitution Goes Wrong (and How We the People Can Correct It)* (New York: Oxford University Press, 2006), esp. 79–122.

35. See Kamala Kelkar, "Electoral College Is 'Vestige' of Slavery, Say Some Constitutional Scholars," *PBS NewsHour Weekend*, November 6, 2016, https://www.pbs.org/newshour/politics/electoral-college-slavery-constitution.

36. Donald Trump, "Donald Trump on Hillary Clinton and the Second Amendment," *New York Times*, August 9, 2016, https://www.youtube.com/watch?v=DE_uCKedvcU.

37. Nick Corasaniti and Maggie Haberman, "Donald Trump Suggests 'Second Amendment People' Could Act against Hillary Clinton," *New York Times*, August 9, 2016, https://www.nytimes.com/2016/08/10/us/politics/donald-trump-hillary-clinton.html., para. 11.

38. ABC News, "10 Victims Dead in Texas School Shooting, Explosives Found, Official Say," *Nightline*, May 19, 2018, https://www.youtube.com/watch?v=e8UX7pKBPpc.

39. For an alternative and compatible rumination on mediated deadlock on gun policy, see Craig Rood, *After Gun Violence: Deliberation and Memory in an Age of Political Gridlock* (University Park: Pennsylvania State University Press, 2019).

40. See Bonnie Berkowitz, Denise Lu, and Chris Alcantara, "The Terrible Numbers That Grow with Each Mass Shooting," *Washington Post*, August 4, 2019, https://www.washingtonpost.com/graphics/2018/national/mass-shootings-in-america/; and Eve Watling, "America's Gun Violence Epidemic: Mass Shootings Getting Deadlier," *Newsweek*, October 1, 2018, https://www.newsweek.com/americas-gun-violence-epidemic-mass-shootings-getting-deadlier-1146879.

41. Brad J. Bushman, "Narcissism, Fame Seeking, and Mass Shootings," *American Behavioral Scientist* 62 (2018): 229–241.

42. For an early analysis of this affective effect as "apocalyptic," see Joshua Gunn and David E. Beard, "On the Apocalyptic Columbine," *Southern Communication Journal* 68.3 (2003): 198–216.

43. Glen Slater, "A Mythology of Bullets," *Spring: A Journal of Archetype and Culture* 81 (2009), https://www.depthinsights.com/pdfs/MythologyOfBullets-GlenSlater-SpringJournalV81-PsychologyOfViolence.pdf, 1–2; for example, see Tim Dickinson, "The Gun Industry's Deadly Addiction," *Rolling Stone*, March 14, 2013, https://www.rollingstone.com/politics/politics-news/the-gun-industrys-deadly-addiction-99443/.

44. "The Demographics of Gun Ownership," Pew Research Center, June 22, 2017, http://www.pewsocialtrends.org/2017/06/22/the-demographics-of-gun-ownership/.

45. Kara Fox, "How US Gun Culture Compares with the World in Five Charts," CNN World, March 9, 2018, https://www.cnn.com/2017/10/03/americas/us-gun-statistics/index.html.

46. Dewey Cornell and Pooja Datta, "Threat Assessment and Violence Prevention," in *The Wiley Handbook of the Psychology of Mass Shootings*, ed. Laura C. Wilson (Hoboken, NJ: John Wiley and Sons, 2017), 359.

47. Benjamin Winegard and Christopher J. Ferguson, "The Development of Rampage Shooters: Myths and Uncertainty in the Search for Causes," in *The Wiley Handbook of the Psychology of Mass Shootings*, ed. Laura C. Wilson (Hoboken, NJ: John Wiley and Sons, 2017), 60.

48. The Black Angels, "Don't Play with Guns," by the Black Angels, track 3 on *Indigo Meadow*, Blue Horizon, 2013.

49. Slater, "A Mythology of Bullets," 6.

50. Slater, "A Mythology of Bullets," 6.

51. Robert K. Merton, "Social Structure and Anomie," *American Sociological Review* 3 (1938): 672–682; also see James Alan Fox and Jack Levin, "Explaining Mass Shootings: Types, Patterns, and Theories," in *The Wiley Handbook of the Psychology of Mass* Shootings, ed. Laura C. Wilson (Hoboken, NJ: John Wiley and Sons, 2017), 47–48.

52. For readers familiar with Charles Schulz's cartoons, this is akin to Linus screaming you can take his blue binkie out of his "cold dead hands," as Charlton Heston once famously screamed about his gun at a National Rifle Association meeting. See Matthew A. Sears, "What the Ancient Greeks Can Teach Us about Gun Control," *Washington Post*, February 21, 2018, https://www.washingtonpost.com/news/made-by-history/wp/2018/02/21/what-the-ancient-greeks-can-teach-us-about-gun-control/?utm_term=.777f4ef24752.

53. See Laura J. Collins, "The Second Amendment as Demanding Subject: Figuring the Marginalized Subject in Demands for an Unbridled Second Amendment," *Rhetoric & Public Affairs* 17.4 (2014): 737–756.

54. For an elaboration of fetish as synecdoche, see Hartmut Böhme, *Fetishism and Culture: A Different Theory of Modernity* (Berlin: De Gruyter, 2014), esp. 309–313.

55. Slater puts this chillingly well: "The power of this fantasy is at the root of the addictive attraction of guns. When you hear from childhood on that you live in 'the land of opportunity,' that you are 'special,' and that you can 'be all you can be,' or you simply see this self aggrandizement [*sic*] all around, then someone or something comes along and clips your wings, the ability to reach for a gun is like having a god-like sense of agency in your back pocket." Slater, "A Mythology of Bullets," 8.

56. Rosa A. Eberly, *Towers of Rhetoric: Memory and Reinvention* (Lexington, KY: Intermezzo, 2018), http://intermezzo.enculturation.net/05-eberly/eberly-ch2.html. Eberly's e-book

is a thoughtful rumination on the relationship between targeted violence and the academy, creatively framed around the case of the University of Texas tower shooting on August 1, 1966.

57. See Paul Virilio, *War and Cinema: The Logistics of Perception*, trans. Patrick Camiller (New York: Verso, 2009), esp. 15–39.

58. For an excellent read of killing imagery and weaponry, see Barry Brummett, *Rhetorical Homologies: Form, Culture, Experience* (Tuscaloosa: University of Alabama Press, 2004), 126–158.

59. Greg Abbott, "Texas Gov. Greg Abbott Delivers Remarks on Santa Fe School Shooting," *PBS NewsHour*, May 18, 2018, https://www.youtube.com/watch?v=LYg3rlNjifw.

60. Erica L. Green, "Betsy DeVos Eyes Federal Education Grants to Put Guns in Schools," *New York Times*, August 23, 2018, https://www.nytimes.com/2018/08/23/us/politics/devos-guns-in-schools.html.

61. Rebecca Keegan, "Jordan Peele on the 'Post-Racial Lie' That Inspired *Get Out*," *Vanity Fair*, October 30, 2017, https://www.vanityfair.com/hollywood/2017/10/jordan-peele-get-out-screening.

62. "It's Not the 'Year of the Woman.' It's the 'Year of the Women,'" CNN Opinion, November 4, 2018, https://www.cnn.com/2018/11/03/opinions/midterm-elections-year-of-woman-roundup/index.html.

63. For an overview of the "#MeToo" movement, see K. T. Hawbaker, "#MeToo: A Timeline of Events," *Chicago Tribune*, December 6, 2018, https://www.chicagotribune.com/lifestyles/ct-me-too-timeline-20171208-htmlstory.html.

64. See Judy Woodruff, "How Florida Voters Are Thinking Ahead of Election Day," *PBS NewsHour*, October 29, 2018, https://www.pbs.org/newshour/show/how-florida-voters-are-thinking-ahead-of-election-day. Also see Luciana Lopez and Michelle Conlin, "Fed Up with Washington, Trump's 'Deplorables' Shake Up the Elite," Reuters, November 6, 2016, https://www.reuters.com/article/us-usa-election-voters/fed-up-with-washington-trumps-deplorables-shake-up-the-elite-idUSKBN1341AB.

65. Patricia Mazzei, " 'It's Just Too Much': A Florida Town Grapples with a Shutdown after a Hurricane," *New York Times*, January 7, 2019, https://www.nytimes.com/2019/01/07/us/florida-government-shutdown-marianna.html.

66. In other words, Trump makes transparent what was already underwriting the US political establishment, a point underscored by his failure to "drain the swamp." See Conor Friedersdorf, "Trump Has Filled, Not Drained, the Swamp," *Atlantic*, September 21, 2017, https://www.theatlantic.com/politics/archive/2017/09/meet-the-new-swamp/540540/.

67. See Carol Anderson, *One Person, No Vote: How Voter Suppression Is Destroying Our Democracy* (New York: Bloomsbury, 2018); George C. Edwards III, *Why the Electoral College Is Bad for America* (New Haven, CT: Yale University Press, 2004); and Kelkar, "Electoral College."

68. Many attribute the aphorism to Carl von Clausewitz; however, this received wisdom is backward; he said, "*War is nothing but the continuation of policy with other means*" (italics in original). See Carl von Clausewitz, *On War*, trans. Michael Howard and Peter Paret (New York: Oxford University Press, 1976), 7, 252.

69. Ginger Thompson, "Families Still Being Separated at Border—Months after Trump's 'Zero Tolerance' Policy Reversed," *USA Today*, November 27, 2018, https://www.usatoday

.com/story/news/politics/elections/2018/11/27/donald-trump-zero-tolerance-policy-border -migrants-families-separated-immigration/2132426002/.

70. David Leonhardt and Ian Prasad Philbrick, "Donald Trump's Racism: The Definitive List," *New York Times*, January 15, 2018, https://www.nytimes.com/interactive/2018/01/15/opin ion/leonhardt-trump-racist.html.

71. Brian Resnick and Eliza Barclay, "What Every American Needs to Know about Puerto Rico's Hurricane Disaster," *Vox*, October 16, 2017, https://www.vox.com/science-and-health /2017/9/26/16365994/hurricane-maria-2017-puerto-rico-san-juan-humanitarian-disaster -electricty-fuel-flights-facts.

72. Mark Hannah, "Trump's Support for Saudi Arabia Contradicts CIA, Subverts National Security and Puts Millions of Lives at Risk," NBC News, November 20, 2018, https://www .nbcnews.com/think/opinion/trump-s-support-saudi-arabia-contradicts-cia-subverts-national -security-ncna938591; also see David A. Graham, "Trump's Effusive, Unsettling Flattery of Kim Jong Un," *Atlantic*, June 12, 2018, https://www.theatlantic.com/politics/archive/2018/06 /trumps-effusive-unsettling-flattery-of-kim-jong-un/562619/.

73. David Crary, "Before Pittsburg Shooting, Anti-Semitic Incidents Were on the Rise," *PBS NewsHour*, October 29, 2018, https://www.pbs.org/newshour/nation/before-pittsburgh -shooting-anti-semitic-incidents-were-on-the-rise.

74. Josh Dawsey and Felicia Sonmez, "Trump Mocks Kavanaugh Accuser Christine Bla-sey Ford," *Washington Post*, October 2, 2018, https://www.washingtonpost.com/politics/trump -mocks-kavanaugh-accuser-christine-blasey-ford/2018/10/02/25f6f8aa-c662-11e8-9b1c-a90f1d aae309_story.html?utm_term=.b439702ff770; also see Betsy Klein, Allie Malloy, and Kate Sul-livan, "Trump Mocks the #MeToo Movement at Rally, Again," CNN Politics, October 10, 2018, https://www.cnn.com/2018/10/10/politics/trump-rally-mocks-me-too/index.html.

75. Julie Rovner, "Timeline: Despite GOP's Failure to Repeal Obamacare, the ACA Has Changed," *Washington Post*, April 5, 2018, https://www.washingtonpost.com/national/health -science/timeline-despite-gops-failure-to-repeal-obamacare-the-aca-has-changed/2018/04/05 /dba36240-38b1-11e8-af3c-2123715f78df_story.html?utm_term=.065e741db44e.

76. Emma Green, "How Trump Is Reversing Obama's Nondiscrimination Legacy," *Atlan-tic*, August 14, 2019, https://www.theatlantic.com/politics/archive/2019/08/trump-lgbtq-rules /596116/.

77. Mallory Simon and Sara Sidner, "Trump Says He's Not a Racist. That's Not How White Nationalists See It," CNN Politics, November 13, 2018, https://www.cnn.com/2018/11/12/politics /white-supremacists-cheer-midterms-trump/index.html; Avesha Rascoe, "A Year after Char-lottesville, Not Much Has Changed for Trump," *NPR Weekend Edition Saturday*, August 11, 2018, https://www.npr.org/2018/08/11/637665414/a-year-after-charlottesville-not-much-has -changed-for-trump.

78. David Smith, "Trump's Solution to School Shootings: Arm Teachers with Guns," *Guardian*, February 21, 2018, https://www.theguardian.com/us-news/2018/feb/21/donald-trump -solution-to-school-shootings-arm-teachers-with-guns.

INDEX

Abbott, Greg, 134–35

Adams, Jason Michael, 67–68

ad hominem fallacy, 74, 100, 104

Adorno, Theodor W.: on autocrats and their supporters, ix–x; cultural criticism of, 38–39, 43; culture industry and speed of standardization, critiques of, 66; leadership, love and, 120

affect: as addictive, 48; demands and, 92–93; emotion vs., 68–82; as force and appetite, 13; form/genre and, 111; *jouissance* and, 88; persuasion and, 118; rational choice model and, 101; recent interest in, 9, 30–31; repression, in relation to, 59, 61; as style, 95

Albright, Madeleine, x

Althusser, Louis, 63

American Dreamz (Weitz), 177n110

American Psychiatric Association: Goldwater Rule, 23, 101, 103, 105; homosexuality, depathologization of, 16

Anthony, Susan B., 135

anthropodermic bibliopegy, 149n19

Arendt, Hannah, 123

Aristotle, 6–7, 34

Arnold, Tom, 97

Ashby, Hal, 127

Augustine of Hippo, Saint, vi

authority, perceptions of absence/decline of: the brave new world of perversion and, 116; erosion of the big Other and, 53–55, 93–94 (*see also* big Other); examples of, 49–51; politics of demand and, 94

autocrats/authoritarianism: Adorno on, ix–x; as intoxicants, x; the mood of our time and, xi; potential for, 116

"Baby Trump" blimp, 84–85

Bachman, Helena, 133

Bacon, Francis, 13, 147n67

Bahrani, Ramin, 47–48

Baird, A. Craig, 101

Baldwin, Alec, 166n60

Bannon, Steve, 107–9

Bardem, Javier, 166n59

Barnum, P. T., 114

Barthes, Roland, 25–26

Beach, Christopher, 128

Beatles, 93

Benjamin, Walter: approach to the patient, magician vs. surgeon regarding, 32; criticism implies participation in dreams/illusions, argument that, 40; cultural criticism

t-compliance